A GIFT OF ISLANDS

BY THE SAME AUTHOR

The Sultans Came to Tea

JUNE KNOX-MAWER is Welsh and was trained as a journalist. After five years in Arabia, she went to live in Fiji where her husband was appointed a High Court Judge. Here she began her broadcasting career, which has continued in this country with her work for the BBC, as presenter for Radio 4's 'Weekend' and other 'Womans Hour' introductions, and for a variety of documentary features. She is currently recording a series on British memories of the South Pacific, 'Tales from Paradise'. Her latest book, to be published next year, is a sequel to her novel of nineteenth-century Fiji, *Marama*

A GIFT OF ISLANDS

JUNE KNOX-MAWER

Living in Fiji

ALAN SUTTON
1984

Alan Sutton Publishing Limited
Brunswick Road · Gloucester

First published 1965
This edition published by arrangement with
John Murray 1984

British Library Cataloguing in Publication Data

Knox-Mawer, June
A gift of islands.
I. Title
919.6′1104 DU600

ISBN 0-86299-196-X

TO MY PARENTS

Cover photograph by G.H. Knox-Mawer

Printed and bound in Great Britain

Contents

Illustrations

All photographs not otherwise acknowledged are by Rob Wright

Acknowledgments

I would like to thank the Hon. P. D. Macdonald, C.M.G., C.V.O., Colonial Secretary for Fiji, for his personal interest and encouragement in this book. To the Hon. the Speaker Sir Maurice and Lady Scott, and Mr. and Mrs. Michael Halsted of the British Council, I am indebted for the loan of houses in which to write, and to Mr. Ian Diamond, Government Archivist, for his expert guidance to source material. Dr. Lindsay Verrier, as to so many other writers, has been of invaluable assistance, so too has Mr. Jack Hackett, Public Relations Officer to the Government of Fiji. The Hon. Ian Thompson, M.B.E., the Hon. Josua Rabukawaqa, M.L.C. and Adi Mei, Mr. George Gray, American Consul, Mr. Q. Weston, Miss Jan Hunter-Smith, Mr. I. Dau and Mr. K. P. Sharma, J.P., have also helped me in a number of ways for which I am grateful. I would particularly like to record my thanks for the kind hospitality of the Hon. Ratu Penaia Ganilau and Adi Laisa, Monsignor Franz Wassner, Mr. and Mrs. David Simpson, and so many others in the Fijian villages I visited.

There is, however, one person to whom this book finally belongs—Peter France. Without him, it could never have been envisaged, let alone written.

Readers conversant with the Fijian language will, I hope, excuse the phonetic liberties I have taken with the spelling of certain words throughout the book, e.g. Th for C, etc.

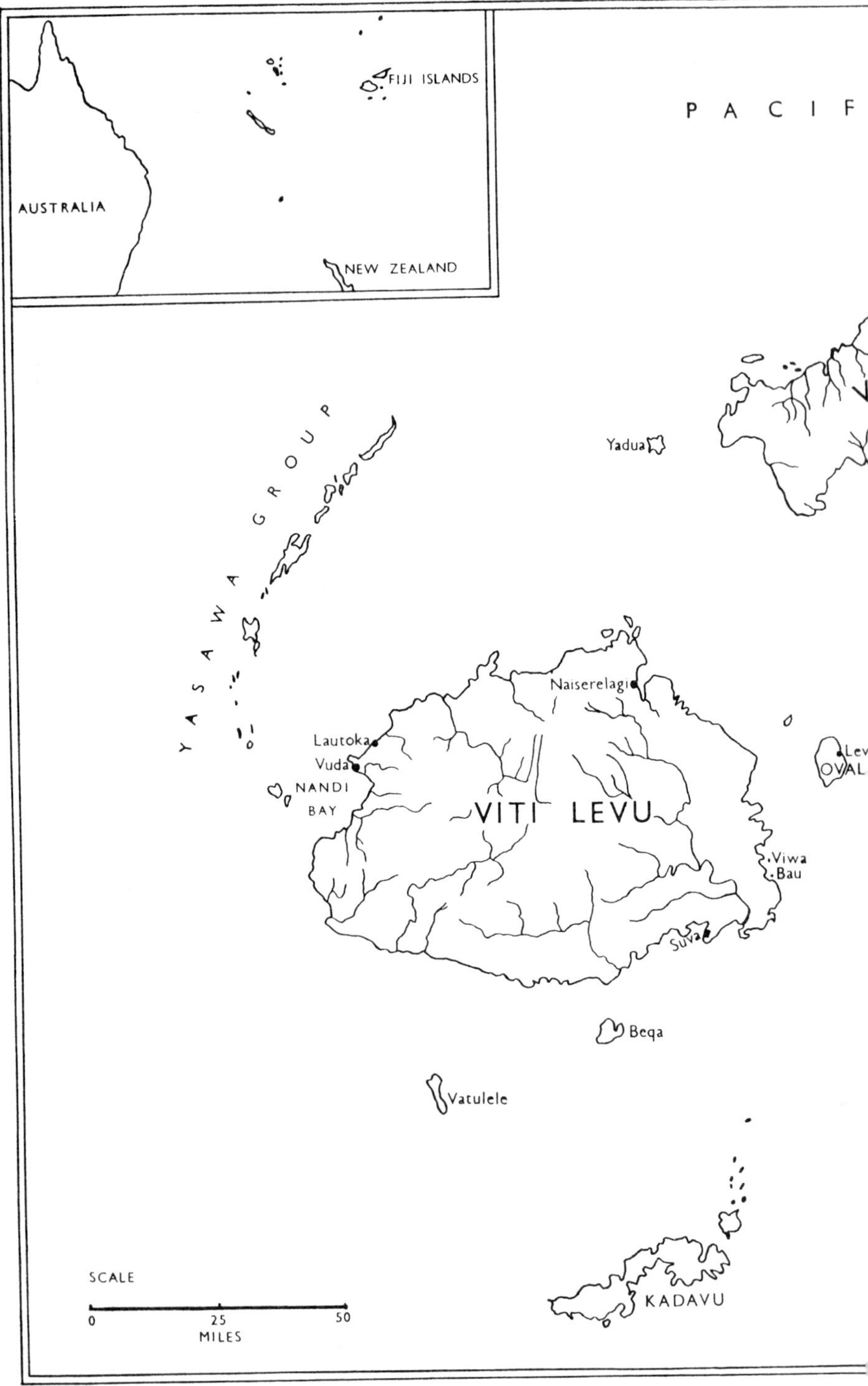

FIJI ISLANDS
AUSTRALIA
NEW ZEALAND
PACIF
YASAWA GROUP
Yadua
Naiserelagi
Lautoka
Vuda
NANDI
BAY
VITI LEVU
Viwa
Bau
Suva
Beqa
Vatulele
KADAVU
SCALE
0
25
50
MILES

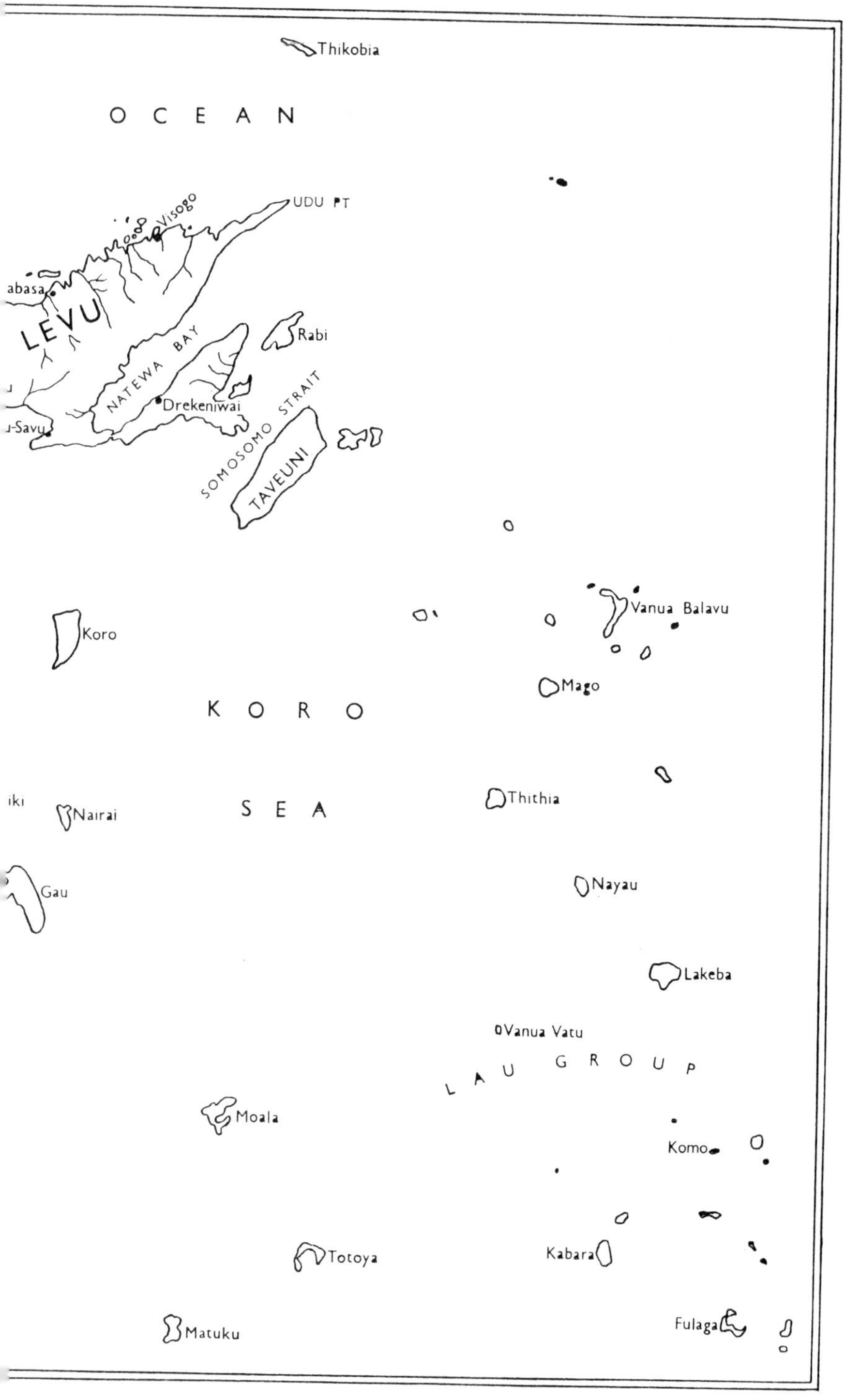

Thikobia

OCEAN

UDU PT

Visogo

abasa

LEVU

NATEWA BAY

Rabi

Drekeniwai

u-Savu

SOMOSOMO STRAIT

TAVEUNI

Vanua Balavu

Koro

Mago

KORO

SEA

Thithia

iki

Nairai

Gau

Nayau

Lakeba

Vanua Vatu

LAU GROUP

Moala

Komo

Totoya

Kabara

Matuku

Fulaga

We give Fiji unreservedly to the Queen of Britain, that she may rule us justly and affectionately, and that we may live in peace and prosperity.

King Thakobau and the Council of Chiefs
August 28th 1874

I

Paradise Street

Waking at first light, I know I am back in Fiji before I open my eyes. The familiar sounds have coloured sleep and dreams without pause—rain showers crackling on an iron roof, the far-away sea-shell snore that was the tide against the reef, the whirr of crickets as constant as if it were the vibration of some machinery by which the whole tropical night revolved.

Dawn filters through the folds of the mosquito net, ghost-grey at first, then gold as the sun rises. Outside, the nearest trees take shape, banyan and coconut palm, frangipani and a lavish breadfruit with half a dozen pale green cannon-balls already ripe among the great dark leaves that glint against the light like serrated shields. The sounds of the dark subside. Everyone is still asleep. I am just drifting off again when I remember that this particular silence is only a pause between movements. Softly the wood-pigeons insinuate a new theme, a purling hyphenated flute note, echoed and re-echoed, until the shrill obbligato of the mynahs takes it up, and then the whole bird population explodes into song, deep-breasted and insistent as a choir of Eisteddfod contraltos. Roosters and dogs and army bugles join in and there is the drone of the first seaplane lumbering skywards from the New Zealand Air Force base at Lauthala Bay.

Resigned and wide awake, I find difficulty in believing that less than two days ago I was still in frozen England. The thirty-six-hour flight had taken us hopping through New York, San Francisco and Hawaii, crossing datelines from yesterday to tomorrow, chasing interminable sunsets, consuming endless dinners that were breakfasts and breakfasts that were dinners before depositing us finally at Nandi international airport on the other side of the main island. It left behind a queer sense of dissociation, this onslaught against time and space. Jet-flung from one pole to the other, one still felt neither here nor there, a shadowy spectator in a kind of limbo suspended between two worlds. This time, too, I had been away for a whole year. I was beginning to realize that twelve months is a long time from a place in which one is still a comparative newcomer.

Two ladies by the name of Miss Gordon-Cumming and Mrs. Smythe were, oddly enough, responsible for heightening this sense of unreality. Each had visited Fiji in mid-Victorian times—fortunately not together as I felt they would have taken an instant dislike to one another—and each had written a book about her travels in the islands. Mrs. Smythe (*Ten Months in the Fiji Islands*) arrived in 1860 with her husband, Colonel W. J. Smythe of the Royal Artillery, following an offer of the islands' sovereignty by the paramount chief to Queen Victoria. The colonel's mission was to advise the British Government on Fiji's suitability as a candidate for imperial possession, a task which he carried out with the severity of a head butler interviewing a young, untried and somewhat unruly addition to the domestic staff. Fourteen years later, despite the colonel's warnings, the cession of Fiji was accepted by the British Crown and, accompanying the wife of the first Governor of the new colony, came a Miss Constance Gordon-Cumming (*At Home in Fiji*).

Almost a hundred years later a musty-smelling, brittle-paged edition of both memoirs was presented to me by an enterprising friend who had come across them in a second-hand bookshop. For the last few weeks of leave I succumbed entirely to the spell of these two ladies. Huddled reading over enormous fires, I began to feel them at my shoulder as real flesh-and-blood—the enthusiastic Scottish accents of Miss Gordon-Cumming who like myself came to the South Seas after a stay in the East (*From the Hebrides to the Himalayas* was the title of her first book), and the more phlegmatic tones of Mrs. Smythe with her sensible holland dresses, her collapsible easel and her travelling stocks of Grimwade's Dessicated Milk.

So strongly did they capture my imagination that I was no longer sure whether the Fiji I was coming back to was mine or theirs. Mrs. Smythe's drawings, for instance, with their dream-like devotion to detail, had quite replaced my own more vapid recollections. Hers was a Fiji dyed in the sad buffs and sepias of Victorian chromo-lithography. Unending storm clouds seemed to loom over those leaden peaks and forests. Steely downpours lashed the coconut trees; a perpetual twilight shrouded the high reed-lined interiors of Fijian meeting-houses in which, on a campstool in the far corner, sat the stolid brown-holland figure of the colonel's lady with her sketchbook.

Then, too, after a prolonged immersion in English attitudes (and I am one of those people who find it hard to believe in the real existence of any place other than my immediate setting) I could sympathize with Miss Gordon-Cumming's introductory remarks: 'Naturally when I announced my intention of really going, everyone replied, "Of course, you're only joking." And indeed even now I myself find it difficult to think of Fiji or anything connected with it in any other light than that of a great joke; its very name has always been considered funny!'

Miss Gordon-Cumming hastened to add though that a cruise on the South Pacific had been one of the dreams of her life. 'And the idea of going actually to live for an indefinite period on isles where there are still a number of ferocious cannibals, has a savour of romance which you can imagine does not lack charm. . . .'

My unopened suitcase caught my eye at the end of the bed. I decided I might as well start to unpack, and tried to imagine Mrs. Smythe cramming into the regulation forty-four pounds not only her sketching things but her stores of quinine, castor oil and laudanum, her books on fern collecting, a few rifles, cartridges, a selection of magnetic and meteorological instruments, some bunting and a box of flags, not to mention half a dozen windows and a couple of doors, 'in case we should find it desirable to have a house run up for us on shore'.

'*Ena gauna thava a kauti koya maikina na wagavuka?*' A piping inquiry beneath the window recalled my attention. 'When did the flying ship bring her then?'

'Last night,' replied a woman's voice. There was the muted crunch of bare feet on the gravel path.

'Whence has she come? *Peritania? Ositeralia?*' (England? Australia?)

'Sst! *E vau mothé tiko beka!*' (Maybe they are still asleep!)

By the time I reached the back door a small group of people was already encamped there. A short, sturdy Fijian woman with square-cut features and the traditional dandelion-puff of black hair, got to her feet.

'*Bula, marama!*' (Your health, my lady!) she began formally, an enormous grin dawning.

'*Bula, Lo!*——'

We broke off to rush into a sudden untidy embrace, then stood back to survey one another.

'You are well?'

'*Io, vinaka.*' It was odd to see again that quick backward tilt of the head that means yes in Fiji.

'This is *Tiu, marama.*' She motioned with impatience to the slim girl behind her. Unlike Lolo who retained the traditional ankle-length *sulu* beneath her European cotton frock, Tiu wore both her skirt and her hair quite short. 'She help the work if you like it.'

Tiu lowered her eyes with a nervous giggle. Lo frowned. Lo is the daughter of one of the first Fijian medical officers and the sister of a *buli* (district headsman). She never giggles, but carries about her an air of iron authority.

Then two bullet-headed boys emerged from hiding outside and were immediately assailed by a small yellow-haired figure that ran out from beyond me. Cries of 'Vanessa!' and 'Vuniani-Charlie!' intermingled at this reunion between Lo's offspring and my own.

'Where is Howard?' they cried.

'School in England!'

'He is big now, eh?'

'He is come back for holidays?'

They disappeared outside while Lo and I exchanged presents.

'*Turaga* stay here long?' she asked dubiously, surveying the cavern of an oven that dominated the gaunt kitchen.

I hastened to reassure her. 'Just a few weeks. This year he has to be Judge'—I used the impressive Fijian word which means literally, He-Who-Speaks-Once—'so we move soon to a nice new house in the Domain.'

The Domain is the communal habitat of the Government official and his family, a bungalow suburb set in a valley of tame jungle on the outskirts of Suva. Paradise Street, our temporary home, was some way beyond the fringe of such *chic* conformity, an old-time settlers' street at the back of town, and Number Two, a shambling wooden house rented by Government as a stopgap during allocation emergencies.

When He-Who-Speaks-Once had spoken, breakfasted and left for Court, I and the house were left alone. Timidly, I took my bearings from what must be the living-room. The stoutly-joisted walls, which stopped a few inches short of the ceiling, had been painted a living turquoise, the door and window frames ranging subtly from stale cream to shop-icing grey. Squares of linoleum, patterned with roses, enlivened the floor-boards. The furniture itself was of the school known to rejectors as 'tropical-baroque'. Cautiously I wove my way round a family of three-legged tables, all enormously heavy and elaborately carved, half a dozen Planters Chairs whose folding arms would extend to receive the outstretched legs of weary planters, and a couple of chaise-longues known locally as lazy-boys, that eerily creaked and wheezed to themselves their tales of past mistreatments. Plant stands, six feet high with legs like cranes, lurked in every corner. Overhead, dusty white china bowls hung suspended on ancient chains as thick as a man's wrist. Spread-eagled across the main walls was a novel decoration in the form of an uncovered electricity meter-board whose exposed clocks and dials served perhaps to remind over-staying guests of the expenses of hospitality.

There seemed to be five bedrooms. Each one housed a cadaverous bed with two tall head-posts shrouded in mosquito-netting. There were several mirrors, poxed with mildew, in which one's reflection loomed towards one like a latter-day Miss Haversham. Opening a corner cupboard, I came upon a very old black mosquito boot, the left one, cracked and bulging to fit the heat-swollen foot of some retired planter. I saw him lying back on the porch in his extending chair, scanning the morning's *Fiji Times*, while his wife with shady hat, freckled arms and gardening gloves tended her orchids and berated the housegirls in her sharp Fijian. In the evening in the lamplight (before the meter's arrival) neighbours would call in to exchange laconic gossip over the whisky bottle, the long silences laden with *malua*, which means by and by and also defines that overpowering air of indolence, that state of gentle stupor, so characteristic of Fiji life.

The rear of the house was a positive honeycomb of bathrooms, murky cells, little penetrated by the light of day and resonant with the croak of toads in the drainpipes. Opening the door of the third of these conveniences, I found myself confronted by the patriarch of the tribe whose explorations had led him out into the bath where he now sat, four-square and hood-eyed, gloating up at my stricken face. Quickly I closed the door again, conscious of a sense of humiliation. Mrs. Smythe, of course, had revelled in domestic wild-life, making enthusiastic plans for a collection of every insect to be found in the house. Even Miss Gordon-Cumming kept pet lizards among the folds of her dress and cherished the large spiders which kept down the cockroaches.

I made my way out into the old-fashioned garden at the back of the house. There was a wide, sloping stretch of grass, feathered over by the shadow patterns of the palm trees which encircled it. The tallest pair stood like sentinels on either side of a flight of worn stone steps leading down to a second lawn. There were no formal flower-beds, but great ragged bushes of hibiscus flared and glowed in every corner—double crimson flowers as softly brilliant as a parrot's breast, single blooms with antenna-like pistals drooping on their stems like giant fuschias, the dark magenta ones that unfold at midnight, the tight frilled petals, a pale peachy-yellow in colour, of the kind called Ballerina.

The smoke of a wood fire drifted across from the yard next door. An old Indian woman was squatting over a huge black cauldron which she stirred from time to time with a pole. This vision from *Macbeth* gave me a toothless gape then disappeared behind the forest of wooden pillars which supported the house some feet above the ground, forming a kind of sinister underworld of old tins and bottles and rubble. The occupants were, apparently, the family of a Hindu schoolmaster.

I wandered down to the bottom of the garden. Through the trees in another backyard a neat Chinese woman was rubbing away at a washboard. She looked up surprised.

'You gonna live here?' she asked, after we had exchanged greetings. Wiping her hands on her tiny hips, she came up to the railings for a closer inspection. Black eyes squeezed out a smile over rounded tallow cheeks. 'Good, good. You got children?'

I told her about them.

'Our girl nineteen now. Study medicine at the San Francisco University,' she chirped.

'Will she stay in America or come back home?'

The smile deflated itself into a flat mask of resignation, touched with sadness. 'We don' know. We leave it to her.' There was a pause. 'We live from day to day here, see,' she explained, turning back to her washing.

From an upstairs window of the house on the other side a plump woman with smooth Samoan features, was beating a mat out with a Fijian twig broom. Catching sight of me, she nodded good morning and smiled, a cigarette in the corner of her mouth.

'The children play together nice, eh?' Voices behind the garage were heard.

'I've been to America, France, Italy, Arabia and Fiji,' my daughter stated.

'Well, you shouldn't really count Fiji 'cos it's part of Britain, see,' came a light rapid sing-song in reply. 'Anyway, I been to Tonga, New Caledonia, Samoa *and* the Ellice Islands. . . .'

2

Sixpence to Sawani

Motor-mowers purred. With a regular muffled thud, the band of the Fiji Military Forces fell upon the opening bars of 'Rule Britannia' in preparation for the Queen's Birthday Garden Party. We were back again in the Domain, a sort of national parkland where that almost extinct species, the British Empire-builder, still lived and bred in a state of natural captivity.

Neat white bungalows containing regulation allotments of Government furniture nestled together on neat green slopes. Their architectural style and situation varied slightly according to the official rank of the occupant. Grade Four quarters usually bordered the road, Grade Three, rather larger, stood slightly above, while on the hilltops rose the stately Grade Two homes of Heads of Departments, fanned by the trade winds of success and with a postage-stamp view of the seas as a crowning privilege.

Driving through in the hush of twilight, such differences seemed veiled. The whole settlement took on the air of a cathedral close, the roof-tops of faithful dependants clustered around the protective shadow of Government House, the legendary Grade One itself. Pipe-smoking men in khaki bushjackets were out in the lanes exercising their dogs and their wives. From lamplit verandas floated the discreet echo of the B.B.C. News from London, clink and tinkle of preparations for small dinner-parties.

It all seemed thoroughly satisfactory. But beneath the surface one sometimes became aware of gathering tensions when it rained for weeks on end in sullen, despairing downpours, when the breeze dropped and the humidity register climbed, when people at parties stayed too long, talking too little and drinking too much, the women's scent mingling with sour undertones of mildew and sweat. On nights like this, dense and starless, the Domain bungalows became low-lying caves of yellow light among the spongy flotsam of the surrounding foliage. Isolated sounds hung on the air, enlarged by the silence. In the distance a mud-bound car grunted and squealed like a stuck pig. Somewhere a door banged. There was a sequence of piano chords, violently struck, and a laugh that spiralled into a cry.

'One of the housegirls,' someone said unconvincingly, pouring another whisky.

As the Colonial Office drily comments in one of its handbooks: 'The climate is usually considered more trying for women than for men. . . . It may be classed as a comparatively healthy colony, but Europeans suffer from a reduction of energy and an increased tendency to functional nervous disabilities of all kinds, due chiefly to the high humidity.'

On a sunny morning though, things seemed different. Escape from the Domain was just a question of turning the corner into the long steeply-sloping hill that was named Thakobau after the paramount chiefly family and led down to the waterfront and the main road to the town. Ahead, glittered the sea, miraculously, calmly blue inside the white furling tape of foam where the oncoming waves breasted the reef. In such weather the Viti-Levu coastline encircled the bay in a grape-coloured frieze of legendary peaks and indentations—Joske's Thumb, The Sleeping *Marama*, the Cockscombs, named by Captain Bligh in 1792. Before rain the thick bush of these slopes stood out in a brilliant green detail. Then under cloud the whole range of mountains seemed to recede behind one another, gauze-grey, and with an oddly flattened transparent effect like a pack of snapshot negatives. Rupert Brooke described them as 'the most fantastically shaped mountains in the world', reminding him of the coast of hell in Greek mythology. To Miss Gordon-Cumming, however, they merely recalled the hills of Ross-shire. 'Every afternoon we explore one or other in the Governor's charming boat, rowed by half a dozen brown beings with great fuzzy heads and wearing a becoming dress of white trimmed with crimson,' she wrote.

Four-square in front of this backdrop, the arched verandas of the Grand Pacific Hotel gleamed pink and white in the sunshine, as solidly elaborate as an Edwardian dessert. Its predecessor, the first Suva Hotel stood on the same site in the early 1870's when Suva was a fishing village surrounded by pampas grass, and the capital of the Fiji Group still at Levuka on the island of Ovalau. According to the Deputy Commandant of the Armed Native Constabulary at the time, a bluff walrus-moustached gentleman by the name of Brewster whose memoirs I had discovered in the Archives library—only competition could counteract the influence of Miss G.-C. and Mrs. S. I decided—it was little more than an ordinary Fijian house. It was built of cane and bamboo and thatched with sugar-cane leaves. There were no windows, but two entrances divided stable-fashion into two pieces so that the lower half could be closed against fowls and pigs. After a meal of salt beef and *dalo*, the weary pioneers would throw themselves down on beds of mats beneath a *taunamu* (mosquito shield) of red spotted handkerchiefs sewn into a rough tent. In those days it was held that ordinary netting was an insufficient protection against mosquitoes and sandflies.

Only a few years later, the traveller rising from his mats would be confronted by an astonishing spectacle on the horizon, in the shape of a large building painted a lurid orange-red. Unexpectedly enough, this flaming vision, ornately peaked and gabled, was Suva's first Government House. The culprit was a colour-blind architect who had performed his task during the absence of the occupier. 'Straitened means prevented my having the work done over again,' wrote the Governor, Des Voeux, irritably. 'So the flamboyant aspect of Government House remained as an apparent monument of our bad taste until the end of our time in Fiji.'

Now, it was the graceful white outlines of the nineteen-twenties model, an imitation of the Colombo Government House, that rose beyond the Botanical Gardens with their fan-palms, crimson bouganvillia and pagoda-like bandstand. No flag was flying from the mast. The new young Governor, Sir Derek Jakeway,whose dynamic brilliance had already disturbed the official dovecotes, was on a fact-finding tour of the islands with his charming wife. The imposing bulk of Government buildings opposite, grey and elephantine and waving a Union Jack in its trunk, added to the general air of patriarchal solidity. Between lay Albert Park, a deserted sweep of green on which the smell of wet, cut grass hung like incense in the sun. On Saturday afternoon there would be cricket here, to the quarter-chimes of the clock-tower behind and the tinkle of ice-cream carts threading their way through the crowds that watched from the shade of the great, pillared banyan trees.

How deceptively ordered the life of Suva seemed from the far end of the city on a morning like this, sedate capital of the South Seas rather than melting-pot of the Pacific. In the first shops the tourist goods were neatly stacked on display—Italian shoes, Siamese silver, Indonesian carvings. Typewriters chirped in second-storey windows, and from the entrance hall of the Fiji Broadcasting Commission's white stucco building came a snatch of a Mozart symphony. Even the Golden Dragon Nightclub was a respectably shuttered ghost of itself, presenting only a vista of yellow cakes and last year's plastic holly, where at night-time the local girls in beehive coiffures and lampshade skirts clustered at the foot of the neon-lit stairs to welcome the sailors, where posses of police roared up in jeeps to round up all drinking ladies not in possession of liquor permits, and the lacquer-haired, rainbow-shirted Paradise Five stumped doggedly on through 'Pennies From Heaven' beneath a notice that warned 'Please Do Not Use the Instruments'. This morning, the only announcement on view was a small poster stuck to the door. It read 'Saturday Dance. An Evening of Tropical Romance. Ties Essential'.

Outside the Town Hall placards were advertising a revivalist meeting of the Seventh-day Adventists. Next week would follow a concert rally of the Church of the Latter-day Saints.

Farther on, at his usual post outside the bookshop, the local prophet, a small bearded Fijian with the glint of a message in his eye, was distributing tracts. 'Last Call To Surrender! Last Great Judgement!' declared the sheet pressed into my hand.

'Thank you,' I said.

He smiled briskly, his eyes on the next passer-by.

It was the *ivi* tree that marked the boundary between the ordered and the haphazard. The *ivi* tree, embedded in a triangle of pavement at the junction of half a dozen busy streets, was one of the relics of old Suva. Long before Europeans came it had been worshipped and feared by generations of the local Fijians as a particularly powerful guardian of the *tevora* (devil spirits) who dwelt among the branches of trees and sprang out on the unwary passer-by at night. Around it, the famous Land Sales of 1880 were conducted when white settlers bid against each other, auction fashion, for strips of the new capital. Now it served as a meeting-place for elderly onlookers who liked to take their ease on the circular bench beneath. Bearded Sikhs, grizzled Fijian elders, Indian farmers in battered trilbies gathered to smoke and gossip, read a newspaper or simply gaze into space deaf to the traffic that rolled in stormy breakers around the island of the *ivi* tree. In his usual place on the starboard side sat an aged European of dignified appearance. With his white goatee, faded solar helmet and black umbrella, he was the prototype of a whole community of old gentlemen, venerable remittance men, retired officials, mysterious Rip Van Winkles of the South Seas, whom one glimpsed patrolling the seafront at regular hours, rocking themselves on the verandas of boarding-houses, turning the pages of last month's London papers in the public libraries, always with the same faintly reproachful air of shades returning to former haunts now changed beyond recall. As I passed, he accorded me his usual formal nod of recognition, then returned to his private thoughts.

Beyond the *ivi* tree, the sedate shop-lined esplanade split away into a tangle of crowded streets that, despite the Australian department stores and the flashy face-lifts to public buildings, still retained the ramshackle vitality of a settler town. Western-style saloon doors swung open on to bar-rooms that were cool and dark and smelt of beer. Chinese card-players in vests sat round on rickety balconies hung with washing. Small boys fished from punts in the narrow creek that ran past the backs of peeling houses and out to sea. Outside the jumble of small shops, selling tinned fruit and butcher's meat, cotton bedspreads, lamps and brooms, cheap talcum powder and white-rimmed sun-glasses and bales of Japanese taffeta, the pavements surged with a lavish mixture of people, slender Indian housewives in butterfly saris, billowing Fijian matrons barefoot beneath their long *sulus*, stout Tongans encased in ceremonial waist-mats, Chinese ladies doll-like in side-split tubes of shiny silk, round-faced Rotuman girls with plaits of thick black hair swinging at their waists and the sway-backed walk of island women.

Squeezed between the shops were the eating-houses—tin tureens of rice and curry in the windows and signboards announcing the Hasty-Tasty, Wing On Chan's, the Ka-Shine (Fijian slang for smart). Farther on came the Kava saloons, the flaking arcades of the poorer cinemas, and the barbers' shops where the Fijians sat to be fashionably crew-cut and the Indians pummelled and brilliantined.

This was the hunting-ground of the young tear-aways, embryo beatniks and Teddy boys, rebels without a cause or employment.

Slick, sulky and unsure, half a dozen of them leaned together in a shop doorway, their thumbs in the pockets of their skin-tight jeans, sweltering with the indifference of martyrs in their Marlon Brando jackets of fake fur and leather. They watched the passing shoppers beneath half-closed eyes with an odd mixture of intentness and apathy.

Then suddenly, there was the sea again, the masts of the trading schooners rising above the warehouse roofs, the smell of salt and sacking and copra overtaking the petrol fumes of the streets. From the far end of the wharf rumbled the strains of 'Soldiers of the Queen'. It was P. and O. day and the Fiji Military Forces Band, a dazzle of scarlet and white and yellow brass were serenading the tourists beneath the smoking battlements of the *Oriana.*

Any day of the week, any time of the day, Suva Market was the hub of the city's life, the focal-point that drew together all the life of the surrounding houses and shops, cafés and docks, even the outlying islands themselves. Outside, under the flame trees, elderly Indians in turbans and dhotis dispensed lemonade from the shade of vulturine black umbrellas. The pavement space around the doors was reserved for the crab-sellers, rough cheerful women from the coastal villages who sat cross-legged on mats against the wall, a fan in one hand, the other holding up for approval a garland of live crabs strung together with grass fibre.

'*Bula, marama!* You see big crab? *Vinaka, vinaka!*' It was good to step out of the sun into the patchwork twilight inside and find it so unchanged—dark faces crowded under a sackcloth awning, eyes and teeth gleaming, the flash of silver between pink-palmed hands. Among the jostle of bodies lay piled the hillocks and pyramids of vegetable flesh, no longer alive but still palpitating with colour, sheened with a faint sweat—all those subtly-planed surfaces of shining green and yellow, paws-paws and melons, mangoes and pineapples, clusters of coppery grapes, the scooped-out orange moons of pumpkins, and knotted together on the ground beneath the trestle tables, the more earthy things, yams, kasava and purple dalo, muscular shapes still bearded with soil.

In the middle of the market, where the sunlight sliced through a gap in the awning, the tables were laid out not with the necessities but the ornaments of everyday living, island jewellery, basket-ware, household decorations. These things had once been growing, but human hands had taken them up, cleaned, beaten, polished, woven, painted or chiselled them, transmitting to them a new life that was immune to the decays of the flesh and therefore to be cherished with a primaeval kind of envy. There were freckled cowrie shells, huge convolvulated conches, bracelets of tortoise-shell, seed-husk necklaces, filigree brooches of mother-of-pearl, reed platters and hampers, clumps of coral bunched together in frozen posies of violet and pink, creamy mats of braided rush fronds, lengths of papery *tapa* cloth beaten from the bark of mulberry trees and printed with branching archaic patterns of faded bronze and black that dappled the fibre as gently as light and shade.

There was always something one wanted to buy. I was just about to awaken an enormous Tongan lady, asleep on a mat under one of the tables, to ask for price of a turtle-shell bowl, when someone called out to me.

A young Fijian named Eroni (Aaron), a Government officer whom I knew well from my work at Broadcasting House, was beckoning me over to a stall near the door. He was standing with a group of some six other Fijians buying *yaggona.* All eyes were concentrated on the twig-like bundles of dried roots, which were being handed around in newspaper, the insignificant looking raw materials of a drink that represents the very heart of Fijian social life and custom.

Eroni looked up as I joined them, dapper in his official grey *sulu* and white shirt. 'There is someone present whom I think you would be interested to meet,' he said in his formal English. 'You have heard of Mr. Baker?'

'Of course.' Everyone had heard of Mr. Baker, a Victorian Wesleyan who in the eighteen-sixties had abruptly met his end in the wilds of Viti Levu, the only missionary to be killed on Fijian soil.

> '*Oh! dead is Mr. Baker,*
> *They killed him on the road*
> *And they ate him, boots and all!*'

sang the village children at the time. Which was, reputedly, just what happened, though the Fijians confessed themselves puzzled by the toughness of this portion of the missionary's anatomy despite continued cooking. 'Eat the boots of Mr. Baker!' was still a well-known taunt much resented by the people of the remote interior where the attack took place. So I refrained from adding this, and merely repeated, 'Of course.'

'Well,' continued Eroni, with a pause for effect, 'this is the great grandson of the man who killed Mr. Baker.'

He pushed forward the Fijian standing next to him, a stocky beetle-browed figure with the craggy features of those hill tribes whom the Fijians themselves called *tevora* because of their savageries in battle, their huge heads of hair and wild appearance. His hair was bushy but cropped, and he wore a pair of khaki shorts and a brightly patterned shirt. Genially, he removed a half-smoked cigar from his mouth and gave me a broad, jagged smile. There was a sociable murmur from the others as we shook hands.

'His English is very confined,' said Eroni. 'This is the first occasion on which he has been to Suva. He is still residing in the same village where Mr. Baker—er—met his end.'

This solved the problem of an opening gambit which had been defeating me since our introduction.

'Is there anything there to mark the spot, these days?' I asked.

Eroni repeated the question in Fijian. There was a brief deep-spoken response with an assured proprietorial air about it.

'He says there is a heap of stones.' Helpfully, he added, 'The axe is in the museum of course.'

'Does anyone really know why it happened though? Surely Europeans had trekked through those parts without harm by the 1860's.'

Eroni nodded. 'That is an established fact. The popular explanation is that he took the comb from the head of the chief in jest. As you know, in Fijian custom it is a very disgraceful occurrence even to touch the head of a chief.'

The Fijian clerk on his other side pursed his lips thoughtfully. 'A political murder, rather, I would say. They believed him to be an emissary of their enemies at Bau.'

'He broke the rule, you see,' suggested another young man in a formal *sulu*. 'In those days a missionary was never to pass beyond more than one heathen tribe at a time, and these people were the second or third in his path.'

The great-grandson of the slayer of Mr. Baker merely smiled to himself and replaced his cigar stump in the corner of his mouth.

'Well, now,' said Eroni. 'Some *yaggona* before we part?'

He turned to the stall-keeper, an elderly Fijian who produced from beneath the table a bowl full of the familiar milky-looking liquid. A coconut cup was dipped in and handed first to me. The queer minty tang caught the back of my throat as I swallowed, in a way I had almost forgotten—rhubarb and magnesia flavoured with sal volatile, was Miss Gordon-Cumming's characteristically Victorian analysis. There was the usual round of polite handclaps from the rest of the group, and from the circle of onlookers who had gathered beyond to see what kind of a party was in progress.

'You are going back into town?' he inquired. The cup had been refilled and passed round the others.

'I told him I was going out to Sawani to the cottage of a friend who said I might use it for writing.

'You will find the taxi rank just outside then.'

'Well, actually, I thought of going by bus——'

'By bus?' There was a disapproving note in his voice. 'You will find it very uncomfortable, I'm afraid. So hot. And crowded too. . . .'

His warnings followed me out to the door. I waved firmly and made my way over to the bus terminus. Being next to the market-place the crowds of shoppers and passengers overflowed into one another to form one big happy crowd in which any stray vehicles, signboards, seats or other conveniences were effectively submerged. No one seemed sure where my bus would arrive. A thin youth in steel spectacles and running shorts stepped out of the press.

'Follow me, mem-sahib!' he cried, weaving his way between an ice-cream stall and a curry-seller's gocart. 'See, mem-sahib?'

Against the pavement was drawn up an elongated tin box on wheels, bright blue in colour and battered-looking. The words Sawani Buss were painted across the chassis, tastefully wreathed in pink hibiscus. Through the front window appeared the head of the driver.

Slowly the procession of passengers lumbered aboard—stout housewives in flowered shifts, bonneted babies swinging from hammocks across their mother's shoulders, two youths entwined in a wrestling match, a grey-haired waddling grandmother, an ancient holy man in loincloth, topknot and beard, who dispensed the touch of sanctity on either side as he made his way to the back.

Meanwhile the cargo rose ever higher in the space around the gearbox. The base of the pile was a vast block of ice, rapidly melting, and on this reposed a stack of freshly-dug vegetables, half a banana tree, several coconuts, a dog in a basket, a bowl of gutted fish and a string of crabs, clicking ominously.

'Okay, folks?' called the driver. He wiped his face and hands with a duster, carefully replacing the frangipani behind his ear. 'Roger and over then!'

Round the first bend we swept and promptly from the driving window sprang a large, white, wooden hand attached to a string pulley. But the third bend proved too much for it and, detaching itself from the main body it lay in the roadway like some hideous amputation until retrieved and wedged back into position. Then off we were again with the broad feet of our pilot tapping out an infectious rhythm on the clutch pedals. One of the younger housewives brought out a guitar. Soon there was singing in the back and, according to the state of the road, radio music from the loudspeaker above the driving seat, sporadic like a dentist's drill.

Through each village, progress slowed down considerably. Beaming faces appeared beneath the palm-thatched eaves, the womenfolk left their yam patches with cries of welcome, naked infants came staggering up wet and gleaming from the village pump. There were parcels to be delivered, messages to be shouted out, social contacts to be made, perhaps even some last-minute shopping to be done at the Chinese store. Window tarpaulins flapping (there had been an unexpected thunderstorm) we roared up to my own stop.

'Sawani turning!'

'She get off here!' cried a dozen helpful voices. Three more people pulled the bell-string which ran down the length of the bus and the grandmother gave me a friendly grip as I made my descent.

Silence fell like a cool hand. I turned to climb the shady side of the steep lane that led to the cottage. A faint breeze ruffled the bamboo thickets on either side. There was the crunch of stones under my feet, a tiny insect voice calling far away across the valley, another replying. Then, round the bend at the top, was the cottage.

It had been built by the Forestry Department and looked like a cross between a log cabin and a Swiss chalet on stilts. A palisade of purple orchids grew six feet high around it, and ranks of pine-like trees that undulated down into the lap of the valley from the chain of mountain peaks on either side. In the distance, the sea spilled on to the land in petal-shaped bays and silvery estuaries, twining away under the hills like those mysterious rivers in the background of medieval Italian paintings. On the very farthest horizon, where the sea and sky met in a great, unbroken, curving rim, a pair of islands glittered in the blue, beautiful as a mirage and as unattainable, the perfect image of the old European dream of a South Seas paradise.

Inside the cottage, everything was just as Peter had left it before setting off for the bush in his Land-Rover at first light. Peter, who had become one of our closest friends in Fiji, was an ex-Oxford administrative officer in his early thirties with an unconventional pre-Service career as repertory actor, beach photographer and farm labourer. The uninhibitedness of his background, combined a magnetic capacity for enthusiasm, an uncanny gift for mimicry (and hence languages), and the mulish bluntness of a Yorkshireman, had made him the *enfant terrible* of Government circles and the joy of the Fijians. On the sofa lay a discarded khaki jacket, his guitar and the scribbled notebook in which he was making a collection of old Fijian songs and chants. The French stage photographs which accompanied him everywhere had been tin-tacked haphazard across the ceiling. The bust of Beethoven with the broken nose brooded from its usual post on the bookcase, amongst the unlikely clutter of *tapa*-cloth, *yaggona* bowls, whale's teeth and other relics of his travels round the islands. Ignoring, in a thoroughly Smythe-like way, the rat I met face to face inside the bureau, I went out on to the veranda.

On this eyrie-like ledge of glass and wood I perched myself at a rickety table, immediately felt I had never been away and wrote spasmodically for the rest of the day, with a break for a picnic lunch out of the fridge. Once it rained, the shadow of the storm clouds trailing across the valley like the hem of a cloak, lifting again with a shaft of saffron-coloured light that flooded the scene with a theatrical, sullen brilliance. Once a hawk came circling down on a nest in the trees a hand's reach out of the window. There was a flurry of golden-brown wings and away he sailed, a small drooping object carefully secured between his talons.

Then suddenly it was time to leave. As I walked down the hill again, the tide of sunset shrank to a single line of gold behind the stencilled trees. Far away, along the edge of the coast, the first lights trembled in unknown villages.

3

A Pride of Chiefs

'So it rather appears we may be a little late arriving at your place,' said the silky, donnish voice at the other end of the telephone. 'Will that be inconvenient at all?'

'Not in the least, Ratu Edward.' Ted Thakabau he might be to his fellow ex-officers at the Defence Club, but the romantic in me rebelled at such de-glamourizing processes. Besides, the chiefly title and full name seemed more than due where a great-grandson of the first King of Fiji was concerned. 'You see, we shall be there too,' I went on.

'Excellent, excellent. In that case we can all make our departures together. Until this evening then.'

The occasion was a hastily convened reception in honour of the members of the latest Commission of Inquiry from London. The problematic but peaceful islands of Fiji—dubbed by the English Press as the colony that wanted to stay dependent—provided a natural haven for these official investigators into anything and everything, from the rhinoceros-beetle scourge, and the banana output, to industrial expansion and constitutional development.

After the party, Ratu Edward together with Ratu Penaia Ganilau, another leading chief and member of the Legislative Council, and his wife Adi Laisa, were due to have dinner with us. Before leaving, I warned Lolo that it would be a late meal. There was a mounting air of drama in the kitchen where half a dozen extra friends and relations were squatting cross-legged in a circle importantly opening up tins and peeling vegetables.

Wiping her hands on her hips, Lolo advanced towards me with an intense expression. 'The serving the dinner, *marama*——' she began for the third time that day.

For the third time I chimed in brightly, 'The usual way, Lo. It will be quite all right.' Fijian custom singles out passing behind a chief and standing while he sits, as the two most serious breaches of etiquette by a commoner. 'Dinner *Vaka-Peritania* not *vaka-Viti!* (Fijian style) Lolo,' I told her.

A wave of giggles from the circle of assistants encouraged me. 'Don't worry. Tiu will be with you to help.' I nodded towards the apparition that had just appeared in the doorway, snowy-headed under a special pre-party application of powdered lime, the local bleach, and wringing its hands in an agony of anticipation.

Lo wavered. 'What about if we put the food on the table before, then go 'way quick?' she suggested. But it was a last half-hearted stand. 'No?'

'No.'

Lolo compressed her lips but nodded her head, and so with a more or less clear conscience we left.

The party was being given by Ratu Mara, who with Ratu Edward and Ratu Penaia formed the central apex of that rigid and complex structure of hierarchal power which reigns in Fiji, with Ratu George Thakobau, a cousin of Ratu Edward, as the paramount leader.

As we drove out to Ratu Mara's house, I was recalling my first encounter with the chiefly side of Fijian life. We were driving along the same road to attend the lying-in-state of Fiji's great man of modern times, the late Ratu Sir Lala Sukuna, also a direct descendant of Thakobau, who had in his lifetime been called to the Bar of the Middle Temple, awarded the Médaille Militaire for service with the French Foreign Legion in the First World War, appointed as an adviser to the Trusteeship Council of the United Nations, finally becoming Secretary for Fijian Affairs and Speaker of the Legislative Council.

Having arrived in Fiji only a few weeks before, I felt nervous and ignorant as we turned in towards the big double-storey house on the hill where he had spent the last years of his life. On each side of the driveway a Fijian warrior stood guard in a kilt of scarlet leaves, a war club over his shoulder, his upper features ceremonially masked in black paint for mourning. Leaving the car, we joined the stream of European visitors who were making their way up to the house formally gloved and hatted in the amber glow of late afternoon. Inside the main door was a great dim room, crowded with people. The authoritative power of the emotion that weighted the air cancelled out one's resolution to make mental notes as something cheap and insignificant. I was conscious only of a soft moaning and sighing; of the heavy scent of sandalwood mingled with coconut oil and thousands of flowers; of a low bier covered with fine mats around which sat many ladies in black whose slow-moving fans seemed to fill the room like the flutter of birds' wings. A single detail burned itself on my mind's eye—the parrots' feathers, incongruously bright, with which the mats were fringed in the traditional style, rarely seen nowadays. As instructed, I stooped and laid my bunch of gardenias among the massed petals and leaves that surged from wall to wall of the long room. Then we passed on between the mourners and out again by a side entrance. The sun had set, the light was fading. Through the open door of an outhouse came the smell of cooking, the bustle of servants preparing the evening meal. In a circle under a mango tree sat the conch blowers, their oiled backs bulging as they raised the great curved shells to their lips. The owl-like hooting followed us down the hill, like a message from the past, melancholy, antique, mysterious.

It all seemed very remote from the scene on which we were arriving—laughter and the clink of glasses on brightly lit verandas.

'Good evening!' called a soft voice from the front steps. Silhouetted against the doorway, the tall, statuesque figure of Adi Lala, Ratu Mara's wife, stepped forward to welcome us, her halo of black hair glinting under the light. A beautiful woman in her late twenties, her natural dignity had acquired a new gloss of sophistication since their recent stay in London. But beneath her *chic* cocktail frock, she still wore the formal ankle-length *sulu* of black silk, and her smile as she squeezed my hand was as unrepressed as ever.

'Ratu Edward is telling one of his stories,' she murmured, leading us in. From the doorway, a familiar sight met our eyes. In the centre of the crowded room, surrounded by a spellbound circle, a superbly elegant middle-aged man in a pearl-grey jacket and *sulu* was discoursing in a low voice to his audience. Everything about him exuded a subtle aura of distinction, from the way he clasped his whisky-glass, the thumb curved to the rim, to the wide Windsor knot of his tie. As he spoke his face remained solemn, with its high bronzed dome of a forehead, its long carved upper lip and sly slant-lidded eyes, but his free hand wore an eloquent accompaniment of its own.

'This lady, you see, wanted to know what exactly was my nationality,' he was saying. 'So I replied, part Fijian and part Scottish.'

There was a preliminary giggle from some of the audience.

'Scottish?' the lady exclaimed. 'Yes,' I told her. 'You see, in my great-grandfather's time a large number of Scottish missionaries arrived in Fiji and apparently they made quite a change from pork.' He paused to allow some of the amusement to subside, then with perfect timing added gracefully, 'Perhaps I should have said Scottish by absorption.'

At the subsequent burst of laughter two other remarkable-looking Fijians joined the circle. One was our host, Ratu Mara, a younger man, immensely tall, with noble, prominent features, horn-rimmed glasses and a slight stoop that gave him a questing, intellectual air. An entirely different type was the other figure, whose massive build and imperial, twinkling glance alone would have proclaimed him a chief apart from his fine head and rugged good looks. This was Ratu Penaia who during the war in Malaya had commanded the First Fiji Battalion, and was now a *Roko Tui* or provincial commissioner with the Fijian Affairs Board.

Seeing them afresh like this, standing shoulder to shoulder for a few moments, I was struck by the impression of Olympic panache and power they gave out. Together they had the effect of making the European men alongside them look strangely puny and unfinished, a sort of rejected first draft for humanity, and beside those bare, muscular calves protruding beneath kilt-like *sulus*, trousers became a grotesque quirk of some outdated fashion. I thought of Britton, one of the first Australian newspaper correspondents to tour the islands, who wrote of the chiefs in the 1870's, 'Their gait is something to marvel at, and the European in walking with them is apt to wonder why he ever allowed tailors to make such a guy of him.'

Pressed to 'tell the one about the menu,' Ratu Edward had embarked upon another story.

'It's a very small thing,' he murmured first with infinite finesse.

The circle of faces closed in eagerly like children's at this time-honoured introduction.

He paused and with a slow hieratic gesture held up one hand as a conductor gathers together his orchestra. It was a very beautiful hand, lean and shapely, with the glimmer of a pale blue stone on the smallest of the long upturning fingers.

'It was on board ship while I was travelling to Europe. I had already been introduced as the Cannibal King. I felt *something* was expected of me. So—dinner the first night. The steward hands me the menu. I read it right through and I ask him,"Is this all you have?"

' "Yes, sir," he replies. "It really looks a little dull," I say. "Also I am rather hungry. Kindly bring me the passenger list instead!" '

A curved and gleaming smile slowly unpeeled itself, like some delicious tropical fruit, in time with his audience's laughter.

'Talking about menus,' remarked a new-comer to the group, a very stout Tongan gentleman encased from thigh to chest over his *sulu* in a traditional waist-mat, the raggedness of which indicated the wearer's aristocratic status. A respectful hush fell. 'Reminds me', he went on, 'of the doctor in England I consulted about dieting. From now onwards only one potato a day was his order. But in Tonga we don't eat potatoes, we eat yams, I told him. "Very well then," he replied, "from now onwards only one yam a day!" '

'I don't quite——' whispered a fair thin lady, a new-comer to Fiji.

'What? Never seen a yam?' cried her neighbour, shaping with his hands the outline of a gigantic tuber. 'Live and learn, don't you?'

The Tongan gentleman had moved out on to the veranda a tall elegant woman in a brocade sheath at his side. I asked a part-Tongan friend who he was.

'It's Queen Salote's son, Prince Tungi,' said my friend, an exceptionally intelligent and attractive woman, wife of a senior Government official and a granddaughter of an English magistrate who married a Tongan lady of noble birth soon after his arrival in the islands. 'He is the Prime Minister. And that's his wife, Princess Mata'aho.'

'Mata-aho.' One always repeated the Polynesian names simply for the sake of hearing again the prettiness of the sound.

'It means Eye of the Dawn.'

A familiar voice broke in from behind.

'Tiuné!'

Only one person I knew called me by this Fijian version of my name. Turning, I was enveloped by the stately presence of Adi

Laisa, the wife of Ratu Penaia and his perfect match. With her splendidly ample physique, rich exuberant laugh and comely features, she looked like the personification of a Fijian Goddess of Plenty. Warmly she took both my hands in hers and cried, 'Welcome back!'

There was a burst of drumming from outside, then the lapping of guitars. We went out together. On the grass in a bronze pool of reflected light, sat a group of young women in the fringed leaf skirts of Lau, Fiji's easternmost group of islands and the home of Ratu Mara's ancestors. Behind them were crouched the musicians, three with guitars, one with a long wooden *lali-drum*. Almost immediately, the women began to sing a low simple, repetitive melody, dense with the descant and counter-melodies of the contraltos. As they sang they rocked gently from their hips, their flower garlands swaying, their eyes lowered and hands in their laps, but made no other movements, for this was simply a musical entertainment not an action *meke*.

When we left, the choir was still singing, the last half of the party bathed in the soporific atmosphere of the island music. Back at home, over dinner, we talked about conversations and encounters at the party.

'I noticed you came in very firmly about Fiji's loyalty to Britain,' I said, referring to a dialogue between Ratu Penaia and the visiting official.

A massive fist was brought down on the table. 'It's all this United Nations business! Questions raised, protests made! What do they know about us there? I think they imagine we are all slaves sold in chains! It's about time they realized that what we want is not separation, but a permanent link with Britain.'

At that moment Lolo appeared in the passage-way with her tray. As she nerved herself to sidle up to Ratu Edward, the situation was resolved by the guest of honour suavely turning round himself to hand up his empty plate and announcing to her with a sly smile, 'If the next course is as good as that, I'm going to take her away to cook for me!'

There was a general laughter, though my own relief was mingled with a slight sinking feeling. If Ratu Edward were, in fact, to ask her to join his household, no European appeals on earth could prevent her acquiescing to this accolade. However, he winked at me reassuringly round the candles and went on to inquire her name and her province. Lolo departed with a look of bridling delight and returned beaming with the main course.

Apart from Ratu Penaia's summons to Vuniani for a dish of fresh-picked chillis from the garden, the rest of dinner passed without incident. Over coffee Ratu Mara and Adi Lala arrived as they had promised to do when their guests had left, and conversation turned to the days when all three men were up at Oxford together. It was just after the war and rationing was still in force.

'I had to have about six mid-morning snacks before I was fit to attend lectures,' groaned Ratu Penaia. 'I nearly died of starvation, I can tell you.'

'And the cold!' Ratu Edward adopted the muffled attitude of a Polar explorer. 'Every morning I'd stick my hand out of the window from my bed and if it was still snowing I'd send Penaia to sign my name for me.'

'What about the ceilings?' Ratu Mara exclaimed. 'They were attic rooms and so we were all in a permanent position of *tu-lo*!' Everyone roared. *Tu-lo* is the phrase—excuse me—used by a commoner as he stoops to pass a chief. Ratu Edward inserted a quick cameo sketch of the three Fijian giants crouching in and out of dwarf-like doors.

'Remember trying to climb the walls when we'd been locked out? We would choose the highest part, of course!'

'And the beer coming up in shaving jugs from the King's Arms?' Ratu Penaia sighed. A rich air of nostalgia settled over the group.

'What about the pear tree?' demanded Ratu Mara.

They started to rock again. 'We were so hungry!' Rata Penaia was explaining. 'There was a pear tree in the middle of the quadrangle and I climbed up one night to try and get some ripe ones. Ratu Edward kept watch at the bottom——'

Ratu Mara sprang to his feet. 'And I suddenly shouted from the top window in a great voice, "*E duae mai butakotha tiko na pea!*' ("Someone's stealing the pears!").'

'I'd fallen half-way down before I realized there was only one person it could be!' cried Ratu Penaia.

Still laughing, everyone took their departure.

'Don't forget your promise, Tiune!' called Adi Laisa from the car.

It was unlikely I would. She and Ratu Penaia had asked me to stay with them the first week of the following month at their house on the island of Taveuni.

Before sleeping I opened Miss Gordon-Cumming's book, now relegated to the bedside table but as maddeningly hypnotic as ever. 'We have had a good many visits lately from different chiefs,' I read, 'several of whom have come to formal dinners and have got through the ordeal in the most creditable manner. I should think that sitting on chairs for two hours, during a long series of courses of strange dishes, eaten with unwanted knives and forks must be very trying to them; but they are so well-bred that they never allow themselves to appear bored, nor do they make any mistakes—and of course the Fijian servants are on the alert to help them out of any dilemma. Besides, at least one of the Governor's interpreters is always of the party. . . .'

4

Passage from India

We sat on wooden benches in an open field, compressed between two layers of heat—overhead the steady afternoon sun, at our feet a pitful of glowing cinders. England was now several weeks behind me and this was the day of the Firewalking Ceremony, held once a year by a sect of the southern Indian Hindus in Suva. Even at a distance of three or four yards the long bed of burning charcoal over which the devotees were to walk, radiated a temperature that licked at the faces of the spectators, the invited officials in the front rows, the tourists with their cameras behind them. At the back, hundreds of Indians were still pouring in from the roadway. There were wiry little women in faded saris, holy men in dhotis and turbans, intense-looking, brilliantined youths in slacks and tee-shirts, and school-girls in pink school dresses and gold ear-rings with arms like antennae, huge febrile eyes and bootlace plaits that dwindled away at waist level in a last trickle of drained energy. Here and there, a group of Fijians laughed and jostled with mock-rounded eyes to see above the heads of the crowd.

'Of course these race divisions are gradually disappearing,' said the Indian politician sitting next to me, a Buddha-faced man in a blue pin-stripe suit. 'I, for example, think of myself not as an Indian but as a Fijian,' he went on, placing a surprisingly small, well-shaped hand on his left breast pocket. 'Our grandfathers came here as coolies. Today we form the majority of the population. And when people ask me which race is to take over the leadership of the country—eventually, that is of course—I say to them never mind who leads as long as we make progress together. We must not be rivals. We must be partners.'

With a frown he waved away a persistent small boy selling monkey nuts and roasted corn. From the direction of the temple in a far corner of the field a succession of drumbeats could be heard, not the aggressive thud of a European drum and stick, but the light, hollow patter, like the beginning of a rainstorm, of fingers and palms against tautened goatskin. But all that could be seen through the crowds was the small putty-coloured dome of the temple roof.

The heat seemed to increase with every minute. Among the ladies fans appeared, and some of the men mopped their faces with crumpled handkerchiefs. It was already half an hour past the advertised time of commencement. When I mentioned this to my companion, he nodded with a cursory smile and continued, 'The only way to achieve this unity is for Government to put into effect a planned policy of integration. They're always talking about it but nothing is actually done. It must start at the very lowest level with multi-racial primary schools. This is very important. Integration. It's the only sensible prospect.'

'Even to the extent of inter-marriages?' I asked.

'But, of course.'

Faintly from the temple there was the sound of singing, the high-pitched chanting of southern India that hovered round the drums in a melancholy, gnat-like counterpoint. At the same time something small and brightly coloured came bobbing and wavering above the heads of the spectators. In the distance it looked startlingly like a human figure. Then through a lane in the crowd appeared a small wrinkled man in a white dhoti, carrying on his head a bronze vessel full of leaves, and following him, four younger men who bore on their shoulders the plaster image of a doll-faced goddess shrouded in salmon-coloured silk.

'That is Maha Mari,' murmured the politician. 'They worship her.'

Behind the priest and his attendants came shuffling a long line of haggard-looking men, naked to the waist, their hair dishevelled. Garlands of wild marigolds, the sacred flower of the goddess, swung from their shoulders, the faint acrid scent tingeing the smell of smoke from the fire. Tumeric powder stained their bodies and faces, yellow as pollen. From a distance it gave them the strangely metallic look of images. It was only as they filed past that one saw with a shock the mutilations they had inflicted upon themselves. Lips and cheeks were skewered with small steel tridents, and several men had the loose skin of their backs and arms pierced by more of these ceremonial barbs. There seemed, at this stage, to be no bleeding from the wounds. Sinisterly, one was reminded of the wax effigies of medieval magic, stuck with pins.

One behind the other the devotees circled the pit, their hands joined in prayer, their eyes dilated and fixed before them like sleep-walkers or men in a state of trance. Heat shimmered in the air above the fire. A current of tension ran through the whole mass of waiting people. Even the politician was silent. The procession had come full circle to the top of the pit once more. The attendants carrying the Goddess drew back. Suddenly, unbelievably, the priest stepped down on to the red coals. There was the sound of indrawn breath among the onlookers as though an unbearable pain had been transferred. Lightly, on bare soles, he started to walk down the length of the pit the vessel swaying on his head, supported by one hand. Still keeping their order the others followed him. There was no change of expression on their faces, no faltering in the rhythm of that steady, gliding walk as one by one they forded the fiery stream. One by one they returned along the bank to repeat the feat and then again until, as is the way with such things, an air of suspended disbelief settled over the audience. Within minutes the sight seemed almost normal.

Then as suddenly it was over. The last walker stepped out on to the grass. In an anti-climax of excitement, they stood together at the far end as though dazed. Some of the nervous exaltation had dropped away from them. Transformed again into ordinary beings, they sweated and shivered slightly in their tattered waistcloths. Yet still there was no gesture of communication between them, nor sign of awareness of the circle of watchers beyond. Each man seemed as remote from the outer world as he was from the sensations of his own body.

It was the reappearance of the goddess and her attendants that brought them to life again. The next minute they were once more in procession and moving towards the shade of the roadway that led to the next Indian settlement. Once more the goatskin drums and the high-strung chanting throbbed and whined then faded away, alien sounds under the breadfruit trees.

Someone threw water in hissing bucketfuls over the remains of the fire. Around me people were getting up to leave, wrapping up the occasion with the familiar comments:

'They say they're drugged, you know, or hypnotized.'

'Of course, an Indian's feet are pretty tough anyway.'

'And then I expect they put on special lotions and so forth first. Even so . . .'

'Saw the rope trick done once—on board ship. . . .'

There was no comment from my neighbour. With the rest of the crowd he had melted back into the great flux of Fiji's Indian life with its 200,000 population, undreamed-of heirs, fire-walkers and politicians alike, of those small bands of labourers brought over in sailing ships in the last years of the nineteenth century. Even as early as the 1870's labour had become one of the vexed problems of the expanding new colony. The ships that plied between the neighbouring Melanesian groups were bringing back ever smaller numbers of volunteers for plantation work and Miss Gordon-Cumming reported (as though discussing a shortage of flour or sugar), 'It is probable that arrangements will shortly be made for importing a large supply of Hindoo coolies from Calcutta, a measure which does not at present meet with cordial welcome as, of course, the cost of transporting them to and fro will add materially to the expenses of the planters who engage them.'

A little later, Deputy Commandant Brewster was noting blandly, 'The Indians have now added considerably to the comforts of the British colonists who are now able to enjoy the services of first-class cooks and domestic servants.'

Unobtrusively, between these two personal observations, had slipped the seeds of an invasion, a bloodless revolution almost, that was to change the whole face of Fiji. In 1879, after a nightmare voyage stricken with cholera and smallpox, 481 immigrants anchored off Levuka in the sailing ship *Leonidas*. Every year more followed with some, such as the inmates of the *Syria* in 1884, enduring not only illness and disease but storm and shipwreck on Fiji's treacherous reefs at the end of the ten-week passage. Although not the 'sweepings of the streets' as is often stated, the immigrants were certainly of the labouring classes, many of them agricultural in origin. The horniness of their hands, examined by immigration officials at Calcutta and Madras, was in fact one of the necessary passports to the plantations of South Seas.

Herded together to live in communal lines on a wage of a shilling a day, these new-comers lost even the small respect accorded them in their hereditary setting and were automatically accorded the lowest place in the social order of Fiji. The normal rites of caste and family life had already been sacrificed to come here. Now the traditional religious ceremonies had to be either abandoned or abbreviated. Gone were the daily household sacrifices. Gone, too, the temples where prayers and offerings could be made. Whatever the difficulties though, the festivals of Muharram and Holi were always celebrated and feasts given out of contributions per head by the immigrants. The fire-walking ceremony I had just seen was a fragmentary witness of the stubborn religious constancy which eventually erected temples for its people, Hindu, Sikh and Muslim, in every Indian settlement. For despite the hardships of life in the lines, few took advantage of the free return passage to India to which they were entitled by Government after ten years' residence in the colony. Repatriation would have also involved the expenses and humiliations of ritual rehabilitation and an often greater degree of personal poverty. Instead, with the same tenacity with which they preserved their customs, they set about improving their material circumstances.

Today, although most of Fiji's Indians are tenant canegrowers for the Colonial Sugar Refining Company, small holders of plots leased outside the Fijian land reserves, or storekeepers and taxi-drivers in town and village, there is also a large and growing intelligentsia—doctors and dentists, lawyers and business men.

In 1936 the Indian people achieved equal representation with the Europeans and Fijians in the Legislature when the Constitution was enlarged by the addition of two nominated members to the three elected ones already provided for. By this time the population mark had leaped to 85,000, nearly 43 per cent of the total population. By 1956, on its way up to today's figure, the score reached well over 169,000.

The familiarity of certain grievances, the tedium of the endless dinner-table discussions around the colony's problems, might for me have translated the people themselves into so many lifeless statistics. Then, too, there was always the possibility that the barriers of language and differing social customs might have reduced them still further to shadowy background figures in one's experience of Fiji. The intense emotionalism of the Fire-walking Ceremony though had stripped away these facades. The statistics breathed; the shadows solidified. I was curious to see, if possible, the temple and the priest of a religion that could still inspire its followers to the ancient excesses of devotion so far from home.

'I shall show them you at a later day,' offered Mr. Lal, a scholarly Indian with a brisk dignity of manner, who was an official of the Magistrate's Court.

And so, at a later date, we drove out in Mr. Lal's Morris Oxford through the hinterland of Suva, a labyrinth of narrow muddy roads lined with matchbox bungalows gaily daubed in sari colours, mauves and greens and apricot yellows, homes of the city's white-shirted army of clerks and shop assistants. Outside one of these Mr. Lal drew up and got out to look for our guide. In the open doorway an old Fijian man, no doubt brought to live in the town by an ambitious young family, sat on the floor, legs outstretched and back to the wall, listening intently with closed eyes to a programme of village songs on the radio. A young part-European woman wandered out on to the next-door veranda in a trailing *muu-muu*, hairbrush in hand, to watch our progress. Deep in magpie chatter, two Indian ladies sailed past with shopping baskets, the white gauze draperies of their widowhood billowing behind.

Across the road Mr. Lal was talking to a lean, moustached Indian in a ragged shirt and dhoti who was leading two bullocks on a rope. Nodding rapidly, the man wrapped the rope round a nearby tree stump and, leaving the bullocks on the grass verge, followed Mr. Lal over to the car.

'He was taking them to plough,' Mr. Lal explained as they both got in. 'But first he will come and show us the temple. He is an assistant priest.'

'Where do you plough?' I asked him.

The owner of the bullocks bowed from the back seat with a dignified smile and waved the question to Mr. Lal.

'He has a field about half a mile away. At night-time he keeps them in his garden.' He pointed to a corrugated iron shed alongside one of the matchbox bungalows. We drove on for a few hundred yards.

'Stop here, Pandit,' directed our guide, bestowing on Mr. Lal the well-deserved title of Learned Man.

We turned into a familiar field, now rain-sodden and deserted.

At the far end was a school building of some kind and alongside it rose the domed roof of the temple.

We got out and walked through the puddles towards a large rectangular depression in the grass. Clumps of wild marigolds were already springing up between the cinders. Quite close was a bamboo flagstaff from which hung a ragged pink square embroidered with national symbols. Flanking it on either side a tall trident of rough iron was embedded in the ground, a large-scale replica of the forks thrust into the flesh of the fire-walkers. Our guide murmured something in Mr. Lal's ear.

'The three prongs stand for the three aspects of God,' Mr. Lal observed. 'The Creator, the Preserver and the Redeemer of the World.'

At the base of the flagstaff the rough stone plinth had been sprinkled with tumeric powder.

'As you will know, it is the principal ingredient for the worship of the Goddess Kali, who is also the Goddess Maha Mari of the fire-walkers.'

We turned to find waiting for us on the steps of the temple, a bent, old man whom I recognized as the priest of the procession. Our guide approached him in an attitude of respect, spoke a few brief words of introduction then unobtrusively took his leave to return to his bullocks.

'The shoes must be removed,' said Mr. Lal, as we paused outside the arched doorway. 'It is the leather that is against custom.' He scrutinized with a darting, anxious glance my waist and wrist, then decreed me innocent with a nod. The priest remained silent, watching us with folded arms and inclined head. His small, nut-cracker face was composed, expressionless, whorled with infinite wrinkles. Yellow against the brown, a small gold stud glinted in the lobe of each ear. A wisp of grey hair had detached itself from the grandmotherly knob at the back of his head. Replacing the end of his white muslin shawl over his shoulder, he gravely turned and led the way in.

We stepped down into a dim stone-flagged room that was a kind of closed courtyard to a smaller chamber beyond. Out of the musty-smelling twilight loomed two life-sized figures of Hindu mythology painted on either side of the dividing arch, as though guarding the entrance to an inner sanctum. On the right stood Lakshmi, the

Goddess of Prosperity, adorned with lotus flowers, a swan behind her. On the left, the sinister elephant-headed figure of Ganesh the Fortune-Teller uncoiled itself out of the painted mortar.

'I can give you literature explaining all these things,' murmured Mr. Lal quickly as we passed through, the stone floor strangely cold underfoot.

The inner room was small, dark and crammed with the impedimenta of worship. In a central niche of the far wall was the altar, a pyramid of rough ledges piled with offerings of bananas, coconuts, marigolds in empty milk-powder tins, bowls of tumeric powder, camphor and yellow *tilak*. A faint odour of decay mingled with the scent of incense-sticks smoking in brass jars and the homely smell of ghee from the open wick-lamp that flickered at the base of the altar.

'It is the Everlasting Light,' said Mr. Lal. 'It never goes out.'

On either side of the altar lining the walls, stood the idols, small dusty figures crudely painted with the solemn black-browed faces of peasant brides. Earthly incarnations of Maha Shakti, mother of all things, The Supreme Power, each one was draped in scarecrow remnants of chiffon and taffeta and lovingly adorned with cheap jewellery. To a European there was a disturbing, almost malignant air about that roomful of stiffly-gesturing plaster dolls, a queer mixture of disused attic and Madame Tussauds, laced with purely Oriental hints of excess, lust and cruelty, the necklaces of tiny skulls, bloodstained knives wielded by serpentine arms, and curly crimson mouths, implacably smiling.

I moved closer then stopped. The draperies of the nearest goddess had seemed to stir. Very quietly and decorously, a small grey shape emerged beneath the hemline of her robe and pattering rapidly across the intervening plain of flagstones disappeared again among the skirts of the neighbouring deity. After a minute or so, another mouse head peeped out from beneath the torn gold fringing but, sniffing strangers, popped inside again. Absurdly, some lines from a poem by Suckling sprang to my mind:

Her feet beneath her petticoat
Like little mice stole in and out
As if they feared the light. . . .

As we stood in silence fresh families, gaining courage, appeared from other corners and nimbly scaled the altar ledges. There was no comment from either of my companions about these tenants who, unlike the proverbial church mice of England, obviously fared well on the provisions left by pious worshippers.

Standing beneath the prayer bell that hung on a frayed rope from the ceiling, the old man spoke for the first time.

'Kali, Amba, Draupadi, Lalita,' he intoned quaveringly, nodding to each goddess in turn.

I told Mr. Lal that if it was permitted I would like to speak to the priest of the Fire-walking Ceremony itself. For example, had he experienced any physical sensations at all as he walked across the pit?

There was an interlude of liquid Hindi dialogue interwoven with rapid gestures. After a few minutes Mr. Lal reported, 'He feels nothing. He is not burnt at all. His spirit is not on this earth, you see. To walk the fire is a proof of devotion.'

'Do any of the other walkers feel pain?'

An expression of distaste crumpled the old man's face as he received this question. 'Only if he has broken the conditions,' was his reply.

'And there are many conditions?'

'For ten days before the walking these are the vows of purification to be kept,' Mr. Lal told me between the bubbling Hindi. 'There is health of body—illness is a defilement—health of mind and spirit—no guilt must block the Light—continence, ritual bathing, Yoga exercises, and sleep to be taken on the ground, stripped to the waist and all those days the walkers must live within the temple.'

I wanted to know who were the walkers. Were they holy men or ordinary people?

'Ordinary people from all walks of life. They are called *Shaktas*. There are farmers, engineers, students, peasants, Civil Servants, all members of the sect. Sometimes children walk, and old women. Sometimes infants are carried in their father's arms.'

'It is their faith that protects them?'

The old man nodded, then after a pause added a few slow, careful sentences to Mr. Lal.

'At times the *shakta* might be sufficiently aware of the heat to run rather than walk. It all depends on the degree of devotion. At all times, though, if there has been no defilement, the feet do not blister. Neither do clothes burn that hang close to the fire. You may not know that it is defilement simply for a *shakta* to be touched beforehand by one who has not undergone purification.'

Through Mr. Lal I learned that many things were laid in the pit according to ritual before the lighting of the fire—fresh limes, dry mango sticks, thousands of prayers written on small scraps of paper, blocks of camphor (symbols of the sun and therefore of purity) and finally warm butter. The first flames were started with the sacred firebowl from the temple, never with matches, and then dogo wood was piled on to feed the blaze. About 40 tons of wood were used which burned for some sixteen hours. It was these embers that the next day were raked to a red-hot consistency for the walkers.

The holy vessel carried by the priest, I was told, was called a *Khalasam.* It contained water, the leaves of the neeb and mango trees, and a peeled coconut pierced by a trident. The pot symbolized the body, the water life, and the trident, once were the three attributes of Universal Power.

'If the Khalasam had been spilt,' said Mr. Lal, 'the whole ceremony would have been defiled and every walker would have gone mad or died within the year. I can give you literature on these things,' he added consolingly, as we turned to leave.

Out in the sunshine we donned our shoes again. Through Mr. Lal I made my thanks to the priest and said I looked forward to seeing him walk the fire once more in a year's time. The old man received this with a smile but shook his head gently and added something half to himself.

'He says', translated Mr. Lal, 'that by then he hopes to be walking in Paradise.'

Back again in the car, we drove back towards the city. But after a mile or so Mr. Lal drew up outside a white arched gateway. 'With your permission I should like to show you a somewhat different temple before we return.'

A gang of Indian children squatting on the pavement over a game of marbles scrambled to their feet and crowded round us as we passed through the entrance. Inside a long flight of shallow steps led up to an imposing classical facade with pillars of ice-cream pink and white set on a smoothly-mown green hill.

'This is the Sikh temple,' said Mr. Lal, leading the way two at a time between the white spidery blooms of wild lilies that bordered the path. About half-way up, I became aware of a visionary figure

A typical sheltered bay

Fishing boats and an island
–one of Fiji's three hundred

The Honourable Ratu Edward Thakobau, O.B.E., M.C.

watching our pilgrims' progress from the topmost step. On level ground at last I drew breath and found myself confronted by the piercing gaze of reincarnation from the Old Testament. Between the snowy turrets of a great gauze turban, and a vast grey sporran of a beard the features that emerged were equally memorable. The eyes were almond-shaped, dark brown, and luminous with a kind of spiritual shrewdness under the arched grey brows. He had a narrow high-bridged nose and the mouth that smiled a cautious welcome was delicately chiselled, firm and humorous. After the smile, he placed both long brown hands together and bowed over them in a graceful *namaskir* of welcome. It was only then that I noticed that the robe of the amber-coloured silk ended, with an unexpectedly athletic effect at his knees and that on his hip hung a great curved dagger, slung from his shoulder in a holster of black braid.

'You are the judge's daughter then?' remarked this apparition in slow, polished English.

'No, no. I am his wife.'

'Ah! He must be a young judge then. And you have children?'

'Just two.'

'Ah!'

'I mentioned to the priest the possibility of our visit,' murmured Mr. Lal, with a touch of nervousness. Once more we bent to remove our shoes. Calmly watching us, as we scrabbled over buckles and laces, the priest resumed his inquiries.

'And your name?'

'Mrs. Knox-Mawer.'

'But your good name?'

'My *good* name? Oh, my Christian name?'

'Yes, your good name.'

I told him. He drew himself up and gazed into space with a dignified twinkle. 'And I am Balvirsingh. It means Master of Strength.' He waved an arm to the doorway. 'Now. You are prepared to inspect?'

Inside was a large airy assembly-room, pink-painted, with more pillars and a linoleum-covered floor. At the far end was a structure like a four-poster bed, a kind of platform surmounted by a fringed canopy. On the platform reposed a large object shrouded in a silk cover.

'This is our Sacred Book. It is only uncovered for holy readings. There are one thousand four hundred and thirty-two pages.'

Here were no untidy offerings, no mysteries. All was sweetness and light. The sole decorations were a few festoons of Christmas paper chains and some coloured balls hanging above the holy book. Tucked discreetly away at the back of the altar was a telephone and a wall switchboard. ('There is connection through to my house,' our guide informed us). Beneath the platform stood a shiny wooden box for offerings of money and two bowls of plastic roses. The only other structure in the room was a pulpit, highly veneered and equipped with a microphone leading to relay speakers in each corner of the room.

Balvirsingh was eager to demonstrate the recently installed fluorescent lighting strips and overhead fans, but I said I was really more interested in the pictures which lined the walls, highly coloured portraits of all the Guru's or Holy Prophets of the Sikh religion, from the first to the last. Behind their beards they looked proud, fierce and exactly alike. There were also a number of battle scenes of frenzied Sikh figures engaged in close combat with enemy forces, armed with swords and shields. Severed heads and limbs strewed the ground amidst pools of blood.

'The Sikhs are a very warrior race,' remarked Mr. Lal quietly, with the same faint note of apprehension I had observed before.

Here, Balvirsingh took over the historical résumé of the intervening centuries in which, like a bizarre echo of the B.B.C. football results, the recurrent phrase was 'Mighty Battle Raged Six–One'—or rather, as I gathered later—'Sikhs won.'

Afterwards he related to us the five symbols of true Sikhdom. 'First there is the hair which is never cut, neither on the head nor the face. Then my sacred comb'—he burrowed in the depths of his turban and produced a small ivory comb. 'Thirdly, there is this dagger which is not for attack, remember, but for the protection of the body. Fourthly, there is the bangle.' He held out his wrist, circled with a narrow silver band. 'This must always be worn so that if one is beheaded in battle, one's body will be recognized as a Sikh body and so given the proper burial rites. And lastly'—he tweaked up his silk shift to reveal a pair of neat white shorts and said surprisingly—'knickers.'

All the doors and windows were kept tightly closed, I noticed.

As we went out again to retrieve our shoes, the hill-top breeze on our faces was a cool shock after the heat inside. Gratefully we accepted Balvirsingh's invitation to retire to his house and drink some tea.

'It is just at the back of the temple.'

Unlike most priests his movements were brisk, decisive, and he marched ahead of us with a straight-backed military tread, muscular brown calves glinting in the sun. The narrow path led past a square stone shelter open at the sides and fitted with canvas blinds. This, he told us, was a place where strangers passing through could lodge the night and do their cooking over a charcoal stove. 'We receive many, and we turn no one away.'

Round the corner there appeared a small house of corrugated iron painted a cheerful shade of blue. A flight of wooden steps led into a tiny living-room almost entirely filled by an enormous rectangular table on which were strewn correspondence, newspapers and various religious tracts. Half a dozen canvas chairs were lined along one side leaving just enough room for a radio and a large electric cooker. On the walls Queen Elizabeth, whom Balvirsingh said he liked very much, rubbed shoulders with photographs of Subhas Chandra Bose, the independence leader, adorned with quotations from his speeches about fighting for freedom to the last drop of blood. There was also an idealized picture of Nehru in his younger days in which the imaginative artist had set him astride a medievally bedizened horse, bearing aloft the green, white and orange banner of India.

'This is where I sleep.' Balvirsingh opened the door on another cupboard-sized room. Behind the door a neat striped jacket and trousers hung alongside a traditional tunic coat of black serge, mandarin-collared and many-buttoned. 'My English suit, my Indian suit,' he said, with a mixture of pride and gentle self-mockery.

We returned to the living-room and sat down in a row on the canvas chairs. The tea, carefully carried in three large cups by a tall thin Indian youth, tasted of ginger and cumin seed. As we sipped it our host, who had downed his in one steady stream, sat watching us with a look of pleasure, stroking his beard—a stage gesture which, reproduced quite naturally in real life, gave one an odd thrill of recognition. He told us he had eight children, six boys and two girls. All of them had obtained either their B.A. degrees or matriculation. He himself had arrived to propagate the Gospel in Fiji four months ago and would return to his family in Punjab in four years time. He went on to say that he was fortunately able to converse in six languages, that Americans spoke very bad English, that he liked Europeans and that present-day Sikhs who cut their hair and forget the Sikh laws were particularly disgraceful men. He added that he read much philosophy and that Tagore was a very great poet indeed.

To prove this last point he took down from the wall a calendar of Tagore quotations and recited with unself-conscious, undulating Welsh-Sunday fervour:

> '*At sunrise open and raise your heart*
> *Like a blossoming flower,*
> *At sunset bend your head and in silence*
> *Complete the worship of the day.*'

After this, conversation would have seemed unbearably mundane, so with a faultless sense of timing Balvirsingh shook hands gravely and escorted us back to the temple door. Descending the steps once more we turned and saw him poised in the *namaskir* of farewell, a sun-burned Moses between the pink pillars and the flagstaff flying the banner of the Sikhs.

Back in town again, Mr. Lal left me at Broadcasting House. It was time for the broadcast of a regular weekly programme called 'English for You', introduced by the education authorities with a view to providing families in country districts with the elements of basic English correctly spoken. In the air-conditioned studio Vijendra Sudhakar, the Indian teacher, spectacled and immaculate in white knee socks, shorts and skirt, was already seated at the green baize table with Epeli Kathimaiwai the Fijian reader, the neatly-typed B.B.C. scripts before them. The red light winked on and behind his glass panel the technician waved us to start. Slowly I read the opening lines for the day and patiently Mr. Sudhakar translated into the microphone and out to the waiting villagers, 'Let us go for a walk in Regent's Park, John, and then it will be time to take a taxi to the theatre. . . .'

5

Comers from the Heavens

Very few colonies can have succumbed to European infiltration so gracefully, so resignedly perhaps, as Fiji. Or so it might seem to the present-day visitor, comfortably buffered by the presence of 10,500 other European citizens and separated by almost two hundred years from the experiences of the earliest *Vavalagi* (Comers from the Heavens) to appear on the Fiji horizons—Cook who left behind him on a rock on deserted Vatoa the first offerings of civilization, a handful of nails and medals and a knife; Bligh after the *Bounty* mutiny stoned and pursued by war canoes off the Yasawas as he threaded his longboat in the path of the trade winds towards Timor, 3,000 miles away; Wilson of the missionary ship *Duff*, lashed and buffeted with hair's-breadth escapes between the sunken razor-edges of the Fiji reefs, sighting vast numbers of armed natives on the beaches and 'smoke among the trees'.

Out of nowhere a spiderly outline named the Feejee Islands replaced the legend 'Here Be Dragons' on the navigation maps. Then in the first years of the nineteenth century an enterprising captain discovered sandalwood among the scrub of Vanua Levu's south-west coast. The ships of the white men followed one another in quick succession yielding axes and buttons, alcohol and disease, and a steadily swelling rabble of beachcombers, deserters, escaped convicts and marooned sailors, the magic of whose muskets had saved them from the earth-ovens and procured for them positions of almost chiefly power among the warring tribes. Obviously the time was ripe for the missionaries.

In 1835 the Methodists, Cross and Cargill landed at Lau from Tonga, forerunners of a gallant band of 'black-coated strangers' who with their wives and families endured incredible horrors and hardships under conditions that seemed hopeless. Yet in 1860 Mrs. Smythe recorded that about 60,000, one-third of the population, had been converted to Christianity. By this time the ordeals of a missionary wife such as Hannah Hunt, who had to close the doors of the house to lessen the smell of cooking bodies outside, seemed legends of the past to Mrs. Smythe and her hostesses, discussing the servant problem over home-made cakes and preserves. 'Nothing can surpass a Wesleyan Methodist tea,' she noted approvingly after her visit to Mr. and Mrs. Martin on the island of Viwa.

Far removed from such cosy proprieties were the lives of most of their fellow-countrymen in Fiji at that period, the white traders of the beaches and gatherers of beche-de-mer. 'He had in fact been gradually reducing the number of his women,' Pritchard reported to one of them, 'and the comfort he felt since he had got rid of *a dozen or two* would, even without a higher motive, be sufficient to induce him to persevere in his good intentions.' The philosophy of another, Pritchard quoted as, 'I works and gets drunk when I likes and gets sober when I likes. I's afeered of no man on this y'ere beach from counsel to darkie. . . .'

Later, when it became known that annexation was being seriously considered, there was a large influx of settlers of a superior type, merchant adventurers of solid English background often, determined to make their fortunes in sugar, cotton or anything else the South Seas had to offer, who brought with them their riding suits, mahogany tallboys, wives, and gilt-framed family portraits. Then with the Deed of Cession, came the first of an entirely different order of beings, the Administrators. Ruling-class Victorians, whiskered and patriarchal and robustly idealistic, they descended on the new colony like gods from Olympus full of splendid schemes for everything. From the capital at Levuka the first Governor, Sir Arthur Gordon, briskly divided his energies between instituting a novel policy of indirect rule through the chiefly system and designing a dashing gypsy uniform for his English staff that dispensed with coat, braces and footwear—('Now all the gentlemen look fresh and cool,' observed Miss Gordon-Cumming graciously)—while in the country districts there was a Resident Commissioner who performed Marriages According to the Flag by waving a Union Jack three times over the heads of the awe-inspired couple.

In view of the ever-increasing number of Europeans arriving in Fiji, some return of hospitality seemed desirable. On a visit to Sydney, the ageing King Thakobau exclaimed, with a curious reversal of the European tradition of a South Seas paradise, that it gave him some idea of what heaven must be. With her usual flair for a journalistic scoop, Miss Gordon-Cumming presented her Victorian readers with a tender cameo of the white-bearded convert who twenty years earlier had celebrated his succession to the ancient title of *Vunivalu* (Chief of War) by having eighteen victims roasted for the feast of welcome. 'The old King', she wrote, 'was never so happy as when the little grand-daughter of the Governor of New South Wales, a pretty little child with golden hair, crept on his knees whispering, "You won't eat me, will you?" '

It was left to an armed detachment of the Native Constabulary to penetrate the civilized world as far as England. The occasion was the Coronation of 1902. During a few crowded weeks, they sang hymns for the sick King Edward under his bedroom window at Buckingham Palace, gave choral performances at Balmoral where they greeted the kilted Highlanders as '*Kai Vata*' (Relations), and thrilled the lady spectators at the Alexandra Palace grounds by spontaneously executing a series of blood-curdling war dances. But for the Fijians the grand climax of their stay came with an excursion to Windsor Castle. Here amidst the splendours of the Throne Room the visitors gained their heart's desire—'to be allowed to turn on and off the glass chandelier which was lighted by Electricity'.

By the nineteen-twenties and thirties there could be few islanders who had not set eyes on a white man. The European had established himself as a permanent and familiar feature of Fijian life, so familiar in fact that in a famous speech of 1939, Ratu Sukuna was able to pin down the typical colonial Englishman once and for all: 'In appearance and manner cold and aloof . . . his colour fresh, his clothes always neat. He is never flurried, speaking quietly in a low gutteral drawl, sometimes exaggerated. He picks up our language quickly enough though he frequently speaks it as if he owned it. He often wears ties of the same device. . . . It is alleged that unless you possess one of these tokens of superiority it is impossible to rise to the higher posts.' In a gentle mockery of an anthropologist's report, Sukuna commented on their 'peculiar custom of toying with tea and cakes' at the hour of four and of the strange rites of a Government House dinner-party for which a chief 'prepares himself' by having a square meal first at home. 'But', he sums up, 'our respect is due to them as they come directly from the country our fathers regarded as the Home of Men.'

In the last twenty-odd years, the increasing impact of press, film and radio has somewhat dimmed the aura of divine authority that surrounded the Englishman in Fiji. The ideas and opinions of the West flood in from a confusing variety of sources. Yet now as then, the immediate personal contact remains the most important influence. Maurice Scott is an outstanding example of this kind of influence—or the Hon. the Speaker of Legislative Council, C.B.E., D.F.C., Barrister-at-Law, to give him his official title. His father, Sir Henry Scott, Q.C., was equally well known. Today, as the champion of Fijian ex-servicemen, for instance, Maurice Scott is perhaps the best-known of all the colony's Europeans, a debonair figure, looking in his full-bottomed wig like a Restoration squire with a Douglas Fairbanks' smile.

Then there are the more recent arrivals. Elderly doctors, retired clergymen, pensioned administrators, they stepped off the English liners of the twenties and the thirties as bright young travellers with the usual letters of introduction, and liked it so much that they never went back. Their activities today rarely disturb the surface of ex-patriate social life. By the outsider, their presence may be glimpsed in a letter to the *Fiji Times*, a faded Union Jack, flying in a front garden, a name repeated like a charm by a yaru-swopping circle of Fijian elders. Officialdom may dismiss them as 'old identities', eccentric hangers-on from the past. Certainly an eighteenth-century delight in nonconformity and personal foible, common to them all, finds room to flourish in the South Seas, traditional refuge for European escapees from convention. Yet this very flexibility, this lack of inhibition has been their key to the guarded Fijian world that lies beneath the manufactured insipidities of tourism and beaurocracy. Like a tropical plant, the charm of this world has entwined itself so closely around the European framework of their characters that it has held them here for a lifetime.

'Of course, Doctor Lindsay Verrier is the one you must meet,' people told us when we first arrived. After a few months we did meet him and continued to meet him with ever-increasing regularity. Our first visit after my return from England followed the time-honoured procedure of all our other visits. At the end of the quiet grass-lined street, Mozart slicing like crystal through the night air that was velvety with flower smells, and a light rapid voice commanding, 'Come along, come along!' The bungalow itself was still invisible behind the giant hedge cultivated by Lindsay to obliterate the hideous neon-lit hulk of the earthly home of the Latter-Day Saints which stands opposite. Then a familiar silhouette, stocky and rotund, appeared at the bottom of the flagstone path, behind him the black embroidery of wrought-iron doors on the gold of the lighted room. A few strands of white hair, the glint of thick-lensed glasses materialized out of the darkness as the doctor turned and pottered in ahead in his Fijian *sulu* and old cotton sweater.

'The Brute! The positive Brute!' he chanted ritually, scooping up a yapping, slavering scrap of Yorkshire terrier in one hand, and pouring out sherry with the other. Around us the chock-a-block trinket box of a roan clustered unchanged. Amidst layers of newspapers, records and books, the familiar landmarks were firmly anchored to the selfsame spots, the cobwebbed silver candelabra and grandfather's German beer-mug on the chest of drawers, the Sèvres candlesticks on the flower-inlaid Dutch bureau, the oval watercolour of a Victorian great-aunt, a Dresden mug of roses. 'And look!' Blue eyes rounding in his pink pendulous face, he showed us his newer toys, the battery pencil-sharpener, the floating vacuum cleaner, the elaborate wiring system that produces alarm bells in every room, an automatic tape-recorder for telephone messages, and a relay speaker like a huge sieve in the middle of the ceiling from which 'The Magic Flute' was floating celestially down. 'Ideal for acoustics, you see!'

'And what do you keep behind there?' somebody once asked him, pointing to the great tapa curtain that hangs across an entire wall. 'Oh, my System! Just my System!' Lindsay piped airily, dismissing with a wave of his hand his life's work in Fiji, the compilation of the entire Fijian population of Vanua Levu. The 140,000 indexed cards in their honeycomb of filing drawers represent a private labour of love begun in 1944 as part of his medical work and built up through years of poring over the ragged registries of the provincial scribes, of questioning and re-questioning the old men in every unheard-of and forgotten village on the island. Dismissed at first as a personal eccentricity, the 'System' is now recognized by Government for what it is—the only definitive record for that area of land-ownership which, under the Fijian system of tribal inheritance, lies at the very heart of the life of the Fijian people and their future.

'I even hear Rumours of Financial Support,' announced Lindsay, now quietly serious from behind his desk with its tape-recorders, typewriters and stacks of files and documents. 'And that means I can start on Viti Levu. I think there'll *just* be time for me to do it. . . .' His voice tailed off into the kitchen where amidst a welter of pans, recipe books, mixer-beaters and all the impediments of the gourmet's shop he busily transferred his attentions to supper. To an accompaniment of chopping, whisking and stirring sounds, interlaced with bursts of Lewis Carroll nonsense-talk or a Gilbert and Sullivan snatch, I inspected the huge stone bread-jar, the print of an eighteenth-century cooking scene, the menu for tonight pinned to the wall alongside the slate bearing a chalked message in Gilbertese for Mr. Noa, the houseboy. 'Plenty of pig left for your supper tonight.'

Sitting later around the ruins of a steak, kidney and oyster pudding and a second bottle of burgundy, Lindsay regaled us with the latest news. He was planning to construct a Roman fountain in the corner of the rose garden. 'I've sent to Italy for plans.' He had consigned to the museum for safe keeping his penny-farthing bicycle, brought out from England in the thirties and ridden triumphantly down Victoria Parade. And politics? 'Oh, the usual thing. We're told to expect at last an *impassione ultimatum* on the future of Fiji in the current meeting of Legislative Council and what do we get?—a heated debate on the possibilities of tar-sealing Gorrie Street.' Before leaving we skimmed through the enormous leather book, crammed with signatures, to bring ourselves up to date with recent visitors to the colony—Noel Coward, Lord Maugham, Sir Steven Runciman, Swedish professors, Tongan footballers, the crew of the Japanese destroyer *Aisake* and a couple who coyly signed themselves 'Stubner, Seattle, Washington—and the Wide, Wide World'.

Sandwiched between these were the names of the regulars. The crimped scholarly hand of Humphrey Evans brought with it a picture of the hawk-faced old man and his house by the sea—both of them perched on shaky stilt-like legs and coloured a faded yellow—where next Sunday we would be summoned to a ritual luncheon of kedgeree and trifle. Like Lindsay, Humphrey Evans had come abroad as a ship's doctor, looking for the South Seas in the Rupert Brooke spirit of the early nineteen-hundreds. Musty snapshot albums show, among the clusters of ordinary faces, a Greek god in blazer and boater, breakfasting at Granchester, punting down the Cambridge backs, picnicking at Henley.

Like Lindsay, too, he decided to stay here for the rest of his life. Rotuma, the tiny dependency 200 miles from the mainland, where he was posted as Government medical officer, was to be his special island, though later journeys led him to almost every corner of Fiji with occasional private sorties through Russia, China and Japan. Now he sits still, surveying the Pacific from his window with hooded, cynical blue eyes, smoking a tremulous chain of menthol cigarettes, tinkling a silver bell for occasional silence from the horde of Fijian infants who overflow from the servants' quarters on to the back veranda. A library of several hundred books, anthropology, entomology, philosophy, withers gently on the shelves around him. Stacked into cupboards underneath are the famous collections of photographs, 19,000 of them and added to every day, the notebooks and drawings of Rotuman archaeology which a paralytic style of illness prevents him from ever transcribing for publication. On the wall, among the Oriental and Polynesian exotica, is pinned an old French corset poster, sole relic of Bohemian youth. The *London Illustrated News* comes every week. On his desk there are letters to be answered from Julian Huxley, C. P. Snow, and Dorothy Tutin, unlikely threads from home. And every day there are visitors from the past, children and grandchildren of Rotuman friends, Fijian families, along with the newer faces who come to sit and talk over the menthol cigarettes, the Tia Maria and the games of Chinese chequers.

Below the signature of Dr. Evans was that of Mrs. Wise who came of Dublin carriage-folk and now, the widow of a Director of Works lived in an ivy-covered house on the edge of a precipice overlooking the wild and misty Tamavua Valley. If Dr. Evans's *metier* was lunch, Mrs. Wise's was tea—China tea. Over the Crown Derby, with a wave of her bridge-coat sleeve and a drawing closer of her long-nosed, rose-leaf face, she would recall hair-raising river trips on bamboo rafts, treks through the bush on horseback, shooting the reef in a sea-swamped longboat—'Me bailin' out with the Commissioner's silver tankard and wasn't the dear man furious!' Bowered in chintz and encircled by a forest of Fijian war-clubs, regimental swords, family portraits and Chinese gongs, one listened entranced while through the stained-glass windows the sunset glowed and faded and the pillars of the miniature Greek temple on the terrace darkened to a silhouette against the sky. 'For such a classical view my husband said there had to be a temple, so he built one.'

Then there was Teddy Johnson who collected chiming clocks, and Pearson-Smith who hunted the islands for additions to his private museum of old ships' cannons. The scrawled names of Aubrey Kinnerton and Michael St. John headed another page. Kinnerton had originally come to Fiji from Africa. Now his Colonial Service trappings were packed away for good in large black trunks—the medals and topees, the antediluvian Emmett contraption he had once demonstrated for me that looked like a canvas sentry-box with an appendage of rusty nozzles and chains and was known as a Portable Safari Shower. Relaxing into a schoolboy's dream of freedom he had, at the age of sixty, bought himself a piano. On this gap-toothed relic, fortified by his familiar tin of Farah's Original Harrogate Toffee and a mugful of sherry, he would pass the midnight hours in stabbing out 'Sleepy-Time Gal', 'Vilia', 'Rose Marie' and other favourites of his youth from the beginners' scores he ordered monthy from Harrods.

More predictably, Michael St. John had bought himself a farm. A beaky, fresh-faced retired D.C., he sometimes invited me to go riding with him. When I arrived he was usually deep in conversation with a caller from the nearby village, the slurred soft tones of the natural Fijian alternating with the incisive narrow-vowelled rhythms of the same language spoken by an Englishman, as curious a contrast as the two speakers themselves standing together on the veranda, the aquiline, stooping figure in jodphurs, the bush-headed profile of the old Fijian upright and intent in his flowered *sulu*.

Once away from the house, the horses always followed the same path. It was a narrow track, steep and muddy, that wound its way between towering walls of undergrowth. White hibiscus, growing wild and fringes of bamboo brushed our faces as we passed. Under the luminous bell of the sky, there was silence except for the creak of saddles, an occasional snort from the horses, the constant reverberation of the crickets. It was an old bridle-path of the 1890's, Michael told me over his shoulder. It led to the rest-house the Governor of that time had had built for him high up in these hills above Suva. Like the buggy processions of moustached and befrogged gentlemen, ladies sheltered from the sun beneath cartwheel hats and parasols, we too followed the corkscrew track until it suddenly opened out on to a small plateau. Among the pampas grass and the tangling vines the rectangle of a *bure* foundation was just visible—all that was left of Sir John Thurston's romantic 'native' eyrie away from the despatch-boxes and the protocol of Government House. Only the view was unchanged, a dream-like sweep of mountain chains and valleys folded deep in trees and in the distance, gold in the evening light, the shapes of the off-lying islands.

Back at the farm again the visit ended with a descent to the 'swimming-pool', a Coleridge-like grotto at the bottom of a staircase of tree-trunks, overhung with waterfalls and framed by orchids and ferns, with a reed shelter at the edge of the pool for poetic reflection. 'Alone in the early morning here', said our host, 'it's like the first morning ever. . . .'

It was at one of these houses on one such afternoon or evening that I met a Catholic priest, a slight middle-aged Austrian with gold-rimmed spectacles and delicate scholarly features, who said to me, 'When you English talk of the European influence in places like Fiji, what you really mean is the English influence. But there are others, you know. When can you come out to Naiserelagi?'

6

The Frescoes of Naiserelagi

'The road gets fairly rough from now on,' called Monsignor Wassner, above the roar of his Volkswagen and the rattle of loose stones as we hurtled out of the last town. 'You don't mind if we go fast.'

It was a command rather than a question. Immaculate in his beige linen bush-jacket and trousers, the country dress of Catholic priests in the tropics, he put his foot down on the accelerator. His thin blond-grey hair floated back in the rush of wind from the open window, the pale, precise profile with its long upper-lip and domed forehead tensed with an expression of pleasurable concentration. From time to time he honked the horn vigorously with a clenched fist, apologized with grave courtesy as we swerved to avoid a pot-hole.

'I enjoy driving!' he said with a smile, his eyes gleaming behind his spectacles.

We had crossed the almost visible line that divided the wet side of the island from the dry. It was like flying out of cloud into sunshine. Now the vegetation was sparser, rough grass and reeds and clusters of hardy shrubs and trees replacing the lush rain forests of the eastern slopes. The tiny wooden bridges that spanned each narrow stream shook beneath us as we bumped across. In their shadows, the women of the villages were beating out their washing on flat stones and naked children darted through the water like prawns. At the sight of the car young boys fishing over the rails raised their hands with cries of 'Father! Father!', smiling transfixed in the swirl of dust from our wheels. And all the way the sea followed us—sometimes near, sometimes distant, always the same sparkling blue in the morning sunshine.

Less than a century ago, in the year before Cession, the whole of this northern coast of Viti Levu was under martial law. A European planter, his wife and children had been brutally massacred on their homestead by a heathen tribe from the hills. A campaign of retribution was organized by the Thakobau Government with its 'Cabinet' of Fijian chiefs and leading European settlers. Recruiting notices with a jaunty Wild West flavour were circulated among the planters, such as the one which read, 'The Major intends to attack on Monday next and invites anyone who is fond of shooting to accompany him.' Six months of this guerrilla warfare followed. Villages were ambushed and *bures* burned. Musket-fire between the detachments of trained native troops and the hordes of long-haired hill fighters rang strangely among the rocky spurs of the unconquered inland regions. Women and children fled to the caves, emerging only to forage for food. In my mind's eye I saw the trailing procession of 1,000 half-naked warriors who, at the end of it all, made their way down to this coast to surrender to the motley band of European 'officers' in their broad-brimmed Tokelau hats and red puggarees.

'There's Naiserelagi!'

Monsignor Wassner pointed to where on a hill-top the grey stonework of a church rose above the surrounding bush. Its red corrugated roof had faded to the colour of lichen. In this wild landscape it had an incongruously weathered European appearance. We turned into a long drive with cropped fields on either side and cattle grazing around the goalposts. 'The children play here after school. It was all swamp land before the Bishop lent us his bulldozer.'

From a clump of banana trees on the edge of the drive a blond man in short sleeves waved a salutation of welcome as we swept by.

'That is Franz. He is from Austria too. He is a lay worker at the Mission. And now, this is where the Mission teachers live—one Rotuman, one Indian, one Australian.'

The Volkswagen climbed up a winding hill past a row of Fijian *bures* with neat gingham curtains. Round the next bend we were out on a plateau of sweeping lawn, the sea falling away silver beyond its rim. Dominating the green from the far end, the church stood solidly four-square, uncompromisingly French with its twin gables, stained-glass windows and broad sweep of steps, the dark granite facade already aged by the climate of the tropics.

'It's only fifty-odd years old you know,' said Monsignor Wassner, with something like pride in his voice. 'The French fathers chose this hill for it—but they had to blast the whole place level with dynamite first.'

We had drawn up outside a long low building of black weather-board. Across the veranda a door stood open. There was a glimpse of a mat-covered floor, a table with an oil lamp on it and a bed behind it. 'That is your room. It is the first time a woman has stayed on her own in the priest's house. No doubt in the old days the Fathers would have raised their hands in horror at the idea—but never mind that!'

'And an Anglican, too,' I added. But Monsignor Wassner only smiled vaguely, unfolded himself out of the car and helped me out from the other side.

A small plumpish woman in her thirties, wearing a brown cotton overall, came up to us dusting soil off her hands.

'I'm sorry, Father—I was just planting some zinnias,' she said quickly in a soft American voice, smiling at me. She had lively brown eyes beneath a calm forehead bare of make-up, rosy cheeks, and brown hair drawn back in a neat plaited coronet. We shook hands as Monsignor Wassner performed the introductions. 'Miss MacPeake is what we call a lay missionary worker. She looks after the dispensary, supervises the running of the house also.'

Together we walked up a flight of low stone steps into the shade of the veranda. From a rope in the ceiling hung an old iron bell. 'It's rung for the Angelus and Mass—and for meals, of course.'

A small boy carried my bags into my room and Monsignor Wassner led me on a tour of inspection. 'This is my study,' he said, opening a door at the end of the veranda. It was a small book-lined room with a view through the window of jagged mountain-peaks and rolling bush. In the corner, caught in a patch of yellow sunshine that made it look as unreal in that setting as a Dutch painting, stood a spinet. He moved across to it and tenderly touched a succession of black keys. Only one frail note shivered and then died.

'It began to fail soon after it arrived,' he said, with a wistful expression. 'It was mine in America. Some of my friends sent it on out to me, they thought I should have it. But in this climate . . . Perhaps one day though I shall find someone who can do something with it.'

Through an archway was another room with a bed in it, a *tabua* on one wall, a crucifix on another. This led out on to a long back veranda that had a comfortable farmhouse air about it with old pack-saddles and harness hanging from pegs on the wall, tall cup-

'Black Christ' fresco mural by Jean Charlot in St Francis Xavier Church, Naisereilangi, Fiji

Fijian schoolgirls

boards half-open and crammed with household pots and jars, a pair of muddy boots drying in the sun. Some chickens were pecking about under the steps and nearby stood a stone water trough, the tap above it adorned with a rough wooden statue of the Virgin.

'This veranda was the favourite spot of Le Pére Helliet, the old French Father who was in charge here before I came,' Wassner told me. 'He became very sick and used to lie out here on his couch, with his *tanoa* beside him.' He pointed out a dusty old *yaggona* bowl in the far corner. 'He always insisted on it being kept full for himself and his visitors.'

We walked on through a large sitting-room, plainly but comfortably furnished with modern cane chairs and Fijian mats. There was a new radio on one of the tables, and Graham Greene and Somerset Maugham on the shelves. 'But this is our real library.' Monsignor Wassner led me to the other end of the room where the tattered but orderly ranks of calf and vellum backs covered an entire wall. Most of the books were French, abstruse seventeenth- and eighteenth-century titles in tarnished gilt, the learned theological arguments within, musty-smelling, and rudely interrupted by insect borings. 'Some were handed down from the first Catholic priests to come to Fiji, towards the end of the last century that is. Others were brought out by the Fathers who built this house.'

From the front veranda came the clanging of the bell. The lunch it announced was a simple meal, slightly constrained by the presence of Franz who arrived from the fields in his khaki shorts and shirt, a gangling tow-headed figure with the face of a Breughel peasant, long-nosed and suspicious. Across the table he watched me with the wary antagonism of one who has been betrayed too often to trust on sight, who has suffered a great deal and now guards his present good fortune with avidity.

'Franz is everything here—plumber, carpenter, cowman, ploughman,' said Wassner, laughing. Even this homely introduction failed to dispel the somehow sinister air of the past that hung about him. In conversation, he occasionally made a reply in English or broke into an odd high-pitched giggle. His whole attitude changed as he bent across to the slight figure at the head of the table and listened with an expression of devoted concentration to some query or instruction spoken in an undertone in German. With Annette, the four of us sat round a long refectory table under a photograph of the Bishop of Fiji, in purple robes and biretta. Two Fijian nuns. their dark faces vivid against their grey cotton habits, carried the food across from the kitchen quarters fifty yards away and we served ourselves to stew, tapioca, and soursop pudding. 'Everything except the meat is homegrown,' Annette told me with housewifely satisfaction.

After coffee on the veranda Monsignor Wassner turned to me, 'And now perhaps you are ready to see the frescoes.'

'People always ask me why Charlot chose to bury such a wonderful painting so far from civilization,' Wassner said, as we walked across the green to the church. He grinned a little. 'Well, firstly, because I asked him when I met him abroad, and he accepted the invitation. No, not seriously. The answer is that these are the people for whom it was painted—the people to whom it will mean most because they have least.' He pointed to the first children emerging from the low wooden classroom buildings behind the house, a chattering bullet-headed crew of six- and seven-year-olds in neat uniforms who as soon as they sighted us came swarming towards us, buzzing with speculation. A few feet away the tide halted.

'Good afternoon, Father!' chanted a well-rehearsed chorus, while twenty pairs of eyes devoured the sight of a European stranger on the compound.

'Good afternoon, children,' replied the Monsignor, stretching out his hand with a smile and continuing his brisk stride towards the church. 'Later, we shall meet—later!'

'We have a hundred and sixty of them altogether, some from villages as far as twenty miles away,' he told me, as we climbed the steps together. 'Those farthest away are boarders, the others walk through the bush to get here each morning—rock-climbs, rivers and all!'

I asked him how many Catholics were in his province.

'About a thousand—many of them too far away to come to church on a Sunday, so the priests trek out to the villages on horseback to give masses at the week-end.'

Above the arched doorway, the word *Venite Ad Me Omines* were carved in the stone. Inside, there was a powerful atmosphere of space and calm, the great nave bare of chairs, our feet silent on the rush-covered floor. I was vaguely aware of Monsignor Wassner pausing at a conch-shell of holy water, before kneeling to cross himself. And then all immediate impressions dissolved at the sight of the fresco itself rising like a dream above the altar at the far end of the church. A crucifixion formed the centre, flanked on either side by a closely-knit cavalcade of robed figures. As I moved closer I saw that these were not the conventional Biblical attendants, but for the most part portrayals of Fijians and Indians, traditionally dressed. The drawing was strong and simple, the colouring curiously pale, with those smoky purplish overtones most characteristic of Fijian settings. That this was a religious work, in a way that many depictions of sacred subjects are not, one felt at once. In that dim greystone interior it shone out with something of the primitive mystery and vitality of a cave-painting.

Standing there, I tried to absorb what Monsignor Wassner was telling me—that the whole composition symbolically intertwined the central beliefs of Catholicism with the lives lived by its converts in Fiji today. Every figure in it was a real person, he said. On the left, the Fijian side, he pointed out the Naiserelagi schoolgirl in her blue uniform, the white-robed priest Father Matatha, whom Charlot sketched while he was preaching and caught in the favourite Fijian gesture of enumeration, one forefinger on the outstretched first finger of the other hand. Alongside the cross came two Fijian villagers, the woman with a rolled mat in her arms, traditional gift of welcome to an honoured guest, the man resplendent in garlands and skirt of bark-fibres crouching to present a whale's tooth, by custom the Fijian's most sacred token of good faith. In the forefront austere and striking in his black robes, stood the South Seas martyr, St. Peter Chanel, in his hands the wooden club with which he met his death at Futuna Island in 1842.

The Indian side of the fresco was dominated by a portrait of St. Francis Xavier, patron saint of missionaries, whose field was India and whose body lies in Goa in a miraculous state of preservation. Wearing the gold and white robes of his priesthood he held aloft the chalice and the Host in the act of consecration, an Indian altar-boy in scarlet cassock at his side. A young woman in veil and sari offered a garland of flowers to the crucified Christ. In the background an Indian farmer led a pair of bullocks through ranks of sugar-cane—in real life he was the local carpenter, Wassner added.

Only the slender figure on the cross remained an enigma. Wrapped in a loin-cloth of tapa, Christ had the purplish bloom of a coloured skin, the narrow head of a European. The features themselves were suggested only vaguely, so that the archtypal sadness and desolation of all humanity seemed gathered there, unhindered by details of individual identity.

'And then,' said Wassner, 'as a special favour, I asked him to make two more panels to go above our side-altars to St. Joseph and the Virgin.' He led me back to the centre of the nave from where we could see, on one side wall, the Christ-Child in the workshop of his father, and on the other, the Annunciation, clear-cut flowing compositions of moving simplicity in muted browns and white and greys. A brilliant *trompe d'oeil* of jagged brickwork, exactly representing the surrounding stones, made each tableaux look like a scene glimpsed through an opening in the wall.

The Monsignor went on to explain Charlot's method of work. The original three windows behind the altar were first covered up and plastered over. The fresco designs, first discussed in correspondence then elaborated on meeting, were sketched on to rolls of newsprint paper which were fixed on to the wall itself to be drawn in scale. Tracings were made of these, the tracing papers pinned to the wall and the outlines pierced through on to the wet mortar with a nail. The long task of the actual painting Charlot performed each day, perched on scaffolding and surrounded by wondering audiences of Fijian workmen and schoolchildren. During his stay, while he was sketching his models from life, he became fascinated by a number of Fijian motifs, the shape of bread-fruit leaves, *tapa* designs, the basic blues and greens of Fijian colouring and traditional adornments, all of which he embedded in his final composition.

'Now I will show you St. Francis Xavier and St. Peter Chanel as we used to know them at Naiserelagi,' said Wassner.

I followed him up to the altar and into the tiny sacristy leading off from it. Inside a Fijian nun was sitting on the floor, her coiffed head bent in concentration, her legs tucked under her grey cotton skirts. In front of her a kerosene burner flared and spluttered and over it she held an instrument like a long pair of tongs with a flat square box on the end of it. I asked her what she was doing.

'I am making the Host, *marama*,' she replied in a low voice, raising the lid to reveal the white wafer of bread, stamped with the insignia I.H.S. She looked up at us with a quick smile on her broad, pretty face. Then lowering her eyes again she resumed her task of scraping the surplus dough from the edges of the box and replacing them in the bowl alongside her.

The Monsignor pointed to two life-size statues of the saints, standing in a corner of the room. Their pink and white plaster faces expressed conventional sweetness, and from their tidy drapes of brown and black and their small, jointless hands were extended in stylized gestures of piety.

'The Sisters are too fond of them for us to part with them altogether,' he murmured as we left.

Coming out we were met by Miss MacPeake who took me off on a tour of the classrooms. These were in three separate bungalows, one for the 'babies' of six and seven, one for the eight- and nine-year-olds, and the biggest for the ten to fourteens. Inside each there were familiar smells of chalk and ink, rows of tiny old-fashioned desks and benches, a few mats on the mud floors, ragged books, health charts, pictures everywhere of the Holy Family and the Royal Family. 'How the Races Help One Another' read one brightly-coloured poster. 'The Fijians—Coconuts and Bananas; the Indians—Sugar; the Chinese—Bread and Vegetables; the Europeans—Big Shops, Schools and Work in Government.' 'We teach them in English from the beginning, you know,' she said.

As we came out of the dormitories she called to the tall figure of Franz ahead of us, a milk-can swinging from each hand. I noticed he had donned a pair of mud-caked boots and a peaked blue-cotton cap of the type worn by German soldiers in the last war. 'May we come, too?'

He shook his head. 'Too muddy.'

'Oh, we don't mind that!' persisted Miss MacPeake, her round face childishly eager.

Franz smiled, shrugged his shoulders. 'All right, we go.'

'You were in the war then,' I said to him as we walked down the path to the fields at the back of the house.

He nodded. 'Hitler's army,' he replied, with a wry sideways look, mock-respect in his voice. 'In Russia that was. A terrible war.'

He seemed to have discarded his former wariness and went on in his halting sing-song English. 'I was wounded. They sent me to France. I was captured at the Seigfried Line—you know the Seigfried Line? Many years I was prisoner of war in England.'

I asked him how he had come out to Fiji. It was through the Trapp family, he said. They were famous singers. I had heard how Monsignor Wassner was working with them in America for many years, arranging their music, their performances? Well he, too, had worked for the Trapps and it was there he met the Monsignor. 'When he left for Fiji I told him I would come too if there was job for me. Ever since I was a boy about ten I want to do missionary work and this is the best way I can do it. As soon as he cable me I take the next boat out!'

He stopped and pulled open an iron gate leading into a muddy field, thick with long grass, a rough shed in the corner. A large bull with a ring through his nose pawed the ground, grunting irritably at the sight of strangers. 'Heil, Selemus,' called Franz. Selemus turned away, appeased and snuffling. From the valley below came a small Fijian girl driving two cows before her. Botu, a handsome brown creature, was the first into the milking shed. 'Good, Botu! Pretty, Botu!' Perched on a wooden box, his head against her flank, Franz now in his element recited nonsense talk to her in a soothing undertone while under his practised fingers the milk hissed and rattled into the pail. 'You are sad, eh, Botu? Your baby has gone. Never mind. Be happy now, Botu!'

It was dusk when we walked back to the house and heard the bell clang out its double-peal for supper. The Monsignor was awaiting us on the veranda. Grace was said round the long table and the four of us sat down to fish and rice in the fading light. I imagined that some calamity had befallen the generator until with an air of quiet authority, our host remarked, 'This is the great advantage of producing one's own electricity. One is enabled to enjoy in peace the brief beauties of the tropical twilight.'

We nodded, carefully prodding our now invisible plates.

'So,' said the Monsignor, waving a white-robed arm towards the bulb hanging over the table. As though in obedience, light sparked and bloomed over our heads. 'And now!' With an airy spring, he rose from the table, crossed himself nimbly and was off through the swing-doors, down the veranda steps and over the green to evening prayers, a fluttering, swiftly-moving white shape in the darkness.

It was not until the following morning that I attended a service in the church. 'Mass is at a quarter to six,' Monsignor Wassner had told me. 'Tomorrow is the Feast of Saint James so there will be plenty of singing from the children if you would like to come.'

It was strange to be woken in darkness by the sound of a bell pealing near by, dressing by lamplight in the small whitewashed room, a crucifix on one bare wall, the shadowy blur of the mosquito-net draped over the bed frame which the local carpenter had shaped to the old Christian design of a cross in a circle.

Outside the air was cool and damp to the skin. Patterns of light fell across the grass from the tall windows and open door of the church, a dark shape against the translucent night sky of the tropics that was still vivid with stars. Slipping in through a side entrance I took a seat among the handful of pews tucked away in the corner opposite the altar to St. Joseph. The place was empty except for the figure of Wassner in his white habit, kneeling at the Virgin's shrine across the nave to make his private Mass, two Fijian boys in scarlet surplices on either side of him. On the central altar stood eight tall candles in upturned coconut shells. The lower walls were lined with lengths of *tapa* and above this the great frescoes thrown into flickering golden relief, seemed to tremble with suppressed movement, like a tapestry hanging or a reflection in a stream.

A nun padded quietly down the nave and opened a small door on the other side. Then one by one the schoolchildren filed through. Except for the rustle of bare feet on the grass mats, there was silence as they composed themselves into kneeling rows until the whole nave was a sea of black cropped heads and upturned soles of dusty pink. Alongside my pew a small girl rubbed her face and stifled a yawn. Another reached out to straighten the crumpled collar of a friend in front. Then like the others they waited motionless, arms crossed Fijian-style with the hands folded under the armpits, eyes closed in prayer or tracing the familiar outlines of the frieze above them.

Suddenly from the compound the beating of a *lali* started up, startlingly close, a compulsive quickening pattern of thuds that still had power to race the blood with a sense of excitement and expectation. As suddenly, at its crescendo, the drumming stopped. From the sacristy stepped a Fijian priest, a young spectacled man in scarlet robes and gold-embroidered stole. Four altar-boys followed him, two holding the hem of his surplice, two behind, and the ritual of High Mass, complex and beautiful, unfolded itself to ringing of handbells and the old sharp smell of incense swung from a silver censer. From the back of the church the catechist led the Fijian prayers. All around us a low rapid murmur, with the Fijian husky sibilence, the blending of m's and b's, rose and fell like the swarming of bees. There was a pause while the Monsignor rose from his seat behind the altar rails and, standing in front of the children, lifted his hand and hummed a chord. One hundred and fifty children drew breath and in perfect unison responded in Latin with first the Gloria then the Credo.

Daybreak showed through the windows. In the half-light of the sacristy the figures of the two discarded saints could be seen facing one another with gestures that looked like the whispered conversation of actors waiting in the wings. Solemnly the Host was raised in consecration. Two of the boys laid a long white cloth over the altar rails and slowly, a line at a time, the children filed forward to kneel and receive communion. One by one, eyes closed, they threw back their heads like fledglings while the priest, with a kind of deft yet reverent briskness, dispatched into each open mouth the morsel of wafer bread. From the seat behind me Miss MacPeake went forward in her turn to take her place at the rail. Sitting there I experienced the familiar Anglican sensation of being shut out from something oddly familiar. It was rather the feeling of a child who is being punished by being quietly ignored, I thought, as we went out together at the end of the service, I following with an awkward bob her graceful genuflexion before the altar.

As we sat down to breakfast I asked Wassner how he had set about teaching these hill-children the complex responses of the mass.

'We go over them line by line,' he said. 'They make progress extraordinarily quickly. Latin is phonetically easy for Fijians, you see, and they are all natural singers.'

We ate French toast, Indian honey and Naiserelagi coffee. Halfway through, a young Fijian man in shorts and *bula* shirt appeared in the doorway, bowed an apology to the Monsignor and took a seat at the table. He was introduced as Father Kavuru and I realized that this was the scarlet-robed priest of the Mass.

'Thanks a lot,' he said with a New Zealand accent, when I congratulated him on the service. His solemn face, broad and spectacled, broke into a smile. 'I'm still not too sure of everything yet, you see.'

His family came from a village near Labasa on Vanua Levu, he told me. He had been ordained only recently. He had received his training in New Zealand where he had stayed with a 'very English family', in a fine big house with a tennis court and a swimming pool. 'Every night they changed for dinner and at the end of dinner there was always the passing-of-the-port.'

After breakfast we sat out on the veranda for half an hour and Wassner, after demurring with his usual modesty, told me a little more about himself. He was born near Salzburg, studied philosophy and theology at Innsbruck and was ordained a priest in 1929. The next three years he spent in Rome, 'working for a degree in Canon Law—and playing the organ at the Austrian church of Santa Maria del Anima! Fifteenth- and sixteenth-century music was my special passion at that time and still is.' It was back at Salzburg, studying in the Major Seminary, that he met the family who were to alter the whole course of his career. Baron Von Trapp, his wife and children were at that time known only locally for their singing. Attracted by a mutual love of music, Wassner became one of their circle and was soon working with them, composing arrangements for their songs which through records, broadcasts and international tours were eventually to become known and loved throughout the world. The singers branched out into a wider repertoire than mere folk-songs. There were performances at the Salzburg Festivals and in 1937 an American manager offered them a contract for a tour of the States where Wassner followed them, just as the Nazis were moving into Austria. 'I was warned that Catholic priests would be among the first to be rounded up.'

The next fifteen years or so were spent with the Trapp family singers. Fund-raising for relief work in Austria was at the centre of almost all his activities. 'It was for this, I think, that my present title was bestowed on me by the Pope,' he said, when I asked him about it.

It was through a meeting in 1956 in Sydney with Archbishop Carboni, the Apostolic Delegate, that he became interested in the idea of mission work in the South Pacific, a field of activity which also attracted several members of the Trapp family. After a trip through New Guinea and the Solomons at the Archbishop's invitation, he came to Fiji, met Bishop Foley and decided to write to the Archbishop in Salzburg for permission to settle with the Catholic mission here. With scholarly zest, he set about learning the language and customs during four months of 'acclimatization' in the Yasawa Islands.

'I don't think the old French Fathers quite approved of me when I first came to Naiserelagi. They were Marists, of course, very traditional in their long black *soutanes*, even in the hottest weather, and I was a secular priest, full of all sorts of new ideas and projects.'

'And still are?' I asked.

'Of course! Of course!' He leaned forward and shifted his spectacles on his nose with a characteristically eager gesture. 'There is so much to do in a place like this. As you probably know the nineteenth-century missionaries tended to prohibit everything native as a product of the devil. Everything had to be done the European way. They installed harmoniums for instance whereas, of course, Fijian harmony is supplied naturally in their way of singing. What I am trying to do is to blend the best of the Fijian world with the essence of the European tradition. Fijian poetry, music, handicrafts, must all have a part in the services. The old Fijian *mekes*, for example, have strong affinities with the Gregorian chants and this is something I am particularly eager to explore. Music, like that fresco of ours, has a great unconscious influence.' He clasped his hands together, his eyes on the church across the green. 'If these children are able to spend just half an hour of every day in an area of dignified religious expression, at least I shall have accomplished something.'

'And are you happy to stay here for the rest of your life?' We both looked out for a moment at the incredible view. The last of the mist which detached the mission plateau from the world beneath circled the surrounding peaks like the haloes of saints in medieval art.

'I would like sometime to visit India. Also I have been asked to return to Rome—a post concerning the arranging and setting of Church music under the new Pope—but my health would not be strong enough, I'm afraid.' He got to his feet briskly, and smiled down at me. 'Besides, the answer to your question is yes. My work is here. This is my place and I am thankful to have found it. And now—as you know, there is much to do today'—he waved his hands round his head, in comic-professor style—'and I am not too good at this kind of organizing!'

The rest of the morning revolved in a bustle of preparation for the visit of the Bishop of Fiji, Bishop Foley, who was calling in on his way to the airport on the other side of the island, the first lap of his journey to Rome to attend the Ecumenical Council. A band of village women arrived with nets full of his favourite prawns for the lunch; white wine was uncorked in preference to the red. His lordship preferred plain oil and vinegar for a salad dressing, some-one said, as the nuns scurried to and fro counting plates and polish-ing glasses.

When the Bishop's black car finally swung round on to the green, it was to the deafening accompaniment of tattoos on the *lalis*, the ringing of bells, and the shrill cries of hordes of children who came surging around from all sides. The young part-European priest who was driving got out and opened the door. A silver-haired man, plumpish and smiling with handsome, alert features, stepped on to the veranda. The purplish stone on his outstretched hand flashed incongruously against his brown bushjacket and trousers.

After the individual presentations, everyone sat in a circle on the veranda and the talk switched to and from the sacred to the mundane with an ease peculiar to Catholic circles and oddly un-nerving to the outsider. As predicted His Lordship selected white wine rather than red, mixed oil and vinegar over his salad, and complimented the household on the size and quality of the prawns. Then puffing genially on a cigar, he strolled across to the class-rooms with the three women teachers, an Australian, a Rotuman and an Indian.

An hour later, amidst renewed clanging and drumming, His Lordship resumed his journey to Rome. Behind the house two of the Fijian priests shook down some green coconuts, sliced off the tops with cane knives and handed round a big shiny gourd to each one of us. For a while we sat on the grass drinking the cool, sweet, colourless *bu*.

'What about exercising the horses?' suggested Father Kavuru. 'You'd like to ride?'

The horses themselves appeared from the other side of the com-pound, galloped bareback by two small boys who urged them on with warlike cries. Andrew, a lean chestnut, was selected for me as a nice quiet specimen. As I climbed up into the stirrups he rolled a lugubrious eye round at me, but picked his way down the hill dutifully enough behind Father Kavuru's horse to the encouraging shouts of the schoolchildren.

'I think we'd better stick to the road today,' said Father Kavuru, as we turned on to the dusty track. 'But next time you come to Naiserelagi, you must come with us on one of our real treks into the bush.' He pointed to a small *bure* on the hillside under a bread-fruit tree. 'The last time we were on our way back home, we'd been riding for about twelve hours and we couldn't go any farther than that house without a drink. So we watered the horses, then went inside for a bowl of *yaggona*. When we came out again the horses had collapsed on to the ground and wouldn't walk another step!'

His story was interrupted by a lorry roaring past us loaded with sugar-cane. Andrew snorted and bucked indignantly in a cloud of dust, then stood stock still for about three minutes by the long grass at the side before consenting to move on again. Round the next bend another lorry went thundering by. This time Andrew reared a little higher and refused to move at all. So it was that I made my return to the mission tethered hostage-wise by a piece of rope tied firmly from Andrew's bridle to the saddle of Father Kavuru's horse. After all these precautions for my safety it was disconcerting for the Father to see me dismount and collapse into a dramatic heap at the foot of a pile of logs on to which I had stepped —and slipped.

'A sprained ankle,' everyone said, helping me inside. The Fijian medical officer was away but Maria would come up from the village to give me massage. Maria was apparently renowned for her proficiency in the Fijian art of *masi-masi*.

Any visions I had of a gentle handmaiden smoothing the pain away with feathery fingers were immediately dispelled by the ancient sibyl in black draperies who hobbled in through the doorway. Summing up the situation without a word she crouched down at my feet, lathered me in coconut oil, then fastening her withered tentacles into my flesh commenced to rake them up and down my leg with the indifference of a sculptor to his clay. Except for a sardonic chuckle whenever I cried out with particular force, the operation was conducted in silence. Despite the anguish I couldn't help being impressed by her professional sureness of touch.

'Ah well,' said Father Kavuru, sketching a lurid mime of cannibal ritual as he spoke, 'We Fijians after all must be expected to have an expert knowledge of anatomy, don't you agree? And now—what about a game of scrabble to take your mind off the injury?' His eyes narrowed behind his glasses and a huge grin spread over his face. 'It's rather a hobby of mine—like to bet I'll beat you?'

For the next three hours this he proceeded to do, while Monsignor Wassner played chess with Miss Naresh, the Indian teacher, and Miss MacPeake read a Graham Greene novel, and then we all retired to bed.

When I limped out on to the veranda the following morning, I found Maria already waiting for me. I told her that as I was returning to Suva in half an hour, I would be seeing my own doctor so perhaps no further *masi-masi* was really necessary. A scowl of disapproval screwed up her wrinkles and she mumbled something to Honorata, the Indian housegirl who was sitting on the steps at her side.

'She says you must stay for further treatment. Maybe one week,' translated Honorata, who had been brought up by Fijians and spoke no Hindi at all.

I asked her to explain to Maria that it was impossible as I had promised my family I would be back today and the children were expecting me.

At the magic word 'children', Maria's expression relented. Soon we were exchanging family histories. Fingering the gold cross she wore round her neck, she fixed me with her opaque, old stare and told me how her husband was dead, her daughter a nun at the mission, while she herself lived in one of the *bures* just below the compound. She treated most of the minor ailments in the village. Lying-ins and laying-outs were her specialities, also the making of medicines from leaves and herbs.

'No bad thing—no bad thing!' she said hastily, breaking into English in her eagerness to let me know that witchcraft or *draunikau*—a word that itself means leaves of the tree—was not included in her practice. 'Old times, yes—today, no!'

I asked her what was her diagnosis of my ankle. 'That part in two,' she said, gesturing, 'all pulled up at back.' This agreed with my own feeling that some vital item of my ankle's anatomy was no longer where it should be, an opinion confirmed later by my own doctor in Suva who told me I had ruptured my Achilles tendon and should be able to walk properly again in about 'six months or so'.

After breakfast the local taxi arrived and with it the time for farewells. Amongst them, it was the words of Monsignor Wassner that stayed with me as we drove away down the hill and out of sight of the grey-stone church with its lichen-coloured roof.

‘When you remember Naiserelagi, which means The Place of Heavenly Singing, remember too that the name of the estate is a necessarily earthly one. *Vunibitu*—The Root of the Bamboo. . . .’

7

Laisa

In true Fijian style no more was heard about my invitation to Taveuni from Ratu Penaia and Adi Laisa in the weeks that followed the dinner-party. Just when, according to European logic, the idea would seem to have been gracefully dropped, a chance remark by a mutual friend made it clear that I was, in fact, expected and at any moment.

Time was limited and two hours by plane seemed a safer alternative to forty-eight hours in a copra boat in what was the hurricane season. Suva's tiny airport, some miles out from the city, had the rustic charm of a village railway station compared to the international crossroads on the other side of the island where I had landed from England. Thin brown cows with horns like lyres grazed on either side of the dusty track that led to the airfield. In the shade of a hangar a mechanic in dungarees with a red hibiscus behind one ear ambled over the shell of a Heron plane to the steady drone of the Fijian choir coming through a radio loudspeaker. Yellow alamanda sprawled over the veranda of the bungalow waiting-room that adjoined it. Inside, a few Europeans, mainly planters in shorts and bushjackets and wide-brimmed hats, sat around on striped canvas chairs reading the *Fiji Times*. There was a peaceful silence marked by the tick of an old-fashioned pendulum clock and the clink of teacups behind the serving hatch. One very small Chinese tourist moved quietly around photographing the blown-up pictures of Fiji pinned on the walls. Then a lean Australian in a white uniform shirt and dark trousers swung out from behind the reception counter, paused to pick up the basket lying on top. From inside it came an alarmed clucking.

'These for Missus Coles?' he asked the buxom, coffee-skinned lady clerk.

'Yea, Missus Coles—and don' forget, eh?'

The Australian put on a cap with gold braid round it and surveyed his passengers.

'Or-right then?'

'Taveuni plane now leavin',' chimed the clerk, clicking out after him, a typed schedule clasped to her bust. It had started to drizzle outside and she opened a multi-coloured golf umbrella over the Indian family who were trotting ahead with nervous haste. At the bottom of the crazy-paved garden path stood an eight-seater Drover plane, poised like a dragon-fly among the dripping flowers. One by one we were squeezed down the miniature aisle into our places. From outside the buxom lady closed the door on us with the satisfied bang of a cook consigning a final batch of cakes to the oven. The rain had stopped and the sun steamed down again. Inside the cabin the heat swelled steadily like a balloon, as we fastened our seat-belts with slippery fingers to the whoop of engines being tested. At what seemed like bursting-point a scream of protest broke from one of the Indian babies behind. Simultaneously, the pilot's face appeared with a reassuring wink in the tiny perspex panel in front. Then we were taxi-ing round to the end of the tarmac ribbon, roaring forward, rising over the meccano control tower, the matchbox buildings of the airport. Two figures in firemen's helmets waved to us and were gone.

Wheeling gull-high, the Drover turned to the sea. I looked out and for the first time saw the South Pacific beneath the wings of a plane. Long slow-motion breakers combed its sleek surface. Over the shallows the colour shifted from squid-blue to jade and turquoise, marbled with the currents, in just the way of the oceans on schoolroom atlases. Sandy atolls floated by like chips of tortoise-shell. Around each island a thread of surf traced the outline of the reefs whose shadows lay clearly visible beneath the glass lid of the water.

Much too soon, land swung up under the wings again. After the vacuum of jet travel one felt the exciting closeness of childhood dreams of flying, skimming at broomstick level over sugary beaches and plasticine mountain ranges, rain forests packed as tight as sprigs of cauliflower, brown thatched roofs in a clearing and a speckle of tiny figures, black on green.

Fiji from the air reminded me of the legend about the gods, Degei and Roko Mouta, as they strolled around the coasts of their

The Honourable Ratu Penaia Ganilau, D.S.O., O.B.E.

Adi Laisa, wife of Ratu Penaia Ganilau

new domain. Wherever the long train of white *tapa*, worn by such superior beings, dragged over the land there appeared smooth sandy beaches, and where the train was carried over the shoulder the land remained rugged and rocky. The outlying islands were said to be mountain-tops transferred by gods and goddesses in their frolicsome moods from the two large islands. 'Degei', Consul Pritchard tells us, 'is represented as having the head and body of a serpent with a tail of stone, together indicative of his keen forecast and everlasting duration.' The Roko's appearance, however, remains a mystery.

Another strip of sea and we were dropping towards a largish boat-shaped island covered with coconut palms that grew as thickly together as hair on a Fijian head. The only drawback was we seemed to be dropping not on to land but into the surrounding water. Then suddenly on the very tip of the island a long, shaved strip of grass tilted up at us out of the jungle, like the flight-deck of an aircraft carrier. There was a slow swooping movement and the wheels jarred on solid ground. Opening my eyes I found we had landed on target. Neither the passengers nor the knot of onlookers outside the tiny ticket-office on the edge of the palms, appeared even slightly shaken by this feat as the plane trundled to a standstill. They must all be Taveuni regulars, I reflected, and sank gratefully into the car that was to take me to the Penaias's house.

For half an hour we drove along the narrow road that followed the undulating glitter of the sea. Sometimes the spray from the waves breaking on the rocks below dashed lightly against the car wheels. Sometimes there was a patch of white beach and facing it a cluster of *bures*, a Chinese store, the corrugated-iron roof of a copra shed. Everywhere groves of coconut plantations stretched back from the road, tall and shadowy, and the rich smell of the husked and drying flesh hung on the warm afternoon air. Occasionally we drew aside to let pass the solitary taxi, a lorry laden with bags of copra, or the island bus.

I remembered that Taveuni was one of the points in the Fiji Group through which the 180th Meridian, the International Date Line, passes. W. S. Gilbert, of all people, had noted the fact too and, ignoring the Uniform Date Ordinance passed for the sake of sanity by the Government of 1879, toyed with the idea of a comic opera. 'In 'Fiji a man may stand with one leg in Sunday and the other in Monday,' he remarked delightedly. 'He may walk decorously to church with his right leg, while his left leg is dancing profane hornpipes. If he cannot kick a bore into the middle of next week, he can easily project him a considerable distance in that direction.'

I myself had heard that a Chinese storekeeper had taken advantage of the situation with a shop that straddled the spot and so provided Sunday sales through a side-door without infringing a single by-law. The driver, though, was at a loss.

'Not too sure where,' he kept repeating. 'I heard about that thing but not too sure where.'

This was a little disappointing—one somehow expected to see the line materialize out of thin air like a rainbow, or at least some kind of science-fiction mist descend to mark the time barrier. But it was certainly preferable to another vision, hordes of sun-spectacled tourists haggling over *tapa* maps and calendars at a souvenir gift-shop, snapping each other on different sides of the week, and toasting the future round a novelty bar entitled 'The Lost Week-end'.

The Penaias's house, being a chief's house, stood high above the surrounding village and to reach it we drove up a narrow winding hill. It was the typical sprawling, one-storey, wooden 'manor'-house of the tropics, with great shuttered verandas and rambling gardens. On the porch Adi Laisa was waiting, a pillar of monumental elegance in a beige and white spotted afternoon dress worn over a brown silk *sulu*.

'Tiuné!'

Two diminutive and shapely hands grasped my own. There was the familiar brown, twinkling scrutiny and dimpling smile. My bags disappeared into the house under the arms of a grizzled bearer in a starched white coat.

There was to be a party that night, Laisa explained, as we went in. Bevies of servants who were already setting a vast buffet table in the inner room, and in the kitchen quarters pots and pans steamed in the lamplight on open wood stoves. From outside came a chugging roar as the generator went into action and electric lights flickered on everywhere. Soon, on the veranda, drinks were dispensed to the arriving guests by the elderly Fijian in the white jacket who had carried in my bags.

'This is Toa,' said Adi Laisa, as he approached us with a tray, a small gnarled man with a cheerful air and a sea-going limp in one leg. 'Mr. Toa has always been with Ratu Penaia.'

Mr. Toa ducked his head, an indulgent smile spread over his battered features, then bobbed away to fetch our whiskies.

A few minutes later the rain stopped and a quarter-moon drifted through the palm trees. At a signal from Adi Laisa, two servants appeared round the front of the house carrying an enormous, glowing fire set out on a strip of corrugated iron and laid on a pair of wooden poles. The conflagration was placed at the bottom of the steps and soon the smell of barbequed steak and sausages floated up to the veranda and smoking platters joined the vast display of rice, prawn curry, Chinese dishes, cold salads, yams and *dalo* that covered the tables.

Afterwards, conversation round the veranda settled into the laconic tempo of people who have seen each other all day, who see each other every day and have long ago exhausted any possibility of untried topics.

But, warmed by alcohol, the old ones rolled along pleasantly enough between the easy-going middle-aged Australian estate-owners and their wives, a couple of bank clerks, the doctor and the schoolmaster. Until the eruption on the scene of a new-comer by the name of Mr. Jackson, a roving representative of the world of commerce.

'Hello, hello, hello!' cried Mr. Jackson, springing into the centre of the room and rubbing his hands as he surveyed the circle, a sharp little brilliantined figure in a too-small striped sports vest and narrow belted trousers. 'Now we can really get the ball rolling!'

'Fred's always the life and soul of the party,' confided the plump planter's wife sitting next to me. 'I don't know what we did without him.'

Within an hour, Mr. Jackson had regaled us with a mouth-organ recital, half a dozen music-hall sketches rattled off in a rasping pseudo-Cockney, several matchbox tricks and a rapid resumé of the highlights of a crowded life, ranging from the beaches of Dunkirk to the palaces of India—'in the good old days, with me faithful bearer asleep across the door'. Then, flagging a fraction, he remembered the records he had brought.

'I've Got Sixpence', 'The White Cliffs of Dover' and 'Pack Up

Your Troubles' wavered out from the radiogram in the corner, now gabbled, now drooling, according to the variations of the generating plant still pumping away in the garden. Mr. Jackson stood and conducted a sing-song in the middle of the room.

At the end there was polite applause from the room behind. The servants and their friends from the village had been slipping in through the back entrance, stooping low and whispering apologies according to Fijian custom, throughout Mr. Jackson's performance. Now they sat cross-legged in a semicircle against the farthest wall, the women in best ankle-length dresses and *salu-salus* of frangipani around their necks, the men with brilliantly patterned *bula* shirts over their *sulus*, the younger ones sporting a hibiscus tucked behind one ear.

'They're going to entertain us,' said Adi Laisa.

'Fair enough!' cried Mr. Jackson. 'And let's have something we can all join in!'

Adi Laisa murmured something in Fijian to the group inside. The women giggled with downcast eyes. An elderly man near the front bowed his head and issued a brief instruction to the others. From somewhere a guitar and a small drum were produced and with expansions of wooden solemnity, laced with just the faintest sidelong flicker of amusement, the party launched into a heartfelt rendering of a current radio pop, 'Sad Movies'.

'That's the stuff,' called Mr. Jackson, beating time with one hand as he turned in his chair and started an anecdote about a party of the previous evening.

Next to me sat the blonde Australian girl who turned out to be the wife of one of the younger generation of Tartes. Everyone knew the Tartes, one of the most successful plantation-owning families in Fiji and the ruling family on Taveuni since the mid-eighteen-hundreds. Now they were a byword throughout the islands for their colourful idiosyncrasies—the huge American cars they brought for which the estate roads must be widened, the cinema they had built for their employees, the amateur films they wrote and produced, the *Gone-With-the-Wind*-type names in which they revelled, Valentine, Darryl, Adrian and Spencer Willoughby Roode-Tarte.

'What a pity Aunt Edie's away,' she said. 'I could have taken you up for tea to meet her. Still I expect you'll be doing the other social rounds,' she added. 'Hats and gloves sort of thing.' Seeing my expression, she grinned. 'In some houses here, you even sign a book. This is Taveuni, you know!'

In the background, 'Sad Movies' had quietly give way to the Fijian version of 'O Sole Mio', which was followed by a well-known song about a girl by the name of Susi, who wanted to ride away with her love in a brand-new *motoka* (motor-car).

The singing then swelled to full tide with a traditional composition about the excellence of the milk from the coconuts of Ovalau. The guitar had been laid aside. Slow, steady and immutable, the chords and harmonies rumbled out to the click of the *lali* and there was silence along the veranda, even from Mr. Jackson, as the guests leaned back in the semi-darkness to listen.

It was, I noticed, a more detached kind of listening, rather unlike the gemutlich affinity of non-Fijians in other isolated parts of the islands. Although the rest of the songs were everyday favourites, with Adi Laisa adding her contralto, there was no actual joining in, no sitting on the floor by the audience here. They would 'know the people like the back of my hand', as they fairly claimed. But between them there was an accepted distinction. Employers and estate-owners, they had standards to maintain. It was this that seemed to give Taveuni its distinctive atmosphere of formality, a place full of carefully preserved observances and symbols, as touching in their tenacity as they were remote from the other Fiji beyond the island.

At midnight, the last guest gone, ease again descended on us. 'Just time for one more record before the electricity goes off,' decreed Laisa. 'My favourite.'

With her characteristic appearance of moving on ball-bearings, she flowed across to the record-player. A silvery voice began crooning, Oriental style, to a string accompaniment.

'It is a love-song,' said Laisa. 'I brought it back from Malaya with me.'

She sat back in an armchair with a sigh of contentment. Around her in a circle half a dozen young women of the household lay flat on their stomachs like cats, glistening eyes half-closed, and listened intently to the strange, bird-like sounds of a girl singing in a Kuala Lumpur night-club.

The record ended and at the same moment, with a dying whirr, the lights went out. From the shadows appeared the Rembrandt figure of Mr. Toa, a lamp in each hand. There was a puff of scented coconut-oil, the rustle of *salu-salus* as the women stood up, still clicking their tongues in wonderment.

'Come,' said Laisa, taking a lamp from Mr. Toa. 'Now I will show you where you are sleeping.'

She led the way through the house, then out down the back steps and along a narrow garden path.

'This will be a surprise for you, I think.'

I agreed, as startled toads went humping away ahead of us to plunge under huge, patchwork leaves on either side.

Suddenly at the end of the path, out of the trees, a peaked outline loomed against the stars. Up three stone steps and we crossed the threshold of one of the most beautiful and elaborate *bures* I had ever seen. Laisa put down the lamp and watched my face with a smile as the yellow glow lapped over the fine cream mats that covered the floor, the walls hung with bark-cloth, the shoulder-high partition of polished reeds beyond which lay two beds, one of them neatly veiled for the night against mosquitoes.

'Ratu Penaia and I mostly sleep here. But I thought you would prefer it to a room in the house. It's yours for as long as you're here.'

There was a discreet cough from outside. Mr. Toa was waiting with another lamp to escort his mistress back through the garden.

'Do you like a shower or a bath?' demanded Laisa from the doorway.

'A shower is quite . . .' I began, knowing that baths and the hot water to supply them were rarities in country districts.

'In Taveuni, you see, they go together.' She rolled her eyes mysteriously. 'When you wake up, just follow the path down the lawn. I'll be there!'

With a wave of her hand, she disappeared.

'*Mothé!*' floated back from the darkness, the gentle Fijian word that means both sleep and farewell. '*Mothé Tiune!*'

But before I could sleep I took the lamp and looked again at my wonderful room—at the foundation pillars of tree-trunks a foot in thickness and bound around with black-and-white *masi*, at the high sloping ceilings completely covered with matting held in place by narrow cross-beams, at the three doorways with their lintels of polished branches hung with clusters of white cowrie shells. The bark-cloth that draped the upper walls was a single length of very old Tongan *tapa*, supple as silk, the traditional patterns of palm-leaves and flowers a faded blur of bronzes, creams and ambers. I put out my hand and encountered the soft, downy surface of a ripe peach. As one moved about, the ground underfoot seemed to have a springy resilience quite unlike a wooden flooring or the usual dried-earth base. Turning back one of the mats I discovered that the whole room was carpeted with a thick layer of tiny pebbles, shells and crushed coral that glinted rainbow-coloured in the lamp-light like hidden treasure. Out of this transported sea-bed, the slender stems of bamboo lining the lower walls rose as though in growth.

Apart from the beds, the only furnishings in the *bure* were a curtained alcove for clothes, a mirror and two long basket chairs. On a low table lay a round feathered fan, dyed in vivid pinks and blues, a ceremonial *bilo* (drinking cup) of half a coconut shell fringed around with the hairy outer husk, and a long-handled fly-whisk of coconut fibre.

Outside the rain was falling again over the rich glut of forest and bush that had yielded this extraordinary tapestry of shapes and textures. As I got into bed I could hear a light regular drip from the fringes of the eaves, and behind, the unbroken shirring of the river and its waterfalls. From under a fold of *masi* a small lizard darted out, froze into a loop in the pattern of the cloth, then slithered back again. There was a faint smell of wet soil and dried fern. I blew out the lamp. It was like falling asleep in a forest at the bottom of the sea.

8

Miss Gordon-Cumming in a Towel

The path down the lawn seemed to end in impenetrable bush—an eye-level mass of twining vines, overgrown ferns and red ginger. It was early morning and there was no sign of life either from the house or from the surrounding garden. But the sensation of wet grass under bare feet and a hot sun on unclothed shoulders gave one a heady confidence. Tightening the *sulu* I wore wrapped round sarong-style—which although practical always made one feel foolishly like wife of Tarzan—I parted a clump of wild orchids and pressed on.

The path reappeared as a winding track. At the bottom, a large yellow towel lay slung over a boulder. Rounding this landmark, I found myself gazing down at a torrent of water which gushed out from the hillside into a kind of Roman bath below, a square stone trough about ten feet across. Suddenly from behind the waterfall emerged Laisa's black head, a pair of plumply gleaming shoulders. Shaking herself she rose to her feet, magnificently sculptured in folds of scarlet-flowered cotton, the wiry pom-pom of hair not really wet at all—it never could be—but glinting here and there with a few scattered drops. She looked up and caught sight of me.

'This will be too cold, even for the English!' she called, with a grin.

It was. After the initial shock it was pleasanter to sit on the moss-furred steps with only one's legs in the water, warming ourselves in the damp, heavy air and shouting across to one another above the roar of the fall that poured steadily out of the rocks overhead like a bath-tap some giant had forgotten to turn off.

'There is one for the servants, too,' Laisa explained, pointing to where the overflow sluiced down into another smaller trough below. All around us the valley fell away in undulations of mist and sun—masked in thick creeper, the outlines of bush and tree only vaguely suggested like furniture under drapes. From a clearing on the opposite slope rose a thread of smoke and somewhere a cock crowed.

As ever on such occasions I heard the voice of Miss Gordon-Cumming at my side recalling, with a fellow-traveller's passion for comparison, her own introduction to the delights of Fiji's waterfalls. 'Of course, we were not always burdened with bathing gowns, but'—a faint ring of bravado here—'a bathing towel and a large white umbrella form an excellent substitute.'

She was still with me as we walked up through the garden again, past the new *bure* that was being built on the far side of the house. Two men were already at work on the roof, squatting astride the thatched gables, and I found myself wondering if they were ordinary villagers or Government prisoners as in Miss Gordon-Cumming's description of a similar house-builder—'one a murderer in heavy chains. Though he looks very happy climbing nimbly about the roof notwithstanding this heavy weight,' she reported, 'it makes me hot and miserable to see him.'

I asked Laisa who the new house was for.

'For Ratu George Thakobau.' Drawing our towels round our shoulders we peered inside under the green uncut eaves of the doorway. The air was damp, the floor still wet and muddy. 'When it is finished they light a fire in here for many days to smoke the ceiling and dry the whole place out.'

'Ratu George is coming to stay then?'

It is Fijian custom to spin a story out as long as possible and persistent questioning is an essential element in the procedure. As we walked back to the big house Laisa told me in instalments that the new *bure* for the Vunivalu, or High Chief, was just part of a programme of preparations for the elaborate ceremonies next month of *Vaka-tara-i-Sulu*. The Casting-Off-Of-Mourning Clothes on this occasion was to commemorate the death of Ratu Sir Lala Sukuna. Properly, the ceremonies should be performed exactly one hundred nights after the chief's death to mark the formal end of the mourning period. But with Sukuna, for various reasons, this had not been done and time had lapsed to the extent of three years.

'Some people say this neglect of custom has brought misfortune to Taveuni,' Laisa said, pursing her lips as we sat down to a large breakfast of cornflakes, tinned orange juice, grilled kidneys and Oxford marmalade. Still frowning she went through the morning mail of Sydney newspapers, invitations to open or attend bazaars, concerts and cocktail parties, and the latest issue of *Awake*, the monthly bulletin of the local temperance movement, while I, not for the first time, wrestled mentally with some of the more striking incongruities of modern Fiji.

'What sort of misfortune?'

'Ah, Ramanu will tell you all about that! We'll ask him up to the house one evening. He is our local witch-doctor!' She delivered this parody translation of a strictly Fijian term with the conspiratorial excitement of a grown-up pandering to a child's expectations, a favourite habit of most sophisticated Fijians.

I reacted suitably but no further reference was made to the subject either on this or any of the other mornings that followed. Each day fell into the same placid pattern—a bathe in the waterfall, a brief inspection of the progress of the *bure*, breakfast, then an hour or so in the garden. Here Laisa, an old print *sulu* wound round her cotton frock, would seize the cane-knife from the garden-boy and, slashing vigorously from side to side, give a practical demonstration of how to keep the pathways clear of undergrowth. Seeing her like this, or watching her swing down to sit cross-legged in a single easy movement, one always forgot Laisa was a large woman. With her upright carriage, the sway of her hips and the lightness of her feet it seemed as if, unlike Europeans of the same build, there was no weight to that luxurious bounty of outline, just softness and buoyancy, a feather-bed quality that was above all essentially seductively feminine. While she disappeared to supervise various household tasks I would feed the families of chickens that scuttled across the lawns. Sometimes I was joined by Ratu Jo. Ratu Jo was the youngest of the Penaia children and the only one not yet away at school, a misleadingly solemn four-year-old with cropped head and enormous eyes, wearing the over-large shorts of an elder brother, the idol of the servants and the tease of his mother's life. Despite Laisa's urgings, he steadfastly refrained from addressing me in either English or Fijian and was always careful to keep a gap of at least three feet between us. Nevertheless, we would walk together in an unbroken but companionable silence, Ratu Jo trailing behind him his favourite toy, a battered tin-can on a piece of string constructed by Mr. Toa, away from the lawns and the herbaceous borders, round the field with the old bull staring over the railings, past the three coconut palms that leaned back at an ideal climbing angle of forty-five degrees, down the steps to the stream where tiny mud-coloured guppies darted in the shallows and a kingfisher on a branch in drab, spiky profile, swooped in a sapphire flash on a lizard in the grass.

Once or twice it rained and indoors it was so dark that the electricity pump had to be started up at noon. Beneath the veranda shutters the view was of a different country—a distant strip of grey sky-coloured sea, the palm trees below clustered together like the umbrellas in the Renoir painting, and against their sombre greeny-blues the foreground explosions of shining red leaves, tall torches of crimson ginger-flowers. Indifferent to the wet, the men still worked on the *bure*, the water gleaming on sleek, oiled backs as they climbed up and down bamboo ladders to put on the last layer of leaves for the thatch. The sound of rain on the iron roof seemed just another echo of the drum-rhythm tempo of Fijian life, a complex counterpoint made up of many small things—the hollow beat of the *lali* from the village *rara*, the chanting of the *bure* workers, the regular smack of axe-blows from behind the house—even the clicking of the garden-boy's scissors, as he walked the flower-beds, or Mr. Toa's absent-minded tattoo with his fingers on the tray beneath his arm as he surveyed the setting of the lunch table.

Around the living-room, china scotties and bunny rabbits stood ranged on small tables beneath knobbled Fijian war clubs and curved daggers from Malaya. Penaia's six-foot-high silver inlaid staff of office as the *Roko Tui* (High Chief) of Thakaudrove Province, shared a corner with his expensive slim-furled London umbrella. Among the ornaments arranged on Laisa's Malayan chest, I noticed a small silver model of a Kiwi bird from New Zealand and a miniature bronze rugby ball, a memento of one of the Fijian team's overseas tours. The wall decorations were even more varied. Whales' teeth (*tabua*), highly polished and yellow with age, hung on cords of sinnet next to Ratu Penaia's framed Order of the British Empire. In the inner room there were photographs of Penaia at the head of the procession of troops returning from Malaya, a portrait in oils in his colonel's uniform and medals, a coloured print of the horse that won him fifty pounds in the Melbourne Cup, and a picture of his youngest daughter in the ceremonial *tapa* robes of a Fijian princess presenting another member of royalty, Queen

Elizabeth, with a bouquet of white flowers on her arrival at the Suva Wharf. Laisa had told me that these flowers were the famous *tagi-mau-thia* which grew on the top of Taveuni's highest peak, and the plucking of them was reserved for only special occasions. Ratu Penaia's favourite books, it seemed from the shelves, were Churchill's *War Memoirs* and lives of the Royal Family, especially the Duke of Windsor. There was also a solid row of *Encyclopaedia Britannica*'s, the laws of Fiji, some Hansard Reports, a number of volumes on colonial policy and, ever popular with Fijian leaders, Bertrand Russell's *History of Western Philosophy*.

A new sound, a low syncopated thudding, had joined the other background rhythms. In the doorway Laisa appeared, beaming and relaxed, a cigarette in her hand. 'This *masi* is going to be very good. Come and see!'

I followed her through to one of the rooms at the back of the house. In the dim light about twenty women were sitting together on the floor, surrounded by the companionable buzz of talk and sewing machines, and a rolling sea of jumbled materials, matting, baskets and babies. One infant was being fed at his mother's breast, propped up by her knee, as she calmly bound a piece of twine round the handle of a newly-made fan. In the corner, two older children were taking a midday nap top to tail on a pile of dried rushes.

There were smiles, low murmurs of greeting, a drawing aside of legs and feet as we crossed to the veranda doorway where three elderly women were bent over a large slab, beating with mallets at several strips of moist, white bark. I had never watched *masi* being made before—it was becoming a rare craft and one never seen in city areas—and looked on fascinated as slowly, like pastry, the material thinned and widened with each tap of the mallet. A few feet away, another group of ladies with soot-stained fingers were carefully stencilling in the traditional glistening patterns, using twig brushes, black dye and shapes of shell and wood, on larger pieces of *masi* which had been joined together with arrowroot paste.

"All this is for Ratu George—the ceremonies next month.'

In the same way, I thought, the great-grandmothers of these women might have sat in 1872 preparing patiently the presentation piece for Ratu Ebenezer Thakabau noted at Taveuni by the English traveller Forbes—a piece half a mile long and, when folded, a solid mass thirty feet long and eight feet high. Being too large to carry away it was left on the beach with a roof over it for protection.

'Isa!' sighed one of the women when Laisa relayed this to them.

'Those days have gone, she says,' Laisa repeated. 'But the women of Taveuni still make the best *masi* in Fiji.'

We went inside again and sat down among the mat-makers, briskly plaiting and stranding from the dried coils of *pandanus* leaf, one to each side of a mat, the dusty coarseness of outstretched feet contrasting with the oiled pink-palmed delicacy of their hands, none of them pretty but the older ones with a fine show of rounded upper arms and Restoration bosoms, a gleaming smile, a pair of slanted eyes or copper-smooth cheekbones to each of the younger ones, and about them all a keen earthy vitality that was in complete contrast to the languors and inhibitions of the harems I had known in Arabia. One of the mats was a bed mat, soft and fine and elaborately fringed with coloured wool. Another had the name of the Vunivalu intricately plaited into the centre of the design in contrasting strands of black and brown. In the old days there would have been sail-mats too, for the canoes, great triangular pieces woven with *voi-voi* from the Yasawas where a dry climate produced material tough enough to withstand the strongest wind and rain.

'These will all be presented to the most important guests at the ceremonies. After the *yaggona* drinking will come the offerings of pigs and turtles. Then, when the feasting is over, the *mekes*.'

'And I shall be in Suva!'

'But at least you can see the *mekes*,' Laisa went on, 'and that is the best part. We are rehearsing this afternoon on the *rara*. You can come down and see the whole thing.'

'*Vinaka, vinaka!*' everyone agreed, as the gathering began to break up to return to the village for the midday meal. On my way out, about to step over the mat in front of me, I was pulled politely but firmly back by a sharp-featured matron with flashing eyes, and so learned one more rule of the mat-making profession—that it is strictly tabu to cross an unfinished specimen. To do so will inevitably result in the mat being misshapen and spoiled.

Sitting on the steps at the bottom of the lawn after lunch, under the huge flowering *ivi* tree that smelt of violets, one could see not only the *rara*, a broad patch of green circled by the shaggy roofs of the village, but the whole of the bay of Somo-Somo. Laisa had gone on ahead and I was waiting for the dancers to appear before I walked down to join them.

There below was the beach, golden in the afternoon sun, where in the 1840's the *Ra Marama*, one of the greatest of Fiji's old double-canoes, had been lovingly and laboriously built as a tribute to the memory of the chief lady of Thakaudrove. A 102 feet long and 18 feet wide, it had taken seven years to complete. Logs had been split with wedges of rock and iron, heavy planks hewn with infinite labour, fitted with lugs and stiffening ribs, bored at intervals to take the sinnet lashings with which they were secured. A deck-house and platform for the chiefs had finally to be completed, before the giant was ready for presentation to Ratu Thakobau. It is reported that though men were clubbed at the keel-laying according to ritual, no blood was spilt at the launching owing to the influence of the missionaries Lyth and Hunt, nor were the customary bodies procured at each place of call on the maiden voyage. But when, at Bau, the great mast was lowered for the first time, the heel slipped and in falling killed one man and injured two others. Thakobau attributed the accident to the wrath of the gods on account of the lack of appropriate sacrifices, and almost immediately twenty-one victims were hunted up to repair for earlier omissions. The canoe was next presented by Thakobau to King George of Tonga, but after three trips it was eventually returned to its original owner. When Thakobau died, the Somo-Somo people took it back and as a gesture of mourning the great canoe was grounded and allowed to rot—on the same beach on which its life had started forty years before.

Beyond stretched the blue silk screen of sea and sky, a single yellow row-boat riding the edge of the tide. In the distance, opposite the Strait, was Benau, the island home of Dakuwaga the Shark-God who lived in a cave below his *bure kalou*, or temple. Everyone knew that Dakuwaga was the god of the fishermen, though from the stories of his kidnappings of beautiful women, he was also the god of adultery. Many were the superstitions that surrounded him. It was tabu to eat shark flesh; sharks with markings on the belly similar to the tattooing of Dakuwaga were released when trapped in the fish fence; when canoes passed over areas of sea he was known to frequent, cups of *yaggona* and morsels of food were thrown overboard to gain his favour. For Dakuwaga was also Dauthina the Light-Giver, and at night would pilot canoes through the reefs by the phosphorescence of his wake.

At a time when such beliefs were lived by, somewhere down there on the outskirts of Somo-Somo Hannah Hunt of Newton-on-Trent and her husband John, the Lincolnshire farm-hand turned Methodist missionary, were setting up house with the Lyths, another missionary couple, in a *bure* lent them by the King of the Reef, Tui Thakau. This was as far as the old man's goodwill extended towards the new *lotu* of Christianity. For this was the Fiji of 1840 where, as Hunt himself noted, 'Cruelty is law', and the people of Somo-Somo were particularly notorious for their savageries.

'The first sight of a Feejee man is very appalling,' he was writing in his journal, as Hannah and Mrs. Lyth counted out the casks of rice and flour watched by jostling hordes of muscular giants with spears in their hands and great heads of hair, two or three feet in diameter, their faces smeared with black and red dyes, their bodies naked except for a loincloth of *masi* or kilt of leaves, and looming behind them the tall thatched steeples of their heathen temples and the jagged peaks and rainclouds of the Taveuni coastline.

Within a week the king's son was drowned and despite the pleadings of Lyth and Hunt the sixteen widows were strangled so that they might accompany their chief to the Spirit World to be his attendants there. 'We were obliged to be in the midst of it and truly their cries and wailings were awful. . . . They took a long piece of Native cloth and tied two knots about the middle and putting one knot on the throat and the other on the back of the neck some pulled at one end and some at another until they were strangled. Soon after they were murdered they were brought to be buried about twenty yards from our house. They were folded up in mats, etc., and were carefully covered over with stones, the cloth which formed the rope for strangling them was hung over them.'

This was followed by the celebration of circumcision rites among the young men. 'When the ceremony was performed, the cloth on which some of the blood had been sprinkled was brought into the king's yard and put on a stick, and the persons who had been circumcised danced round it. Their dancing consisted in walking and jumping and singing and shouting and yelling, etc., a most heathenish affair to be sure and continued several nights. . . . In connection with this ceremony many females and some men had one of the joints of their fingers cut off. . . .'

Throughout a nightmare year Hannah saw enemy captives slaughtered, roasted and eaten by the Somosomans at cannibal feasts held only a few yards from the mission fence, where the king's house stood opposite. On one occasion, 'the King came in during the time the bodies were cooking and enquired why we had closed all the doors of the house. We told him the true reason which was because we hated the smell of the bodies which were cooking at which he was not pleased. We went into Mr. L's study where Mr. Lyth and Mrs. Hunt were sitting, and as soon as Mrs. H. saw the King she began to cry. We spoke strongly to the King on the conduct he was pursuing, etc., at which he became angry and among other things said if we did not cease to reprove him he would kill us. I think he was partly displeased because Mrs. Hunt wept.'

But the school-lessons and the translations of texts and the sermons continued, attended by a handful of converts, and shortly after Hannah's twenty-seventh birthday she and Mrs. Lyth joined in the Sunday service unseen as they lay nursing their new-born sons behind one of the matting partitions that divided up the great reed house. Both children were to die, Hannah's of dysentery, only three days later. They buried him there in the garden, the first member of a missionary's family to lie in Fiji, and the King sent his carpenter to build a small house over the grave according to custom.

Hannah herself, despite her always delicate health, was to survive her husband, returning to England and Newton-on-Trent as a widow after his death on the island of Viwa in 1848 at the age of thirty-six.

Mr. Hunt is dead
The people of Viwa mourn.
The preaching day came
They wear black dresses
Dresses of reverence
He is carried to the chapel.
His face was lovely
—ai-ee! ai-ee!

So ran the *meke* composed to mark the grief of his people. . . .

tation of Whales' Teeth—the Honourable Ratu Mara, O.B.E., in the ceremonial dress of a Paramount Chief

Traditional costume for a women's *meke*

The royal island of Bau from the air
The preparation of *yaggona*

Mrs. Hunt has not eaten
She only drinks warm water
The black cloth is opened
Black is stitched to her bonnet
And serves as a covering for her face
—ai-ee! ai-ee!

What would she feel now, I wondered, as I sat looking down at the somnolent English scene of clustered thatch and deserted green, the neat wooden schoolhouse with the Union Jack floating in the compound, the drone of a multiplication table rising from the veranda. Farther along a copra lorry trailed a cloud of dust past the white limestone church whose square turrets and low walls glinted in the sunshine.

At that moment, from the Council House at the head of the green, a group of men emerged and settled themselves down in a closely-packed circle outside. There was silence broken lightly, insistently, by the clicking of a single *lali,* faint as the chirping of a cricket from where I sat, and as incisive. It was a summons that brought from the shadow of the trees on the other side, a flutter of movement as with delicate swaying steps a seemingly unending line of women unfurled itself from this hiding-place and rippled slowly across the grass. Tiny figures with round black heads and stiff wide skirts of black and white *tapa,* they glided jerkily forward like a string of wooden dolls kept in motion by the clockwork ticking of the drum. Drawn up in a line across the *rara* they turned to face the Council House. The *lali* stopped. The women waited. There was a brief pin-drop pause, against the low hum of the heat-laden air and sea. Then from the men, a solitary voice, shaky with age, began to chant. Pitched on one high note in a minor key, the succession of level long-drawn monosyllables tolled out across the green with the weird solemnity of the pronouncements of a seer or a trance message from another world, punctuated only by the bony rattle of the *lali* sticks. Another deeper drum joined in and around it rose the voices of the others, solidly interwoven, and the rhythm of hollow hand-claps, as with one accord the women raised their arms and broke into a vigorous, sweeping series of gestures matched in perfect unison by the swaying of their bodies, backwards and forwards, from side to side.

At such a distance, the dance resolved itself into a single, concerted pattern of action. In this dimension one saw the dancers as they really were, inseparable elements of their setting, behind them the trees and birds their arms and hands were sketching, before them the sea whose surfline seemed to mirror the surging ripples of their ranks as they advanced and retreated and tossed their heads, releasing an eddy of long white streamers to the breeze. This was what the *meke* was, I thought, as I turned to walk down the hill—not a display of personal grace and skill nor an escapist entertainment, but a translation, a living record of the scenes and events in men's lives most worthy of commemoration, familiar poetry that was the vital sap behind the workaday world's coarse, outer husk.

By the time I reached the *rara*, the first part of the *meke* was over and the women were resting in the shade of the Council House. There were words of welcome from faces I now knew and hands reached up to take mine in greeting as I made my way across to Adi Laisa, sitting in state on the kind of fine mat which was *tabu kaisi* (forbidden to commoners), in the centre of the gathering. One other person shared the mat, a pleasant-faced, middle-aged lady who was introduced to me as the wife of the present Tui Thakau. Then Laisa said something to the circle of men who were providing the musical accompaniment. Stern, beetle-browed persons, mostly of venerable age, they nodded gravely at me over their shoulders, then turned back to their conference.

'That is Ramanu,' whispered Laisa, indicating a particularly wrinkled old man with a spray of drooping fern behind each ear. 'It is he who has composed this *meke*.'

A loud handclap interrupted her. A stout, glistening man with an unmistakable air of authority stood up and issued a brisk command. At once the ladies were on their feet, brushing down their papery crinolines, one or two of them pinching out the cigarettes they had been puffing—brown cheroot-like affairs made locally—and all of them assuming the intense, abstracted expression of performers about to go through a particularly complex routine.

'It is the story of the life and death of Ratu Sukuna,' was all she had time to add before moving off with the others.

Once again the old voice pronounced the theme—it was Ramanu's of course—and once again in time to the chorus the women took up their urgent semaphore of gesture and movement, this time in rows of six. As they danced, the stout man walked rapidly up and down the ranks, marshalling and curbing their patterns with the controlled ferocity of a sheepdog on the heels of his flock. Occasionally, to draw attention to some fault in the composition, he blew a short sharp blast on a whistle, a sound even more startling because of its incongruity. This was corrected smoothly, without pause, the concentration of the dancers unbroken even by the intermittent fighting between two scrawny village puppies who snapped and rumbled round their ankles throughout the rehearsal.

This time I tried to connect the dance with the events of Sukuna's life. Sometimes one would recognize from the movements, say, the pulling away of a boat, the actions of farewell, the swaying of a lamentation, tantalizing as the glimpse of a familiar outline in an ancient script. Mostly though, for the outsider, it remained a spectacle, with the sombre ring of the chant, the grave, almost priestly expressions of the women, the general air of dedication as surer indications of the solemnity of the subject than any interpreter's *sotto voce*.

The *meke* over, the performers sank to the grass again and there was a respectful silence while the Master of Ceremonies, discarding his whistle, addressed them in tones of command.

He was telling them, Laisa murmured next to me, which women were to prepare *yaggona* for the singers at the next rehearsal, which to bring food. The start of the practice would be announced by three strokes of the *lali*. Anyone coming late would be required to pay a forfeit in kind, the nature of which would be decided at the time. The triple handclap of respect followed these pronouncements. There were grunts of approval from the old men, and everyone collected themselves to leave on a wave of farewells and reminders. Two young girls with frangipani in their hair rolled up Laisa's mat and followed behind us as we walked back through the village.

'We must hurry,' Laisa said. 'Penaia will be back for dinner.'

Dusk was falling with the faint, rapid rustle of the tropics. A group of young men stood leaning their elbows on the little wooden bridge. Cooking fires were springing up in the narrow compounds between the *bures* and lamps glowed in open doorways. In one of the gardens they were picking mandarin oranges and called us in to have some, so we went and stood under the branches with their small dark leaves and pale globes of fruit while they threw the ripe ones down to us, and the children ran round with baskets gathering them up for presentation.

As we were leaving, again there came the roar of a jeep on the road behind us and a squeal of brakes.

'So this is where you are!' rumbled the voice of Ratu Penaia. '*Meke* practice again, eh?'

A hulking figure in white bushjacket and khaki-green trousers climbed down from the passenger seat and sent the driver off again with a flap of his hand.

'Come! We shall walk up together. I shall be glad to stretch my legs after the plane.'

Amidst the detonations of the reversing jeep, a volley of exclamations from Laisa and delighted giggles from the girls with the mat, we started to climb the steep drive up to the house. Taking his wife's elbow in one hand and mine in the other, Penaia strode between us humming to himself the tune of 'I Belong to Glasgow', one of his favourite compositions. Half-way up, the sound of other voices, singing in Fijian, drifted down to meet us. Turning the bend we found ourselves face to face with about twenty men stripped to the waist and carrying cane knives, villagers returning home from work on Penaia's plantations. There was a moment of medieval grace when, simultaneously, the men sank to the ground, some squatting, some bent on one knee, those on higher ground creeping forward until they were on a lower level than their chief. With easy gruffness, Penaia stepped forward to greet them, arms akimbo. Through the trees the last shreds of sunset illuminated the expressions of unselfconscious pleasure on the ring of upturned faces around him as, correctly hesitant, they answered his questions, laughing softly with lowered eyes at his final joke. Then with a nod and a movement of his hand he passed on, Laisa and I following behind. There was the mordant, musky smell of cooling sweat, the awareness of a scrutiny that was short and sharp. Out of sight, the singing rose again, more loudly cheerful than before and laced with the shouted exchanges of news and greetings from the first of the village *bures*.

Three canvas chairs had already been set out on the porch. Penaia sank into the largest of them and gave a kind of friendly bellow. Before it had time to die away, Mr. Toa was at his side with a tray of whisky, ice and glasses in one hand, the familiar lamp in the other.

'Mister Toa!' exclaimed Penaia, clapping him on the back and breaking into a stream of questions in Fijian which caused the little man to wheeze and hunch his shoulders in delighted protest as he laid the drink and glasses out on two small tables, then stumped away, still shaking, back into the house.

'Ah!' After a deep initial gulp, Penaia sighed with relief and stretched his legs in front of him. Bonzo, the household mongrel, sprawled down between them. 'A terrible place, Suva. One can only relax in the country.'

'How was Legislative Council?' Laisa asked. 'Anything interesting?'

Penaia turned the glass in his well-shaped hands before replying, his eyes slit against the lamplight that burnished the outlines of the handsome face with its heavy jaw, small curved nose and backward-sloping Thakaudrove head.

'The usual things,' he said at last in a slow, tired voice. 'The usual things.'

We sat in silence for a few minutes. A half-moon came skimming up through the clouds. By its light a small figure flitted across the far edge of the lawn and was gone.

'Eh!' shouted Mr. Toa, who was refilling the ice-bucket. Breaking into a string of denunciations, he shuffled down the steps and peered indignantly after the intruder.

'Never mind, never mind,' soothed Penaia. 'It is a very bad thing in Fijian custom to cross the house of a chief,' he explained for my benefit. 'But this is just some child taking a short cut in the dark. There are still one or two elderly rulers in remoter parts who treat such trespassers with the end of a rope, though—but don't worry, I'm not one of them!' He chuckled, stretched himself. 'And so—no more of politics! Tell me of the constitution of the piggery, Laisa!'

They both laughed at this well-known family topic, and Laisa reassured him that the distant relation who was in the habit of removing pigs from their piggery during Penaia's absences and presenting them to the people on his behalf, seemed to have reformed his ways for the present.

'And the girls must go out to catch prawns next Monday,' he

went on. 'Some Defence V.I.P.s from Australia are touring Fiji and want to see Taveuni, so we must feast them. Remember the Commission of Inquiry?' he asked me. 'I brought a hundred people from Kadavu to do *mekes* for them when they came here. I think they enjoyed it. But that kind of thing is not possible at present, I'm afraid, with next month's ceremonies to prepare for.'

Throughout the conversation Laisa had been in and out of the kitchen two or three times, thus letting her husband know tactfully that food was ready whenever he should decide to call for it. There was no Eastern air of submission about this. Rather, the preservation of harmony, a polite outward deferring that masked the basic power wielded by most Fijian wives, even those like Laisa whose marriages had been arranged as a form of alliance between two chiefly families, with prolonged and delicate consultations between the elders and no meeting of bride and groom until the actual ceremony.

'To soup then,' he called suddenly, rearing to his feet. With a gallant bow he offered one arm to Laisa, and one to me, and together we went inside.

'I have been admiring this,' I said, pausing before the Roko Tui's staff-of-office in the corner of the living-room.

'Ah, my staff,' replied Penaia quietly, touching one of the silver bands with his forefinger. 'You were not here for the installation ceremony, the swearing of the oath?'

'No, it was before we came to Fiji,' I told him.

' "To the people over whom you are placed, be as a father," ' he repeated, still in the same gentle, almost tender voice. ' "Lead them, teach them, feed them. Take heed not to oppress them and in all your acts remember that strict and solemn account which you must one day render at the Judgement Seat of God" '—'It is a very old Fijian form of ceremony.' He broke off and laughed briefly. 'Hardly a fashionable one these days, don't you agree?'

Over dinner he was relaxed again, consuming vast helpings of his favourite dishes and regaling us with topics ranging from *Rigoletto* ('a marvellous thing—I saw it five times running when I was in London.') to the serving of crayfish in New Zealand hotels ('You won't believe it but they never eat the heads over there, so I always had plenty!').

At the end of the meal he surveyed the depleted table with a sigh of regret. 'Do you know, I'm certain they had bigger appetites in the old days. Take snakes, for example. Snake was always a food reserved for the chiefs—I'm quite fond of it myself in moderation. But for my grandfather, a good fat three-footer nicely stuffed and baked would be just an hors-d'œuvre.

'Ugh!' shuddered Laisa, rolling her eyes. 'Not for me!'

'And as for *bokola-Vuaka Balavu* or "Long Pig" as one of the old chiefs called it once in joke,' Penaia went on, still with the same solemn expression. 'In the time of my ancestors there was one whole tribe whose sole responsibility was to keep the cooking-pots of the Chief and his family filled with samples of the highest grade. This tribe originally came from Bega. They arrived at the island and told the Chief they were fishermen. "From now onwards', said the Chief, "you can hunt for men instead." Or, so the story goes. . . .'

Mr. Toa, whose enjoyment of each of his master's quips and idiosyncrasies had continued undiminished throughout the meal, now moved towards him from behind Penaia's chair and crouched to murmur something in his ear.

'Ah—we have a visitor!' Penaia announced to us. 'Not for too long, though,' he added in an undertone, as he led the way out to the porch again. 'I'm sleepy—and this one can talk for ever!'

At the bottom of the steps, on the edge of the pool of lamplight, an old man was sitting with his legs folded neatly under his ragged *sulu*. By the ferns behind his ears I recognized Ramanu, though he had, I noticed, substituted fresh sprays for the ones he had worn in the afternoon.

'Here is someone from Wales where they have *tevoras* (familiar spirits) even bigger and better than your own,' announced Laisa loudly, by way of introduction, as she and Penaia settled themselves back in their canvas chairs. A pair of hooded eyes, milky opaque like mother-of-pearl, peered swiftly up, not so much at me as round and through me. Then, having reassured himself of the patent fraudulence of this claim, he gave me a slow, toothless smile of magnetic charm and a hand to shake that was as dry and papery in mine as a dead leaf.

'He is very deaf as well as a little blind,' Laisa murmured. 'I think it will be better if I translate between you.'

'Please tell him how good the *meke* was and ask him how he composes such things.'

The old man accepted the compliment with a grave nod and carefully selected his reply, grey head bent against the light, his hands clasped loosely in his lap.

'He says the forming of the words takes time, especially as they must be set to the special *meke* style of our forefathers. One must be in the right mood for such work.'

The old man spoke again and so the conversation ran—Ramanu's Fijian interleaving Laisa's English in a low husky counterpoint, a sound one grew used to like the rustle of pages being turned or the hiss of an old gramophone needle.

'Sometimes, though, it carries one away into another world where certain things are shown one that otherwise remain hidden. As with a *meke* he was composing a few years ago, imagining life in different parts of the globe, far from Fiji. When he came to Ceylon, he suddenly felt "something is wrong with this place—something terrible is going to happen here". He became very cold and could not continue with the *meke*. And, just three months later, Ratu Sukuna died suddenly on his way to England as the ship was passing this very spot.'

'Can he influence the future in any way, by making of spells and so forth?'

The old man looked stern.

Not *draunikau* was the answer. 'That is for evil men who wish harm to their neighbours. But those who say there is no such thing today are fools. Even in the towns in the hospitals a man will sicken and die, not because of what the doctor writes on a piece of paper, but because something—a small section of bamboo perhaps containing trimmings of his hair, or scraps of his clothing or food, together with certain roots and leaves—has been hidden somewhere in his house, and the secret words repeated over it. A man with an enemy will pay much money for such things to be done by a *vuniduva*—a sorcerer—of that kind. To defeat it, the spell must be "pressed down" by another, more powerful one. This is his—Ramanu's—special gift, the setting of a good charm. Like the one he cast for Ratu Penaia when he went to fight in Malaya.'

'It is a fact that although the Communists often tried to get me, they never succeeded,' Penaia himself confirmed. 'The jeep in front would be ambushed, and the jeep behind, but never the one in which I was travelling.'

He nodded and smiled at the old man, who smiled back almost sheepishly. In the flicker of the lamp flame, the threadwork of wrinkles seemed to tremble across his face like a spider's web in a current of air, as he turned and spoke again to Laisa.

'It is the same kind of power that he uses to protect himself when he walks through fire.'

In the way of the famous fire-walkers of Bega, I suggested?

A scornful shake of the head met this remark.

'That is simply placing the feet on hot stones. What he does is to dance through the middle of a large fire without the flames touching him. This I have seen too,' Laisa added, 'and wouldn't know how to explain.'

The old man sighed and murmured something.

'But he hasn't done this lately. It can only be done when one is seized with the spirit, and with age this declines.'

'And the bad luck you were speaking of because of the delay over the ceremonies for Ratu Sukuna . . . what does he say of that?'

This time Ramanu replied with gravity and at length.

'Many things have gone wrong,' Laisa translated. 'Because the proper honours were accorded neither at the correct time nor the appropriate place, our ancestors are displeased with us. Ratu Sukuna's sister suddenly dropped dead this year after no previous illness. And, stranger still, the sharks around this coast have all at once become hungry for human flesh. Only a few months ago a woman was taken a few feet from the shore at a point where such a thing had never been heard of before. Now he has warned that no one must go swimming until the ceremonies have been performed, or there will be more tragedy.'

'This is very strange for Taveuni,' Penaia explained. 'People here say they have seen sharks basking near the rocks at the north end, rubbing themselves against them to remove the barnacles from their skin.'

'And if it is a big one forty feet long,' Laisa said, smiling, 'that will be Dakuwaga himself. Some of the old folk tell you they have actually fed him and scratched his back for him with sticks—eh, Ramanu?'

She turned to the old man. But at the mention of the god's name his face had suddenly become blank and now with closed eyes he sat rocking himself gently, murmuring in an absent, conversational way, '*Wai-lei!—Wai-lei!*'

'Well, we are all tired then,' she said. She came down the steps to help him to his feet. Out of nowhere a small boy appeared and took his arm. After saluting his hosts, Ramanu took my hand once more in his, then drew his shawl closer around him and with characteristic dignity made his departure. At the corner of the house, he turned to call out something to Laisa in a faintly querulous tone, as he pointed to the rolled-up mat left leaning against the wall by the girls.

Laisa laughed and shook her head. 'He says there are enough spirits around this house without inviting any more! The old people say that a mat left out like that at night is the favourite hiding-place for a *tevora*.'

We stood for a moment, watching the old man and his escort disappear into the darkness, carefully skirting the great shadow of the *ivi* tree on their way.

'Is this house really haunted then?' I asked her, as she took the hurricane lantern to lead me down the path to my *bure*. Together we waded knee-deep in its golden stream between swinging banks of shadow.

'I believe so,' she replied. 'The local people won't come near alone at night, you know. Even in the daytime they keep very quiet around the place. They say it has such a heavy air of *mana*—chiefliness.' Her voice dropped to a murmur alongside me. Three *Tui Cakau's* have lived there at one time or another, you see, and two have died there.'

The lantern's circle melted into the glow of the *bure* lamp as we mounted the steps. In the doorway, Laisa paused for a moment, her face intent. 'Quite often, sitting in the living-room, one is aware of someone close, watching. Once even, though Penaia never smokes and we were alone, the smell of Fijian tobacco was suddenly so strong it was as though someone had puffed a cheroot right into my face. And I'm told that both the old chiefs who died in the house were very heavy smokers.'

She came closer and grasped my arm. 'Will you believe me when I tell you I can't sleep in my bedroom alone while Penaia is away? Either the children or the servants must be with me. It's always the same sounds one hears. Footsteps coming in through the front veranda—old, slow steps—along the passage, right up to the bedroom door. The handle is turned. There is silence, then, slowly the footsteps go away again.' I shivered. With a laugh, Laisa changed her expression.

'Well, at least I managed not to tell you until just before you leave! Anyway,' she reassured me, turning to go, 'it is the house I am talking of. Nothing to do with the *bure*! *Mo-thé*, Tiuné!'

'*Mo-thé*, Laisa!'

I must have believed her because I slept heavily and without dreams, so heavily that next morning I almost missed my plane. To awaken someone by force is considered by the Fijians to be not only impolite but positively dangerous to the spirit, and everyone would have been happy to let me lie on indefinitely.

However, the jeep roared up alongside the landing-strip just as the pilot, glancing at his watch, was about to step up into the cockpit.

'Nearly gave y' up this time!'

First the waving figures of Laisa and Penaia, then the airfield with its tiny tin-roof buildings, and finally the whole green floating-dock of close-packed palms that was Taveuni, dwindled away beneath the wings. An hour later I was in Suva.

'Today is very busy,' said the Indian taxi-driver, as we glissaded through the rainy streets. 'Methodist Rally *and* cruise ship.'

On Albert Park the massed, white-clad heirs of the Hunt's mission to Fiji were marching with banners to the singing of *Tuberi Au* ('Lead Kindly Light'), while in the doorways of all the leading stores—as bait for the tourists—muscular warriors in full regalia of paint and club paced the grille-lined alcoves with the sulky bravado of caged lions, today's tame replicas of the real-life apparitions that had struck such dismay in the hearts of Hannah and John one-and-a-quarter centuries ago.

9
The Castaway Capital

Levuka. The castaway capital. A town of ghosts, I thought, standing at the rail of the little launch as we throbbed past the seafront stores and shanties, marooned at the foot of the hills like a string of old railway carriages in an overgrown siding.

Steeply behind rose the island of Ovalau's incredible peaks and cliffs. Glimpsed on the horizon between bucking sails and masts, it was a sight that meant 'civilization' to the nineteenth-century traveller, the approach to the old settlement of the white men of Fiji—the beachcombers, the runaway convicts and gatherers of *bêche-de-mer* who came first; the small traders and boatbuilders of the mid-century, precarious dependents of the Fijian chiefs, burned out by the savage inland tribes, deported by the King for political reasons and admitted back again after an exile of four years; the solid fortune-seekers of the cotton boom of the 'seventies and the Cession supporters and administrators that followed.

I was glad that the only way to get there was still by sea, even though the crossing had been a rough one. Boarding the launch that morning, some thirty miles up the coast from Suva, the weather had seemed calm enough, the painted name of the *Jubilee* on the prow grazing gently against the end of the rough stone jetty, scales of bright sunshine on the water's skin. Around the boat there was an excited jumble of passengers simultaneously embarking and disembarking. From among the large-bosomed *maramas*, babes in arms, the hordes of skirt-clutching children, muscular youths in ragged shorts, Indian business men with a clutch of pens and pencils in their shirt pockets, His Lordship the Bishop of Polynesia cleft his way down on to land, a large, striking figure in a white linen suit, a golden crucifix dangling against his vest of purple silk, and on his head an enormous sombrero from the Cook Islands—the perfect picture of a South Seas cleric with a parish of eleven million square miles. 'Most of my parishioners are fish, though,' he had once reassured me.

On board the two European couples, middle-aged tourists, had taken the small deck seat with an air of divine right. Inside there were two cabins, one on each side of the engine-room, about six feet by six with a narrow bench running all the way round. We looked first in the fore cabin, crammed tightly with passengers, suitcases, and a bucket in which someone had already been sick, and decided on the aft one.

'Today they have twice as many people,' said Mr. Lal, from the court, who was travelling with us. 'Yesterday, you see, they had to turn back half-way because of a tropical storm. This is very rare,' he added tactfully, noting our faces.

The Fijian family on the opposite bench gave us smiles of welcome—a grizzled, simple-looking patriarch, the mother younger and plumply unlined, two teenage daughters, a boy of about six, and twin babies in swaddling sheets and red woolly cardigans, although the heat below was intense. Mr. Lal settled himself next to an Indian merchant and like his neighbour was soon immersed in a highly-coloured Hindu periodical.

Above us ran a slatted rack, too shallow for luggage. At eye-level, through the open window, a row of boots, sandals and bare feet swung down from the youths who were sitting on the cabin roof. There was half-an-hour's interval while luggage was thrown aboard, rolled mats, baskets of clothes, cooking pots, kettles and buckets, and the neat, brown cardboard suitcases of the Indian merchants. Suddenly, a bell like an alarm clock went off. The engines rasped into life, the ropes were hauled in, and with a jerk we began to move away.

Once outside the bay, a wind sprang up that curled the sea into high toppling waves and sent the little boat reeling from side to side like a fairground swing.

With desperate concentration, Ronald had engrossed himself in the book he had brought—Harold Nicholson's *Some People*—pointing out from time to time some particularly graceful witticism as a continuous lurching line of passengers disappeared and emerged through the small door behind him.

Suddenly the largest wave of all came pitching in through the window opposite, and a sheet of water cascaded over the Fijian mother and the right-hand baby.

'Eh!' With an exclamation of surprise she rubbed her fingers over her face and mop of black hair, shook out the skirt of her soaked dress. The dripping child was sleeked down with an old *sulu*, produced from a basket, and promptly went to sleep on his stomach looking like a small wet seal. The father meanwhile, smiling admiringly at the tempest, crossed one leg to form a cradle for the second twin, and the rest of the family settled down to a packet of damp biscuits, also retrieved from the basket.

Next to me, the Indian merchant brought out a bag of betel nuts. Just when the grinding drill of the engines seemed about to penetrate the innermost corner of the skull, the smell of diesel oil and copra from the hold to overpower the last whiff of fresh air, the outline of a large steep island appeared through the legs at the window. With a cry of joy, I started to get my things together.

Mr. Lal leaned across the Indian merchant. 'We are now half-way there!' he shouted triumphantly in my ear.

In fact it took almost an hour to round the far headland, a lion-coloured bluff of sandstone whittled by the weather to an edge like the prow of a ship. The sea was calmer now and I watched from the hatchway steps as the Levuka side of the island glided past. Soon I was joined by a small elderly Fijian in a neat grey *sulu* and shirt who had been fast asleep in the lifeboat. He sat down next to me, carefully placing in his lap a shabby little case in which he had been collecting church subscriptions. Then with a courtly flourish he opened a large umbrella for shade above my head and held it there by its broken catch, despite my remonstrances, for the rest of the journey.

'God will be pleased,' was his only remark, delivered with an enigmatic nod which seemed to include the caseful of money, the good deed and the whole transfigured morning around us. Women or mermaids with nets, thigh-deep in marble water, turned and raised their hands to the passing boat that meant no more than a certain time of day. Behind them lay deserted beaches under awnings of palms and, rising sheer above, thickly-wooded cliffs and peaks with here and there the downward smoke of a waterfall or the raising spiral of village fires.

Then came the first signs of Levuka itself. The twin towers of the

Catholic Mission, the Catholic church—rose-coloured stone of an oriel window facing the sea—a Doric column on a plinth (commemorating what? or whom?), hill-climbing bungalows, neat and trim on the foreshore, drab and peeling in the background, two Martian-like erections, steel tents on stilts, which turned out to be the harbour lights, another church with a homely clock-face, the weatherboard verandas of the Royal Hotel, the Commissioner's house with the Union Jack flying from the green-painted roof. Finally, from one end of the seafront to the landing-stage stretched the long road of silent shops and stores. Some seemed mere wooden shanty buildings. Others were gaunt caves of concrete with the brave legend 1954 or 1956 across the front, epitomizing, like the vanished pearl-button factory, the one-time pineapple cannery, the sheep-farming project and a dozen others, that recurrent surge of optimism to which Levuka, like Mr. Micawber, was prone.

'Never changes!' said a wrinkled part-European at the rails to one of the tourists, in the affectionately indulgent tone applied to a favourite black sheep of the family. 'She never got room to change, see.' He indicated the narrowness of the shelf on which the township was perched, the steepness of the land rising immediately behind.

It was midday now. Apart from a couple of copra schooners, the harbour was empty. Engines off, the launch drew alongside the wooden jetty, a rope from the deck was thrown over a capstan. There was a smell of warm tar. Outside the customs shed a few elderly Fijians in battered peaked sailing-caps sat on their haunches against the wall, talking in undertones. Otherwise the place was as still as the town in the classic Western when everyone waits behind closed shutters for the Sheriff and the Lone Ranger finally to confront each other, guns drawn, at either end of the square. Except that there was no tension here—only a permanent, peaceful doze.

Yet in its heyday this was the port whose citizens boasted that a ship's captain had only to follow the thickening line of floating gin bottles to chart his course into harbour, where drunken chiefs and brawling whites fought among the grass huts on the beach, where—in reality—the long street rang with the pistol shots of rioting settlers and the price of a Fijian 'wife' was a pair of muskets. Even towards the end of the eighteen-sixties, a Dr. Messer, staff surgeon of the visiting H.M.S. *Pearl*, described the smell of Levuka as being 'like that of some filthy Chinese or Turkish village,' with horses and cattle, pigs and goats roaming at large among the ramshackle buildings, the beach and tracts of waste land strewn with offal and rotting vegetables.

Mrs. Smythe, however, in their new house on the hill farther along, just beneath Mrs. Binner's *jardin anglais*, was daintily elevated above such horrors. 'The walls are lined with white calico and the windows have neat white muslin curtains looped up with scarlet braid. As I look up, a dazzling line of white catches my eye. There it goes running along the outer edge of the roof. The ground between us and the beach is filled with coconut palms. Beneath them broad-leafed bananas wave lightly to and fro; while lower still green grass and ferns are bidding welcome to the sweet fresh air.'

In 1876 Miss Gordon-Cumming reported that mud and broken bottles still formed the beach, but of Levuka itself, went on, 'We had imagined it was still the haunt of uproarious planters and white men of the lowest type described by visitors a few years ago, instead of which we find a most orderly and respectable community of about 600 whites inhabiting 180 wooden houses. We are told that the reformation of the sobriety of the town is partly due to the Good Templars who here muster a very considerable brotherhood.' The houses she dismissed as 'all alike hideous being built of wood (weatherboard is the name) and roofed with corrugated iron or zinc on which the mad tropical rains pour with deafening noise; or else the burning sun beats so fiercely as wellnigh to stifle the inmates to whom the luxuries of punkahs and ice are unknown and even baths by no means a matter of course as in other hot countries'.

Turning to more picturesque topics, she glanced out of the Government House windows at the view of the harbour and wrote: 'There is an occasional man-of-war or merchant steamer, and always native canoes passing to and fro with great three-cornered yellow mat sails, and brown men who often sing quaint *mekes* as they approach the town with an odd sort of accompaniment on their *lali* or wooden drum. The chief's canoe carries a flag and sometimes a fringe of streamers of native cloth floating from the sail; and the canoe itself is adorned at both ends with glistening white shells like poached eggs (*Cyprea Oviformis*). . . . The eye that loves exquisite colour can never weary here.'

Yet on another day the seafront reflected the tragic precariousness of life for such Europeans as the young planter returning by steamer from a short business trip to a nearby island, having left his wife and new-born baby both making good progress. 'All the flags in the harbour and the town were flying half-mast for a funeral and when the captain of the steamer hailed the nearest vessel to ask who was dead, the poor fellow heard his wife's name called back in answer.'

Now there were neither flags nor steamers, just a couple of shabby single-masted copra boats and the daily launch from Viti Levu whose disgorged passengers stood around the jetty in aimless groups as though gently drowning in the somnolent Levuka sunshine, like flies in syrup. The eruption of two taxis from out of nowhere broke the spell. The first one, an old Chevrolet, collected the tourists and we climbed into the other, a Buick driven by a lean young Indian. This bizarre cavalcade of hand-me-down American opulence then trundled over the rails of disused copra-cart tracks, down the dusty road of shops and sheds, and over the bridge to the hotel.

Inside the porch, the proprietor and his wife emerged to greet us from behind a forest of tropical ferns and plants in enormous urns —he robust, blue-eyed, typically Australian, though in fact half-French and a *Kai-Viti*, she an island mixture of another kind, dark, pale and once-beautiful.

'We were quite busy last week-end—the Suva–Levuka Launch Race you know—but it's quiet again now,' she said, leading us up the old shallow staircase. On either side of the passage-way, doors stood open for coolness, revealing Edwardian butlers' bedrooms, neat and narrow, with elderly gentlemen napping on sprigged counterpanes, china hot-water jugs under lace-covered dressers. Ours, being the honeymoon suite, had a three-cornered wash-basin, a double bed and a dividing door on the veranda which encircled the whole of the upper storey. As on a ship, this was the communal meeting-place for visitors with its weather-beaten cane furniture and sloping boards, deserted now except for a languidly sweeping Rotuman girl and a middle-aged lady in a kimono drying her hair.

We went down to the dining-room where one of the visiting couples, the New Zealanders, were already seated at a corner table. The other pair came in from their gin-and-tonics and established themselves unforgettably as English, as the Elizabeth

Ardened wife, squeaked piercingly, 'Oh! Do we *have* to share?' as the Rotuman waitress, with a non-comprehending smile, nodded and went on ushering them into the two empty chairs at the New Zealanders' table.

Resolutely, after lunch, the tourists set off—the English to the left by car, the New Zealanders to the right on foot. Feeling like old-timers, we slept. An hour later, I changed and went out to walk down to the post office. On the bridge outside the hotel, a small shock-haired Tongan man I had seen in the kitchen doorway at lunch, stood leaning over the parapet.

'I am Kasi the cook,' he said, as I stopped to watch a shoal of small fish swarm round the hunks of pork chop he was throwing them, a smile of childish delight on his face. 'This meat no good any more. I think maybe fish don't care 'bout that.'

All along the sea wall the land had been reclaimed and grass now covered the beach of the settlers' first camps. Little groups of children and women in saris sat under the trees on mats, families of the Indian traders who kept the shops on the other side of the road. The smell of drying salt came strongly up from the hot stones below. The sea was out. A rusted anchor, a few spars of wood, empty bottles marked the brown line of high tide.

Down the long street the only car in sight was our taxi of the morning.

Here and there, above the level of the shops, the blurred imprint of Edwardian prosperity was still visible, in a balustrade of carved plaster, or the scalloped pelmet of an upper window, now scarred and flaking amidst a patchwork of weatherboard and corrugated iron.

Crossing over, one saw only the shabby close-up of present-day existence, the roughly-painted signs 'Hot Beans and Cold Drinks', 'Cocoa, Fruit and Biscuits', and 'Elite Restaurant' in windows that were pathetically bare of anything except a pile of lemons and a bowl of curry.

I went into one of the general stores to buy some postcards. On the shelves lay the usual accumulation of cheap Western goods found in poor tropical towns, gimcrack mirrors and tins of talcum, rolls of coarse cotton, and exercise books with the Queen and the Duke on the covers. The Indian behind the counter, sleek and thin with fervent eyes, said, spreading his hands, 'There is no work for anyone here, you see. In the old days, this place was the centre of everything. Even when Suva became the big place, we still had the copra—boats calling here from the islands every day and life for the people. Now they have stopped that too. They almost all go straight to Suva instead. So what is there left?'

'All the time people come in to buy without paying,' murmured his wife, seated at a sewing-machine in the corner. 'They belong to our church. So what can we dc but sell on credit, hope that things will come better soon?'

He gave me the cards. I passed him the money. There was nothing more to say. The big Australian branch-store next door, where the European residents bought their glass and china and household goods, looked equally bare but with an atmosphere more of amiable torpor than desperation. Two pretty part-European assistants stood gossiping at the cash-desk. An elderly red-faced gentleman in a shabby white topee, white shorts and plimsolls waited at the counter and under a chair a shaggy dog panted and scratched his ear.

Past every two or three shopfronts, an alley-way gaped like a rotten tooth, passages to the houses behind where sombre fires of coconut husks smoked among the wild marigolds and overgrown steps twisted up under low-spreading flame trees. Old relics lay half-hidden in the grass of these entrances, an old-fashioned grinding-stone, a discarded *lali* lying on its side full of rainwater.

Suddenly down the street a stream of children erupted like a shoal of minnows, on their way home from school. Brightly ribboned, gleaming and chattering, buttoned into starched regulation shorts and shirts, pastel dresses with neat white collars and cuffs, Indians, Fijians and part-Europeans, they flashed purposefully past—towards what future remained a mystery—and were gone.

Only one of the schooners, the *Meri,* now lay at anchor on a millpond sea. A line of washing had been draped across the boom and a young Fijian was sluicing down the deck. In the doorway of the copra-shed opposite, a cavern of coconut-scented gloom, a European overseer nodded the time of day to me as he watched two men unloading the sacks from a handcart like a railway porter's luggage-barrow. Two youths sat cross-legged on the post office veranda, one strumming a guitar, the other humming the tune. Inside, a sleepy giant took my cable to London, deliberating for some minutes among piles of yellowing forms as to how much it would cost. Behind the other wire grille, an olive-skinned girl with a beehive of fluffy black hair was manipulating the switches of the Levuka telephone exchange, greeting each caller personally.

'Mr. Powell—I jus' seen you on the road goin' up to your place so I put your call through to Suva right away, eh?'

'Sorry, May, Mrs. Ashley's still out, dear!—You get the fish Eddie bring las' night?'

Outside, the two American cars were drawn up waiting. One, I noticed now, was labelled across the door 'Paradise Taxi', the other simply 'Better Taxi'. Selecting the latter, I got in and we turned and jolted back down the main street.

'How many cars in Levuka altogether?' I asked the driver.

'Just we two—where would anyone drive a car here? . . . Oh, and the bus, too—we have one bus here.'

A scheme that would certainly have appealed to Miss G.C., I thought, as I got out at the hotel. In 1876 she wrote that, apart from wheelbarrows—'which the Fijians first carried on their heads with great care'—there were no such things as wheels in Levuka. Furthermore, she went on irritably after a particularly hot slog along the rough mile of village footpath, 'There is no means of being carried such as we are accustomed to find in all Eastern lands, palanquins, sedan chairs, etc. . . . The highlanders here are just as strong as the hill-men of India, but the idea of carrying a lady has not yet occurred to them.'

Relief, however, came in the footnote, 'Before we left the isle, Captain Knollys succeeded in drilling a set of men to carry Lady Gordon in a wicker chair, and on the occasion of certain special festivities in the town a second chair was rigged up for me. So probably future residents will have chairs and bearers as a matter of course.'

Soon after, however, a road was made along the beach and a covered cab transported residents from the farthest point of the settlement to the Government offices at Nasova, a distance of two miles, for sixpence a head. . . .

Back at the hotel the lounge room had been transformed. Fijian mats had been laid over the flowered linoleum, pillars twined with palm leaves, and *salu-salus* hung around the walls, some of fresh hibiscus, some of plaited silver paper. Friday night at the hotel, the proprietor told me, was Island Night. There would be an entertainment of Polynesian dancing for the guests, and everyone should dress as informally as possible.

Promptly on time the visitors came down the stairs, attired as requested, with careful nonchalance, the men in linen slacks and flowered shirts, the ladies in sun-frocks and peeling shoulders. Most of the hotel residents were already seated in a semicircle. An anti-mosquito coil smoked beneath each chair. The queer acrid smell mingled with the Blue Grass and Old Spice anointments of the Europeans—and then the whole mixture succumbed to the over-powering scent of coconut oil as with a sudden rush, bare feet pounding, hands clapping, the room seemed full of rustling, swaying, closely-packed yellow grass. The next minute the cornfield resolved itself into twenty or so male and female bodies in ankle-length hula skirts, their modesty *sulus* of scarlet cotton glinting through like poppies, the women with bodices of the same material.

For a moment they were still. Then arranging themselves in two rows in front of us, they began to sing in the liquid, Oriental-sounding language of Rotuma, matching the story with the movements of their hands. Most of them were typically Rotuman in appearance, the men lithe and slant-eyed with high, flat cheekbones, the girls beautiful in a solid way with full, rounded arms and heavy heads of hair, smoothly plaited over one shoulder. Here and there a Tongan or Samoan face stood out and in the centre, melodramatic as a Victorian missionary print, the blue eyes and creamy skin of the proprietor's daughter, a beautiful girl of about seventeen. In the end, it was she who dominated the dance, hips rotating in one continuous flicker of movement, each limb and muscle shivering in rhythm with the drum, her face ardent, while the sweat rolled down between her shoulders from under the long thick rope of yellow hair and even the Rotumans stood back to applaud.

Between dances her mother, laughing shyly, circled the dancers sprinkling talcum on each one's shoulders—the modern remnant of the old custom of anointment with scented oil as a token of thanks. Turning, I saw her take her place again at the back of the room with a group of other middle-aged women who had slipped in from the kitchens. Some were fat, some worn, with only the remnants of good looks, for beauty dies quickly in the islands. Yet as they leaned forward to watch, their faces were lit with an intense delight, a kind of transferred pleasure mixed with private recollections of the past, an expression of mischievous contentment that was a world away from the dissatisfied eyes of wall-flower matrons in Western society.

Meanwhile, the European visitors sat self-consciously tapping their feet just out of time with the drum-beats, with the eager yet baffled look of grown-ups watching a children's game. Then came a general free-for-all which ended the display. 'Come dance!' cried the girls, but regretfully they shook their heads. The naval commander, however, had no choice. In a flash he was swept up by two buxom ladies on whose arms he hung with rigid determination, a glassy look in his blue eyes, as they bounced him relentlessly through a Polynesian Lambeth Walk, choking back their laughter in a supreme effort at good manners, nimbly avoiding his large, high-polished, black shoes.

Then it was time to rest for a while. Out in the lamplit garden the younger ones sat on the steps or stretched their arms to cool themselves up into the white-starred branches of a frangipani tree. The musicians, hidden till now, moved forward and strummed for some of the women to sing—an old blind man who beat with the flat of his hands on a barrel-shaped drum, a young boy playing a wooden *lali* with two short sticks, a couple of older women with ukuleles, and an incredibly handsome young man with the profile of an Egyptian king who flicked at his guitar and cast sidelong glances of encouragement at all the prettier girls.

The dancers refreshed, half a dozen records were jammed on to the player and the entertainment continued with the electrifying Polynesian version of the twist. The outstanding performer was Rameses the Second who led one partner after another flying through a series of gyrations that were as formalized as a ballet.

When it came to my turn, the slow waltz provided for the benefit of English guests was playing, so he had breath to tell me that his name was George and he worked as a carpenter for his father. Studying the profile that M.G.M. make-up artists toil to reproduce for those Hollywood stars of Biblical spectaculars not favoured with doe-eyes, perfect noses and sculptured cheekbones, I asked him whether he had ever wanted to leave Levuka.

'No, I don't think I'll ever want to take off,' he said. Then, after thought, 'Except maybe to Suva, now and then.'

'Everyone gets to love this place,' explained his sister Emily, who was one of the dancers, a handsome broad-faced girl with a thick mane of black hair. We were all sitting together at one of the tables afterwards. 'I used to write poetry in school, y' know, and all my poems started off with something about the hills of Ovalau.'

A girl passing on the dance-floor called out something to her with a grin.

'You know what she is saying?' Emily asked. 'She is saying I am a horse! Fijians always call us Tongans horses, nobody knows why unless, they say, we used to eat them over there!'

He and his sister were not whole-Tongans though, George added. 'Our great-great-grandfather and his brother were Welshmen. They were both bad boys, see, and they decided to sail to the South Seas to find themselves Polynesian wives as they had heard that they were the most beautiful women in the world.'

'So of course they chose Tongan ladies,' Emily put in.

Their father had kept all the letters and records of these things, even a copy of the family crest, they told us.

On the floor the Limbo Rock gave way to the steady slow march tempo of an even better-known British composition and the party, too, was at an end.

Upstairs, along the dimly lit passages, the hotel seemed more than ever like some old blunt-nosed ship, timbers creaking on either side, crickets whirring as steady as a distant engine-room and always in the background the hiss and lap of the sea.

The veranda was in shadow, deserted. From beneath came the leisurely click of billiard balls, occasional laughter, the rattle of glasses. Then gradually, a strange traffic-less silence in which the voices of the last passers-by floated with a detached, eerie effect, unaccompanied by footsteps.

' 'Bye, Frankie!'

'You people coming then?'

'*Mothé* Joe!'

The soft, sing-song snatches dissolved into the trill of a guitar. Dark shapes in the roadway strolled away, noiseless on bare feet. In faint counterpoint from the room next door, we heard.

'Seems terribly dull. And so *hot*!'

'Tiresome. Very tiresome.'

Moonlight emerged for a moment, laying a powdery finger on the white fluted column of the war memorial beyond the seafront, the site of the old town's gallows, they said, where the famous story of Filipino Looey had been enacted, the condemned man who had escaped with his life. According to the historians, Looey was convicted of the murder of a fellow seaman, but the execution was postponed for a day owing to the illness of the sheriff's wife. In typical Levuka fashion the rope was left out on the gallows all night and by the following morning was so swollen with rain that it would not run in the noose. Hanging for ten minutes after a drop that instead of tightening only stunned, the victim called to the bystanders to shoot him and end his misery. Instead, he was cut down, returned to his cell, and eventually reprieved with provision to leave the country. . . .

Across the water the harbour lights made pinpoints in the dark, two yellow and two turquoise that shone out clear and steady, one winking diamond-white, a floating signpost that marked the narrow pathway home through the reefs.

The moon went in again, and so did we.

10

Dragon-Whisky and Crocodile-Gin

Waking in the morning, one captured again those small, elusive pleasures of childhood awakings on seaside holidays,—the flicker of sea-reflected sunlight on the ceiling, the smell of salt in the distance dry as snuff, the scuff of bare soles on gritty oilcloth already warm in stripes beneath the shutters. From the veranda came the clink of early-morning teacups. Downstairs the first bell rang for breakfast.

Everyone I had spoken to in Levuka had told me, 'You must see old Arthur Robinson!'

Who *was* Arthur Robinson, I wanted to know.

'He's been a trader round the islands for years—a real king of the shell-backs.'

'Prospecting for gold at one time.'

'Great gambler on the Stock Exchange, very rich."

'Owns a couple of plantations.'

'Ran a butterfly farm.'

'Had a big automobile works in Australia. . . .'

The house of this genie, they told me at the hotel after breakfast, was just above the playing-fields. The proprietor pointed to a white bungalow perched like an island among billowing waves of jungle, about half-way up the mountain-side.

With some trepidation I put on a pair of walking shoes though, as it turned out, all I really needed was an extra lung. I followed the road round to the base of the climb and was met not by a track through the bush but by an unending spiral of stone steps cut out of the undergrowth. Pausing for breath on one of the grassy landings thoughtfully provided for the expiring visitors, I caught glimpses of other carved stairways twisting up through the greenery towards isolated houses. It seemed that in the same way that New York solved its expansion problem by building sky-scrapers, Levuka town-planners had hit upon the scheme of building streets entirely of steps.

I learned later that social status in the town was judged to a very large extent on the height of one's house above sea-level, and the number of steps required to reach it.

Starting to climb again, I was trying to form a composite image of the multiple personality described to me, when quite suddenly I looked up to see a lean, white-haired figure in khaki shirt and shorts confronting me beneath a mango tree.

'Out of breath?' he chuckled, raising his eyebrows over his spectacles. 'Yes, I'm Robinson. Come and see what I'm doing.'

A pair of muscular brown legs, mysteriously tattooed at the calf and ending in a pair of faded blue plimsolls, twinkled ahead up the garden path.

'All this was strawberries a few years ago. Apples over there.' He twirled his stick from one side to the other, then leaned on it in an attitude of mock-elegance. 'I feel a bit of a Burlington Bertie with this,' he murmured in the Edwardian vocabulary one kept coming across everywhere in Levuka. 'But it's damned useful.'

We stood back and admired the tangled landscape of hibiscus and snapdragons, flox, canna lilies, clematis and ten-feet-high purple orchids. 'And this!' He darted down a side avenue and prodded at a rose-bed neatly encircled with half-buried beer bottles. 'This is something you haven't seen before—a rose that changes colour. Starts off as cream, then goes all the way through to crimson in three days.'

Round the side of the house we came to the bench where he had been working. Small strips of mother-of-pearl, delicately painted in red and white patterns along the back, lay everywhere.

'Spinners!' cried Mr. Robinson triumphantly. 'Catch twice as many fish as those nickel ones you buy in the shop. And do you know why?'

I confessed I didn't.

'Because mother-of-pearl's something they're used to—so they've nothing to fear, have they?'

He had a light fishing boat, he told me, made specially for him of plywood. 'You and I could carry it up those steps between us.'

I feared that this statement was to be put to the test, but the next minute he had set off again, this time towards the house along a path lined with silver-painted troichus shells. It was the typical settler's bungalow, a long, rambling, wooden affair with peeling green shutters half-raised against the sun. Inside, above the shabby cane furniture, the walls were a chequer-board of old snapshots—rigged schooners at anchor, fierce mop-haired native groups posed like prep school elevens, Edwardian ladies with even larger coiffures and fiercer expressions, all faded to a ghostly khaki and set in tortoise-shell squares and ovals. Cheek by jowl with these hung the Fijian trophies—whales' teeth, canoe paddles, long curved war-clubs black with age and murderously spiked at the top.

'Pineapple clubs, they call them. You can't pick up any like that, nowadays.'

My host pranced on from room to room, one hand in his pocket, the other pointing out the gems of his collection.

'These are a pair of antlers from a Wakaya deer—that island, just out there—you knew they had deer there, I suppose. And these tusks here, these belonged to poor old Johnny. Johnny the Pig.'

We sat down finally on canvas chairs on the front veranda and he sketched his career for me, beginning in Victoria, Australia, where he was born. He pointed out among the nearest photographs a handsome fair man with a noble moustache and chin-high collar. 'That's my father, Paymaster in the 21st Lancers.'

He first arrived in Fiji in 1906 at the age of eighteen as an assistant in the trading firm of Henry Marks and set up stores for them in the Yasawas, the remote and lovely pattern of islands off the western coast of Viti Levu. There he stayed until 1921, with only three other Europeans on the group, and these rarely seen. 'Often, there was never a word of English from one year's end to the other. And the Yasawas dialect is quite different from ordinary Fijian, you know.'

In 1921, tiring of such an isolated life, he went back to Australia and started his automobile works, which crashed and went into voluntary liquidation along with so many others in the big depression of '22. So, back to Fiji he came, cutting copra this time on a piece of land given him by his old friend Ratu Sukuna. He worked first with his own hands, then gradually built up a labour force and took on another plantation on Natewa Bay in Vanua Levu, settling in Levuka. From there, he could travel to both places by launch.

Bored by this factual account, Mr. Robinson broke off, flung out a hand at the view below us. 'Ah, Levuka in those days! It was a different world! See the playing fields down there?' He pointed a bony brown finger at the neat rectangle of green, fringed with palms. 'That was an encampment when I first saw it. Samoans, Tongans, Wallis Islanders, half-castes—or part-Europeans as they're called these days—all living together in old shanty weatherboard houses. And as for the harbour!—' He glanced across the glittering bay at the two solitary masts, swaying above the jetty. 'Used to be thick with schooners coming and going round the islands. Every planter had his own cutter. And in the evenings we'd have some parties, I can tell you. Dances and dinners at the houses of all the big planters, the heads of all the business firms, a lot of them Germans in those days and living in style. Suva may have been the Government centre, but Levuka was still the capital of commerce and social life all right.' He rubbed his chin, smiling, emotion in his voice. 'No radio, of course, but we'd swing round to accordions and concertinas, and the Edison wax discs on the gramophone. The Royal and the Poly—that's the old Polynesia Hotel—those were our hunting grounds, dear me, yes. . . .'

His blue eyes widened in a zestful sideways glance at me. 'Oh, the gambling and the drinking that went on, not to mention the feuding and the fighting! Then there'd be concerts at the Town Hall, sometimes the old Collins's Variety Show from Sydney. At the week-ends we'd have canoe races across the bay and foot races round the town. I had the record, y' know, for running and jumping too.' He massaged a muscular calf and grinned. 'Not too bad even now for a seventy-five-year-old, eh?'

'Mind you,' he went on, 'the Fijians were much more sociable in those days. You couldn't walk past a Fijian house without someone calling you in for a bowl of grog—*yaggona*, that is.' He got up suddenly, beckoned me into a sort of study. 'Ever seen these before?' He slapped his hand on an enormous round-bellied pot of red clay about four feet high. 'This is what they did their cooking in years ago. Baking in the earth oven, boiling, or rather steaming, in this, d'ye see.'

We sat down again on the veranda. 'Yes, the Fijians were different when there was just them and ourselves. 'Course, all that's changed now.' He gazed reflectively out at Levuka again. 'Laziest place in the islands. You know what they say about people here—too tired even to wake up. Fortunately I like a quiet life. Mind you with this Japanese fish-freezing plant starting up, I reckon things are looking up at the moment. Well!'

He clapped his hands on his knees, sprang to his feet again. 'You'll be wanting to hear the story about Apolosi, of course!'

With a business-like air, he disappeared through the inner door to fetch, I imagined, some personal relic of the notorious Apolosi Nawai, the Fijian impostor of the 1920's, who caused havoc with his hoaxes and plots and who became accepted by extraordinary numbers of fellow countrymen as a latter-day Messiah come to lead them out of darkness and into the glory of Fijian domination and prosperity. Not knowing Mr. Robinson I prepared myself for the usual third-hand anecdote that people liked to tell about this bizarre figure.

With a flourish, my host bounded into the room again. It seemed he had merely removed himself to assume a different character. Cutting short further preliminaries, he set the scene with an actors' vivid gestures and a power of recollection gloriously unblunted by television or cinema's re-hashes of other people's dramas.

'Apolosi had fled to this island in the Yasawas, d'ye see, and we were after him in the Government cutter—the *Lady Ascot* it was called—the magistrate, a posse of special police, myself as interpreter. We'd seen smoke rising from the trees, people running across the beach. Then suddenly, there was Apolosi himself with his cane and his Norfolk suit.' Mr. Robinson stuck out his chest and strolled up and down, twirling his stick. 'Apolosi almost always wore European clothes. And at the back of him, a solid pack of Fijian warriors, about five or six hundred of them, spears in their hands, their faces blackened with war paint. Well, the dinghy took us ashore and out we got.

'Not the King nor the Governor will take me alive,' called Apolosi. 'One hand on me and you'll all be torn limb from limb!'

'The magistrate started to move towards him with his warrant of arrest. The Fijian spears moved too. I whispered to the Government party to stay where they were. These people meant business. I had my eye on a fellow a few feet away with a great knife at the level of my throat. Funny, though, I didn't get the breeze up at all at that moment.

'Then the Fijians began calling to us. "The *lovus*—the ovens—are ready for you." '

'I looked to one side and saw an enormous pile of firewood about twenty feet long.

' "Take your uniforms off!" they called to our native policemen. "Do you want to be cooked with the white men?"

'The only thing to do, I told the magistrate, was to go back to the mainland and organize an armed arrest party on a more suitable scale. So back we rowed to the *Lady Ascot*. But we couldn't cast off, y'see, until daybreak. All that night we lay offshore while our friends on the beach went through a mime in dance of what they would do to us if we landed again.' Mr. Robinson leaped menacingly into the air, his stick transformed into a weapon of death, his long, baggy features twisted into a fiercesome grimace. Frozen in this pose, he went on in a hushed voice, 'It was low tide. Bright moonlight. Backwards and forwards they sprang, waving great flaming torches above their heads and stabbing their spears into the ground as they called, "That's for you, Magistrate!" and "Come ashore, Robinson, this one's for you!" Before we sailed at dawn, we must have each been killed, cooked and eaten fifty times over or more.'

'What did happen to Apolosi?' I said, collecting myself.

'Oh, they got him in the end. An armed party went out from the *Renadi* and the *Lady Ascot* in whale-boats with muffled rowlocks and they caught him in the hold of his own ship preparing a get-away to one of the other islands. He got three years, I think it was. Then the Government had to keep deporting him from place to place. As ugly as sin he was, but the tongue of a wizard. The bigger the lie, he once told me, the more they'll believe it.'

There was a brief interval between acts. I reverted to a more peaceful topic. 'What about this butterfly farm people tell me about?'

'Oh, I saw an advert in an American paper about someone wanting to buy a species of butterfly called the Monarch. As it happens, there were hundreds of these around my plantation feeding on the ipecuana plant. So instead of catching them with nets, I got the caterpillars, put them in wire-gauze cages, fed them on the leaves and turned out hundreds. After killing them you had to fold their wings in tissue paper ready for packing up. Yes, I made a bit on that.'

'What about the——'

'That was after the mushroom farm, of course. Didn't make such a go of the mushrooms.'

'—the gold prospecting?'

'Ah, yes! Got a bit in Vanua Levu, but couldn't find the source, unfortunately. It was while I was digging around there that I found the stones, y'know, those prehistoric things. Hold on a minute, I wonder if I can . . .'

He came back with some snapshots of a group of fallen boulders, engraved with various odd symbols.

'The Naukiniba stones, they're called now. Pretty famous with the tourists. Pre-Fijian carvings, they say. I was just sitting by a stream, eating some lunch and scratching around, when I started to uncover them from under the bush.'

He sat down and fixed me again with his histrionic, blue gaze. 'You've heard of people reading their own obituaries in the newspaper, perhaps?'

I nodded, mesmerized.

'Well, there's a Fiji version of that story and it happened to me. I'd been in hospital, d'ye see, laid up for six months with a rotten leg. Trod on a stone-fish and had the spine broken right off inside my foot. That's what started it. They didn't expect me to pull through. Then, all of a sudden, I made a complete recovery. Came out and set off for my store at Tamasua, this little place in the Yasawas. When my Fijian overseer saw me coming in the dinghy he fell flat on his face in the sand. There he was, screaming at the top of his voice that it was the spirit of Robinson come back to the islands!'

The flesh-and-blood Robinson went down on his knees here to convey the scene more graphically.

'Well, I finally got him to touch my feet to convince himself it was really me and he starts blubbing all over again. After a bit he managed to believe it and then he told me that today was the ceremonial Tenth-day after receiving the news of my death. At this very moment, in the village, they were preparing my *borotu*, the death-feast—and off he started again. I told him to cheer up, all would be well, and we set out to the village. When we'd rounded up all the villagers who'd gone screaming off into the bush at the sight of me, we all sat down cheerfully enough to a terrific feast of yams, pig, fowl, *dalo* and so on, and at the end *I* was presented with the pile of mats that should have been divided among the mourners!'

He brought out a packet of cigarette papers and a screw of tobacco and nimbly rolled himself a smoke.

'Then there was the time I was looking for sea-snakes——'

The sound of the bell from the Catholic Church dragged me back to the present at least an hour later. I made my farewells. Then, at the top of the steps, Mr. Robinson announced, 'But, of course, you haven't met Atetha!'

Round the back of the garden a tall, handsome Fijian woman finished pegging out a line of Mr. Robinson's khaki shorts, then came over and shook hands with me.

'This is Atetha, my wife.'

Somehow or other, we found ourselves in the house again with Mr. Robinson tugging open the doors of an enormous cupboard.

'What do you think of these?' He indicated the shining rows of glass pots inside, chutneys, pickles, jams of exotic dappled appearance. 'All my own work!'

Atetha slid me a smile of amused complicity.

'What'll you try?' he invited, holding up a jar that seemed to contain a pair of perished rubber gloves. 'Dried octopus? Or what about this?' He brought out from the back a tall, murky bottle and held it up with an expression of pride. Peering forward to read the label, I recoiled again rapidly. Through the glass there gazed impartially back at me, imprisoned in liquid like a zoological specimen, either a very large lizard or a very small alligator.

'Dragon-whisky?' cried Mr. Robinson jovially. 'A Chinaman gave it me for backaches. To cure 'em, that is! Still a drop left in the bottom!'

One of Mr. Robinson's jokes, I decided, accepting with relief instead a bowl of preserved, home-grown ginger in syrup. The church clock chimed half-past one. Late for lunch, I said good-bye again and rushed out into the sizzling sunshine, my head throbbing with visions of red-hot *lovus* and cannibal spears, death-feasts and Chinese dragons.

'Hey!' called a voice from the door. My host stood waving the famous bottle. 'If you don't believe me, meet me at the Ovalau Club at four. I'll buy you a dragon-gin!'

An interlude of calm was obviously essential before the appointment. The Town Clerk, Captain James Whittle, would surely provide it, I felt. A neat white-bearded figure, I had passed him several times on the hotel stairs when he had formally invited me to pay him a call at his office. 'In the Town Hall,' he had said. So, after lunch, I walked round the corner and over the bridge to the grey stone building that announced itself four-square across the arched entrance as the Levuka Town Hall. Immediately beneath this, however, was spread a tumultuous film poster entitled *Four Men and a Gun*, with a postscript adding, 'We will show the finest films in town'.

Inside, the door on the right said *Library*, the one on the left *Town Clerk*. Out of curiosity, I went on through the main entrance and found myself in an old-fashioned assembly hall. It was a big, echoing, musty room with rows of straight-backed chairs and benches, denuded gas-chains drooping from high-raftered ceilings, the paint peeling round windows that were ominously high and barred. I stood in the middle and tried to picture it in the days of its glory—the turbulent meetings of settlers and chiefs, muskets at the ready against the newest raid by the Hovoni hill tribes; patriotic gatherings on the birthday of those sovereigns whose portraits formed a faded arch of triumph over the proscenium; mixed quartets amidst the potted palms holding their music sheets up to the flicker of the gaslight to render, above the boom of the over-zealous pianist, 'Come Into the Garden, Maud', and a selection of the latest gems to arrive from the firm of Chappell in London; the dancing, in a crush of gin-fumes and wilting plumes, and all those other Levuka occasions with their heady blend of nineteenth-century decorum, pioneer recklessness and South-Seas sensuality.

Now, the old stage had been filled with rows of dusty velvet tip-up seats, the upper gallery of the cinema that the hall had become, the screen suspended at the other end above the doorway. The footlights were covered over. In the wings some ragged back-drops leaned askew among the ropes and pulleys. From the projection room at the back came a rustling and the murmur of voices. As I left they began a practice run-through of the evening film and the shadows of outlaws with guns flickered over the screen, transparent in the daylight as the ghosts of Levuka's shooting men of a hundred years ago.

In the doorway a printed notice, framed in glass and signed by Captain Whittle, sternly admonished the cinema-manager to 'see that the audience are always suitably dressed and well-behaved'. Outside his own door another of the Captain's missives met my eye, to the effect that anyone interested in making suggestions for the forthcoming summary of the town's by-laws should communicate with him immediately.

'Come in,' remarked a courteous, elderly voice at my knock. A large desk and a pair of official, horn-rimmed glasses almost concealed the resident of Room 13 who greeted one on the stairs at regular times of the day. Then he stood up to shake hands, a slightly-built little man with a white goatee and the precise, pared-down appearance of his name. He waved me into an old revolving chair that stood in the centre of the floor, slightly tilted as if supporting on its axis the whole structure of the room with its paper-crammed shelves, its dim brown walls and comfortable inky smell.

'Well, now,' said Captain Whittle, eyeing me over his glasses with an air of gentle shyness. 'And what do you think of Levuka? Lovely place to live, don't you agree? A wonderful lot of people.'

I asked him how long he'd lived here.

'Now let me see, I first left England'—he thought carefully for a minute or so—'ah yes! just after the South African scrap it was. And I finally settled down here immediately following the cessation of hostilities with Kaiser Bill!'

'How did you come here in the first place?'

'Quite simple. I was with the Fleet when we visited Fiji. That looks like the place for me, I thought to myself, and here I eventually landed. Oh, I've done all sorts of things around the islands, mostly with boats. Colonial Service in the New Hebrides, Shipping Superintendent for Burns Philp. I had my own boat for a while, two-fifty auxiliary schooner, taking Government officials, cargo and so on round the Gilbert and Ellice. That was in the days when young Grimble was D.O. there. Knew him well, a splendid man.'

His present job, the Captain went on to explain, he'd only undertaken two years ago at the age of eighty-four, so it was still fairly new to him. 'Plenty to do, I can tell you, plenty to do.' He poked at some files in front of him. 'Never any real trouble though. Just ordinary scrappin' from time to time.'

With his air of jaunty formality he got up to switch on the overhead fan, then remembered that the electricity had been cut off for repairs that afternoon, and sat down again.

'Do you ever feel you'd like to go back to England?' I asked him.

He shook his head sternly. 'In my opinion England could learn a lot from a place like this, for all her age and sophistication.'

Did I know Australia at all, he continued. He'd been on a visit four years ago to his family living in a city suburb and the thought of living among those unending rows of red-tile roofs had given him a pain. He kept in touch with news of home, of course, listened to the B.B.C. news and so on. 'Just to see what foolishness they're up to next.'

I got up to look more closely at a picture on the wall behind him which had been intriguing me for the last few minutes. Inside a single large frame were crowded hundreds of miniature photographs, row upon row of moustached and bearded gentlemen, each carefully numbered.

'No, not a criminal record-sheet,' chuckled Captain Whittle, coming up behind me. 'They're the original Levuka settlers, almost a complete gallery, I believe.' He took it down and pored sadly over a patch of damp in the left-hand corner. 'Roof must have been a bit leaky at some time or other. If you're interested, I've got the list of names somewhere.'

He bent down to open the door of an old-fashioned safe in the corner. After a few minutes of shufflings and rustlings, he produced several pages of bleached copper-plate, fastened together with a rusty clip. It would have taken some hours to have gone through the whole list, matching each numbered entry with these bold, faded faces of the past. They were all there, the familiar Fiji names, Hennings and Kaad, Bentley and Joske, Raddock, Storck, Tarte and the hundreds of others. Regretfully I folded it up and handed it back to the Captain who with tender care returned it to the safe, and the picture to its hook.

On another wall were lined the dashing figures of Thakobau's Special Police Guard of the 1860's, hirsute swashbucklers in the peaked caps known as 'cheese-cutters', cast-offs, according to Brewster from the old 65th York and Lancaster Regiment serving in New Zealand, cunningly collected and resold in Fiji by an enterprising trader named Cripps.

Alongside the photograph hung two elaborate prints in black and white. According to the plaque on the frame, they commemorated

Fiji's first royal visit in 1881 when Prince George, afterwards George V, and his elder brother the Duke of Clarence called in at the new colony during a world cruise in H.M.S. *Bacchante*. 'War Dance by Electric Light' was the arresting title chosen by the artist, Lieutenant Percy Scott, R.N., for his first sketch. In the full flood of a searchlight beamed on to shore from the *Bacchante*, a horde of bedizened warriors pranced and whirled their spears on a beach surrounded by dark, massed trees, a full moon overhead. Watching from unnervingly close quarters sat two grave young men in naval caps and brass-buttoned jackets. Behind them clustered a retinue of formally-dressed gentlemen and in the forefront five or six ladies in full *décolleté*, with pearls and fans and high-piled hair. One could almost hear the reverberating thud of drums and the hoarse yells of the dancers, the polite rattle of applause and clipped murmurs of English interest among the onlookers.

In his other sketch Captain Scott had depicted an even more famous incident of the visit, the royal *yaggona* ceremony. This time the scene was a more composed one—the cup-bearer advancing solemnly towards the royal pair between rows of squatting Fijians, their hair plastered to their heads with white lime in the old-fashioned manner. According to tradition, it was on this occasion that the Duke of Clarence had firmly declined to drink, while his younger brother swallowed the mixture at the prescribed gulp. In those days the root was not pounded in the preparation but chewed by mouth, and thoughts of tuberculosis, the scourge of the islands, may perhaps have flashed through the mind of the heir to the throne. Ironically enough, he was to die an early death in England, a tragedy at which the Fijians later expressed little surprise. They had in fact predicted that a young chief who failed to play his proper part in so solemn a ritual could never be king.

Through the open door I glimpsed a familiar figure in the roadway, waving a stick. I explained to the Captain I had an appointment to keep. Quite, quite, he nodded. He'd enjoyed our little chat and time flew past these days. He shook hands and stood closely observing my departure with an impatient Mr. Robinson.

The Ovalau Gentlemen's Club turned out to be just next door, a simple wooden construction but still with an impeccably gentlemanly air about it, rather like an English cricket pavilion, with flagstaffs at the ready, fore and aft.

'Two crocodile gins!' called Mr. Robinson to the elderly Fijian who limped forward as we entered. The Fijian nodded without surprise and disappeared into the back quarters.

'This is the Ladies' Lounge,' said Mr. Robinson, as we sat down at one of the tables. I wondered why as I looked round at the sagging canvas chairs, the uncompromisingly upright piano, the piles of old copies of the *Fiji Times* in the corner. 'We have to have somewhere for them to sit when they're brought in by a member,' he explained.

It was in the hidden inner regions then, that all those legendary club scenes were enacted—that moment at the end of an evening when with a shout of 'Boy!' a certain seasoned veteran would pass out backwards neatly caught by the resourceful bearer; the dramatic ejection of the remittance-man of noble English family who removed his shirt to play billiards in a heat-wave. And so on.

The elderly Fijian came padding back. Silently he placed before us two tumblers, a jug of water, and a large bottle in which reposed, bathed in colourless liquid, the brother of Mr. Robinson's crocodile. This one, though, had a glassily reproachful eye. Trying to evade it, I inspected the label. 'Ha-Kai-Chiew', it read. 'Long famous world renown.'

Mr. Robinson, pouring me a cloudy half-glass to which he added a dash of water, informed me that originally the bottles contained rice whisky. When this was finished, any kind of spirit could be substituted and the beneficial qualities of pickled crocodile would remain unaffected.

I took an apprehensive sip. It undoubtedly tasted of gin, but gin with certain musty and mysterious overtones. Before I had plucked up courage to try and define them, Mr. Robinson drew up his chair and seized my attention again.

'I didn't tell you this morning, did I, about our *tevora*, our ghost?' he began. 'A Fijian, a big man, with two front teeth missing. Every single time he'd disappear again into the very same spot in the floor. . . .'

We'd just got to the crucial point where the Bishop had advised him that the ghost might have something in the house he wanted to show him and the former owner of the property had asked to buy it back again at a surprisingly high price, when we were joined by a new-comer.

'J. R. Wigglesworth, British Columbia,' announced the dapper white-haired gentleman who sat down at the table with us. Mr. Wigglesworth with his Edwardian charm, his immaculate grey knee-socks, and his Whittle-style goatee, was apparently another of those octogenarians who in Levuka seemed to flourish like fifty-year-olds.

'Dead as a door-nail, of course,' he drawled gently. 'But the prettiest place on the map.' The Fijians, he thought, were 'out of this world', though some of the Europeans were a bit limited.

'Would you believe it, not one of them plays bridge,' he protested. 'And I haven't had a game of chess out of anyone yet!'

Nevertheless Levuka, Mr. Wigglesworth had decided, was the place for him. His family were all grown up, he had set out on a world cruise, discovered the place and returned to take a bachelor flat just outside the town ('only forty steps up') which he hoped to keep for good if he could get a permit to stay.

He had just embarked on the story of his youth in Canada when someone else arrived. This was the positively juvenile figure of the Reverend Whansbon-Ashton, Archdeacon of Polynesia and a Levuka resident, who was himself, he told me, a mere sixty-four. A short, incisive-looking man in white drill trousers and jacket, he sat down in the fourth chair and, eyeing the dragon-gin, ordered himself a squash. Then, settling his steel-rimmed glasses on his nose, he started to talk of the recent visit of the novelist Robin Maugham, who had bought the mystery ship *Joyita*. Maugham had requested the Archdeacon to exorcise the evil spirits said to have been troubling the *Joyita* ever since she had been found drifting and abandoned in Fiji waters in the 1950's.

'Of course, I couldn't comply with it just like that. He was writing a book about it, you see, and I thought it might well be a stunt. Besides, the ceremony of exorcising evil spirits is a fairly complicated business, and a very serious one. For instance——'

The final interruption came in the shape of a stout, red-faced gentleman in a white solar topee, who announced that the key to the bowls-room had now been located and the game could start.

The gathering began to break up. I felt, however, that at least one story should be completed.

'So what did you find under the floor, Mr. Robinson?' I asked, getting to my feet.

'Under the floor? Ah, yes, our *tevora*! Well, actually we haven't looked yet. But I'm sure we'll find something when we do . . . must get round to it, sometime.'

I left them ambling towards the bowling-green at the back. Outside, Ronald was waiting on the bridge. Leaning over the balustrade, one suddenly realized that Levuka was full of bridges, elegant little arched affairs that spanned the narrow river at regular intervals ahead and behind us with a dream-like, willow-pattern effect. Beneath the gardens of private houses all along the curve of the bank, a series of miniature classical columns rose out of the water. It was a view that had nothing to do with the tropics. In the solidity of the stonework, the ornateness of architectural detail, one felt only an exile's devotion to things English, a determination to reproduce somehow, somewhere, in however minor a key, the atmosphere of home. The very incongruity of the scene was a reflection of bracing Victorian optimism, full of plans for the progress and expansion of a brand-new British possession.

Together we walked on through the winding lanes that lay behind the seedy fronts of shops and shanties, a world apart, the nostalgic English-village capital of the colonists. The sense of hardship and insecurity faded here. In these cluttered bungalows that were more like cottages, with their flagstone paths and cramped, flower-filled gardens, people of equally cluttered and easy-going descent were living in content, if not prosperity, on family work, odd jobs, allowances of one kind or another.

It was not more than five but in the shadow of the hillside the light was already dimming. Inside, low-watt bulbs flickered on in bedrooms filled with brass bedsteads, in porches overhung by swags of pale roses and torn frills of iron lacework.

In the garden behind the hotel, among the hibiscus trees, the washing and the chickens, four or five of the Rotuman girls were sitting in the shadows on the steps, singing softly and intermittently as though practising something new. They looked up and there was a shy silence until we had passed. On the left stood the Courthouse, a white-timbered building with lawns of closely-shaved perfection.

'The prisoners mow them every day,' says Ronald.

Farther along, the grey tower of the Catholic church appeared above the greenery. A wicket-gate stood open on a narrow path leading to the back entrance. In the darker twilight inside, a few stained-glass windows gleamed ruby and sapphire, and an oil lamp burned, suspended on chains from the ceiling, blurring the threadbare red capet up the aisle, the shabby wooden pews. There were the usual clam shells of holy water. Someone had crowned the plaster Madonna near the altar with a coronet of white hibiscus. Most of the building was cream-painted timber, but the clock-tower itself of grey stone, much older. A bell-rope dangled in the porchway. Standing beneath the shaft of the tower one heard the regular hollow thud of the clockwork, like a heart beating in an elderly ribcage.

We went on then towards Nasova, the original Government headquarters and the site of the signing of the Deed of Cession. Under the mangrove trees, the beach road was deserted, the silence broken only by the exhalations of the sea, the crepuscular shirring sound of daylight contracting like a fan. Out of that half-light one expected to materialize any or all of Levuka's legendary characters—the beachcomber Paddy Cornell, one of the first Europeans, runaway convict and Irish wit and father of fifty children, shambling along to the King's *bure*, for Thakabau had appointed him court jester and expected a nightly supply of entertainment; or the sinister Colonel Thomas Woolaston White, revolver at his belt on his way to Keyse's Place, a long, low building stretching out into the water on piles, for a meeting of the Klu-Klux-Klan, the white die-hards of the 1870's, of whom he was president. Or in more sociable mood there might go past in his four-in-hand the monocled cotton-planter known as the Marquis of Koro, or Mrs. Otty Cudlipp alias the Duchess of Levuka, wife of the auctioneer and leader of fashion and society, who personally designed and stitched the royal standard for the King. (A white dove under a crown was the final choice, after His Majesty had rejected the original design of a dove on a red escutcheon as being 'too like a fowl boiled in a three-legged pot'.)

There might even be glimpsed the vision of Miss Gordon-Cumming herself, swaying by in her cane-chair with Lady Gordon on their way to the Queen's Birthday Race Meeting a few miles down the coast. The main runners in the race that year were the butcher's horse, and two ponies belonging to Sir Arthur and a certain Captain Olive. 'Nearly one hundred boats, cutters, and canoes had arrived from Levuka and along the coast. Europeans and Fijians formed picturesque groups beneath the cocoa palms and other trees, while a grandstand had been erected for the *élite*. . . . Later we had dinner on board H.M.S. *Sapphire* with a *pièce de résistance* of larks stuffed with truffles.'

Out on the horizon lay the string of islands whose names ran like an incantation, Koro, Batiki, Wakaya, Nairai—smoky cloud shapes in an oyster-coloured sky. In the foreground the gaunt silhouette of the *Joyita*, riding at anchor some fifty yards from shore, haunted by the ghosts of either a spiriting or a massacre, no one knew which. Somehow, in its Levuka setting it seemed perfectly appropriate that she should have been bought on a whim by an English lord who was also a writer and a nephew of Somerset Maugham. Would he come back for her, people asked? Was it true she was to be used for a film? Once again, nobody knew, but the rumours, the suppositions, the Miss Havisham-like *Joyita* herself, had all become an essential part of the local scene.

Then ahead of us, to one side of the road, a Union Jack drooped from a tall flagpole. Beneath it, on a smooth green handkerchief of turf, hedged round with hibiscus stood the Cession Stone, a large boulder in which was embedded a plaque reading: 'The instrument ceding to Queen Victoria, her Heirs and Successors, the possession of and full sovereignty over, the Fijian Islands and the inhabitants thereof, was signed here on the 10th October 1874.'

That October 10th had been a morning of driving rain and wind so the ceremony had been postponed and it was not until 2 p.m. that the citizens of Levuka, dressed in formal best, crowded round to watch two hundred sailors and marines of the warships *Pearl* and *Dido* form up outside the Government Buildings. After the formal signing of the Deed by the Governor of New South Wales, Sir Hercules Robinson, acting on behalf of the Queen, by the King, his Ministers and Chiefs, the flag of the Thakobau Government was lowered and the British royal standard was raised to a salute of twenty-one guns from the warships.

'The guard of honour', wrote the historian, Derrick, 'presented arms as the *Pearl's* band played the National Anthem; the marines fired a *feu de joie*, and cheers were given for Her Majesty the Queen and for His Excellency. Sir Hercules Robinson then called for cheers for Thakobau, *Vunivalu* and *Tui Viti*, and for the Commissioners; and the ceremony ended with general handshaking and congratulations.'

Yet the focal point of all the day's pomp and ceremony had been an old wooden club embellished with silver ferns and doves, a silver crown at the head.

'Before finally ceding his country to Her Majesty the Queen of Great Britain and Ireland, the King desires, through Your Excellency, to give Her Majesty the only thing he possesses that may interest her,' read out Mr. John Bates Thurston, Chief Secretary and Taveuni planter, as Thakobau made the presentation to Sir Hercules. 'The King gives Her Majesty his old favourite war-club, the former, and until lately, the only known, law of Fiji. In abandoning club law and adopting the forms and principles of civilized societies, he laid by his old weapon and covered it with the emblems of peace. Many of his people, whose tribes, died and passed away under the old law; but hundreds of thousands still survive to enjoy the newer and better state of things. . . . With this emblem of the past he sends his love to Her Majesty, saying that he fully confides in her and her children who, succeeding her, shall become Kings of Fiji, to exercise a watchful control over the welfare of his children and people, who, having survived the barbaric law and age, are now submitting themselves, under Her Majesty's rule, to civilization.'

From behind us, a young Fijian policeman in white serrated *sulu* and navy-blue shirt walked silently over the grass towards the flagstaff. Briskly, he saluted the flag. Then with neat movements he lowered it to the ground, folded it under his arm, remounted his bicycle and gracefully pedalled off into the dusk.

11

Island of Kings

'He was busily engaged with some European sailors cutting out sails for his schooner among grandchildren and children, and listening to the tales of a fisherman who was the court story-teller. A large musical box which he called his Jew's Harp, played "Home, Sweet Home". Later he read from a Bible wrapped in a silk handkerchief, his spectacles on his nose. . . . During prayers he exclaimed at intervals, "*Ndina! Ndina!*" (True! True!).'

Britton's picture of the celebrated Thakobau, *Tui Viti* and *Vuni valu* (King of Fiji and Chief of War) at home on the royal island of Bau in 1870, was an idyllically Victorian one. Selecting a different role, the great man made just as vivid an impression on Mrs. Smythe ten years earlier at the first official meeting between the Colonel and the King.

'William was in full uniform and so, I might say, was Thakobau, for when we entered his house we found him seated in a chair, dressed in a naval officer's blue coat with brass buttons, item a blue silk waistcoat, a white shirt, black cravat and trousers, and coarse shoes and stockings. In spite of his ill-fitting clothes and his unaccustomed seat, the chief looked very dignified.'

'My first impressions of Thakobau', wrote Emma Small, the young wife of a Methodist minister, who arrived at Bau in 1879, 'were of a very tall, magnificently made man with splendid limbs, a strong determined face and penetrating black eyes. How I shuddered when I took the Chief's once-cruel hand in mine, a hand that had once caused so much bloodshed in Fiji.' At Methodist meetings, Emma added, Thakobau's prayers were outstanding for their originality and beauty.

It was this bizarre Jekyll and Hyde element in the situation that so titillated the Europeans who met him. The more lurid stories of his past were well known to everyone. At the tender age of six, as the young Seru, nephew of King Naulivou, he had clubbed his first victim—'a boy slightly his senior'. By middle age he claimed to have eaten of one thousand human bodies. His treatment of a personal enemy who had betrayed him by word of mouth was to drag out the man's tongue with a fish-hook as far as he could, then cut it off and eat it raw in front of him. When the missionary Hunt warned him of the hell fires awaiting him if he did not repent, Thakobau replied nonchalantly, 'Well, it's a fine thing to have a fire in cold weather!'

'I shall still pray for you with a good mind, although you treat the subject so lightly,' Hunt replied.

'Go on with that!' said Thakobau.

Such prayers, combined with the political pressures of the period and a succession of defeats to both prestige and power, met with dramatic results on Sunday, 30th April 1854, when Thakobau publicly became a Christian, renouncing the gods of his fathers and his old way of life, and exclaiming, 'I have been a bad man. I have scourged the world.'

I looked up at the enlarged photograph hanging in the reception-room of the house at Bau where we were sitting. The Thakobau of the last years, the trusted counsellor of Governors who, 'with painful care' could write his own name on a piece of paper, stared heavy-lidded past the camera's eye and mine, a Roman emperor in a *tapa* waist-cloth and a striped cotton shirt with a tired old warrior's face, fierce, imperious and sad, framed in a Victorian beard of startling whiteness.

The man sitting under the picture poured out whisky for his guests.

'And in Las Vegas, Ratu George,' prompted one of them. 'How did you get on there?'

His broad, saturnine features curved in a smile. 'Oh, I ran out of money, of course. I told them—look, I'd wager the Fiji Islands instead but my great-grandfather gave them to Queen Victoria!'

Everyone laughed while Ratu George Thakobau looked up at the face in the frame that, though older, was so like his own, then quickly round at the gathering.

'He seemed extremely affable,' Britton had written of the first Ratu Thakobau. 'But when the attention of the visitors was diverted, I noticed that he took in the whole party with a searching feline glance from out of the corner of his eye when for an instant the courteously genial expression of his face was changed to an unpleasantly hard and cold expression; which though it only lasted a second seemed like an index to an entirely different character.'

Ratu George's glance was neither hard nor cold, merely wary. Yet it had in it this same quality of detachment, an extra reserve hinting at stronger, more complex feelings beneath the surface that distinguished him from other Fijian chiefs of whom he was, paramount. The face was striking, with the inscrutability of an archaic idol, a *tikki* in rubbed-out stone, the eyes prominent, heavy-lidded, the mouth wide and full under a flat Melanesian nose. When he came into a room, his square-cropped, grizzled head, bull neck and massive shoulders combined to produce an air of primitive power that extended beyond the physical. One began to understand the almost superstitious respect of the European guests for his great-grandfather. Generations of absolute authority left their mark on the most democratic successor, and Ratu George's *mana* seemed to have survived the process of change almost intact, despite his New Zealand university education, his tours of Australia as captain of the Fiji rugby team, his wartime experiences fighting with Fiji forces alongside Americans in the Solomons and on Bougainville. In 1946 he had visited England as a member of the Fiji contingent in the Victory Parade and went over again to represent the colony in 1953 at the Coronation.

Yet with Europeans his manner was still a disconcerting mixture of shyness, geniality and chiefliness, except with a few old friends who liked to call him George and with whom he enjoyed a game of snooker in a Suva club in the evenings. In the political world he remained an independent figure. Although employed by the Government in various advisory capacities, in Legislative Council he took his seat as the representative of the Council of Chiefs. To me, he seemed very much the nineteenth-century chief who cared little for the conference tables and cocktail parties of modern colonial policy, his day-to-day life still closely linked with the traditional past. His inauguration to the title of Vunivalu in 1959, a traditional ceremony revived after 106 years, was attended by more than 3,000 Fijians. He had walked to the *vakatunaloa* along a specially woven mat, more than 200 yards long, to receive the *tabua* from his first cousin, Ratu Edward Thakobau. For the feast each tribe of the Tailevu Province provided a stack of food 6 feet high, 3 feet wide and 5 fathoms long. The gift of the Tongans was a length of *masi* measuring 30 yards. Altogether it was an occasion of feudal proportions.

This table, Ratu George turned and told me now, indicating with his small, almost feminine hand, the one with the drinks on it, was the very table on which the Deed of Cession had been signed. A huge whale's tooth, almost 12 inches long, hanging on the wall by its cord of sinnet, had also been handed down from that period, he went on in his husky, hesitant voice.

The rest of the party claimed his attention again on the subject of his visit to America, where he had been the guest of the U.S. Government on something called a Leadership Course. I was pondering to myself what old Thakobau's reaction would have been to such a project when Adi Lelea, Ratu George's second wife, slipped quietly into the chair next to mine and we began talking together in undertones of domestic affairs. A small stolid boy of about two followed her in and stood at her knee. He was her youngest, Adi Lelea told me. They had called him Epenisa (Ebenezer), the name chosen by Ratu Thakobau for his public baptism in 1857, three years after he had *lotud.*

Adi Lelea murmured on in her perfect English and light high-pitched voice while I privately admired her extraordinary prettiness. In the days of its glory, the island of Bau had always extracted a tribute of handsome women from each kingdom it defeated. 'Hence could be seen at Bau the prettiest women in Fiji,' delicately remarked the Rev. Joseph Waterhouse in 1850. Lelea, a Bauan girl, was the perfect product of such traditions. She was very young with a small, slight figure and a creamy skin that was almost as pale as a European's. Fluffy dark hair, cut short, framed a heart-shaped face. When she smiled, two dimples and a flash of teeth like white shells appeared, and her widely tilted, black eyes lit up under arching black brows. Her manner, too, was delicate and gay with a Jane Austen sort of demureness and a gentleness that was unusual in Fijian women. In Suva she drove a small shiny car to do her shopping and, wearing the decorous ankle-length *sulu*, made tentative small-talk at the official cocktail parties. Here on Bau she was relaxed, cossetted, at ease, first lady and wife of Thakobau, safe in the heart of the Fijian hive.

Where we were sitting now, Adi Lelea told me, was Ratu George's reception house for the entertainment of guests with talk and drinks or *yaggona*. There were adjoining bedrooms at the back. According to custom, food was served and eaten in the second house, just opposite. Both houses were of modern frame construction, but the mats and wall coverings of finest Fijian work. She brought out some photographs and we looked at Ratu George, magnificent in chiefly *masi*, presenting the ceremonial *tabua* to the Queen at the Fijian welcoming ceremony, and Lelea herself adorned for the occasion with a superb necklace of shark's teeth.

'That came from Kaba, the peninsula off the mainland quite close to Bau,' she said. 'The people there have special allegiance to Ratu George. Every year on Boxing Day they have a fish drive in some lagoons that are reserved for the *Vunivalu* and he asked them to catch the biggest shark they could for my necklace. When they caught it and hung the jaws up on a pole to dry, they were big enough to go round the heads of three men. And fifty teeth altogether, the finest I've ever seen.'

A small boy in neatly patched shorts came stealthily in from the back door and dropped on to all-fours. Clapping his hands three times, he murmured something in Adi Lelea's ear, then crept away again, his eyes fixed on Ratu George who was absorbed in talk. Adi Davila, it seemed, was ready for us so we took our leave, shaking hands with our host and hostess, carefully skirting the circle of elders gathered round the *yaggona* bowl in the corner, and the very old man squatting on the doorstep, his gaze fixed out to sea, his cane in his hand, a servant since childhood of his father's, Ratu George had told us, who still regarded it his special privilege to guard the chiefly entrance.

Adi Davila's house was a large *bure* down by the water's edge, with great stepping-stones of coral leading up from the sea to the doorway under the spreading shadows of bread-fruit-trees and Tahitian chestnuts. Adi Davila was the wife of one of Fiji's political leaders, a remarkable man with no chiefly rank, who claimed descent from one of the first Negro slaves to escape from a passing American whaler and settle in Fiji. In the Fiji of today, Ravuama Vunivalu (*Vunivalu* here as a name, not a title) was an outstanding member of the Legislative Council, a leader revered by the people for his cleverness—smartness, as the Fijians say—his forthright ideals and brilliant oratory, and we had known and admired him since we first arrived.

From under the eaves a tall matriarchal figure stepped across to meet us—Adi Davila, another lady of Bau, with her lively clear-cut features and huge expressive eyes. She was a teacher at the Fijian school just opposite our house in Suva and now she exclaimed, with a schoolmistress's enthusiasm, 'Come, let us see Bau first before we have our food. Ronald can go in and talk to Ravuama.'

I said this was just what I wanted to do. So far, my only glimpse of the island had been as we were poled across from the mainland after our twenty-five-mile drive from Suva. A toy island, it had looked from the boat, this tyrant kingdom of yesterday, less than 400 yards across and perfectly round like those fortifications of sand that children build in a shallow pool with neat little inlets for the sea to fill in, pebble breakwaters and matchbox houses under sprigs of palm. Crossing the village green with Davila, the past seemed even more unreal. The grass had been smoothly trimmed and neat bushes of hibiscus and gardenias flowered among the encircling *bures* that sloped down to the shore. Here in the South Seas, history left few ruins behind. Nature or the missionaries covered its tracks too quickly. The palaces of the kings, woven from palm and reed and branch to rear their great peaked gables some fifty or sixty feet into the air, had rotted, decayed, returned to the earth from which they came. The twenty pagan temples, tall pagoda shapes shrouded in thatch and leaf where to ecstatic shakings the hereditary priests spoke to the people in the voices of their gods, had been burned down and destroyed. Beyond the trees a few tumbled boulders at the water's edge were all that remained of the massive stone canoe-docks built by King Banave at the end of the eighteenth century to accommodate the royal war fleets, the vessels of neighbouring states come to pay tribute to the conquerors with gifts of the land, as well as the flotilla of two hundred small canoes that glided in and out at all hours, serving the needs of the three to four thousand people who thronged the cramped space of the island.

To the earliest Europeans such barbaric splendours must have seemed the exact realization of every traveller's tale or explorer's dream of the heathen islands of the uncharted Pacific. A mysterious unknown seaman from the wrecked *Argo* of 1800, known by the Fijians as *Na Matai* (the Craftsman) was the first white man on

Bau. The pieces of broken plate and a few buttons that came with him from the wreck were a nine-days' miracle on the island. Soon after a Bauan canoe sighted a sandalwood ship near Koro Island and to support their tales of the wonders they had seen the crew brought back with them some hatchets, a monkey, and what may have been the original ancestor of Fiji's cat population. Successive castaways were not permitted to wear European dress, but given instead the loin-cloths of *masi* worn by the Fijians. And so they lived, half-wild relics of another world, spinning out the years by petty trading and the gathering of *bêche-de-mer* for the trading ships, mending muskets, telling yarns, and following the beck and call of the chiefs.

Here, on a day in May 1808, had come the most notorious beach-comber of them all, a ragged young sailor named Charlie Savage, brought by the Fijians to Bau off the wreck *Eliza* to be the Vuni-valu's white man, *na nogu kai papalagi* (my European). Within a few days he had demonstrated to the King a strange new weapon. It sounded like thunder and felled a man from a distance with no visible effort, a piece of magic that would make him the terror of his enemies. On the strength of the *Eliza's* muskets, Savage lived on at Bau for the next five years, dividing his time between his many wives and the bloody campaigns which laid the foundations of Bau's political power and earned him the title of *Koroi-na-vunivalu* (a kind of Knight of the Vunivalu's). His death was as violent as his life. Ambushed by a horde of enemies on the mainland, he grew impatient waiting with the rest of the group on their rock refuge and, confident of his ability to handle all Fijians, went down to treat with them. He was immediately seized, suffocated head down-wards in a pool of water, cut up, cooked and eaten before his com-rades' eyes. As a final insult, his bones were later made into sail needles. Ironically enough, the others finally reached their boat in safety, holding before them an enemy priest as hostage.

I asked Adi Davila if any of Savage's descendants still survived. There was a daughter living at Rewa about the middle of the last century, she had heard. 'But of course the Bauans were careful to eliminate any of his male children whose mother was of high rank.'

We had reached the entrance to the Methodist church on the far side of the green. Inside, it was cool and dim with floors of polished hardwood and rows of straight-backed pews. The walls, Davila told

K

me, were built of the foundation-stones of the old temples. In the same matter-of-fact way of a housewife demonstrating economy with left-overs, she pointed out the unusual looking font, a tall blunt stone, whitewashed, with a cup-sized hollow for holy water in the top. 'This stood outside the largest temple. It was the killing-stone. The warriors dashed out the brains of their captives on it.'

Outside, I looked for the site of the earth-ovens where bodies were then cooked, the portions wrapped up in leaves, placed over hot stones and sealed again with earth to preserve the heat. The cannibal feasts of Bau were notorious and it was the boast of the people that their ovens were never cool. After the sack of a neighbouring town in 1839 the bodies of 260 men, women and children were distributed among Thakobau's friends and allies. In 1875 Miss Gordon-Cumming had noted that the ground here was marked only by the greener grass. Today that final evidence, too, had long since disappeared with the rest—the well where the bodies were washed, the wooden drums that summoned the people to the feast, 'now used', she had remarked approvingly, 'to call them to church and school'. But the huge ironwood tree near by, its trunk scarred and pitted with age, was I felt sure the one mentioned by both Waterhouse and Miss Gordon-Cumming as being the sole survivor of the original sacred grove cut down by Thakobau on his conversion, 'covered with notches to record the wretches whose skulls were dashed against the temple stone'.

In the bright sunshine of a mid-twentieth century afternoon it was all unimaginable. Standing there alone and at night, though, I thought, one might find the comfortable present blown out like a candle in the space of a heart-beat. For darkness was the true element of this place, the peculiarly dense darkness, clouded and moonless, of the tropics, studded with the flare of flaming brands, the coppery reflections of the cooking fires on ranks of gleaming faces and, more eerie than any of these, the pallid luminous glow which, according to the earliest travellers, rose from the bodies of men still warm from the ovens. 'Mr. Harding asked his cannibal acquaintances why they used forks for human flesh only. They replied that human flesh when cooked emitted in the dark a peculiar halo which, according to their description, resembles a phosphorescent or magnetic flame. The utensils or saturated wrappings containing it, or the hands of anyone manipulating it, present the same appearance; and therefore it is that, being much afraid of this they used the well-known "cannibal forks". . . .'

A flock of mynahs scattered noisily into the air as some children, laughing and calling, ran on to the grass kicking a ball between them. Between the *bures*, lines of washing perched on poles of split bamboo flapped like flags in the warm wind. Women's voices rose and fell under the trees where they sat round on a mat plaiting shiny green food-baskets out of coconut fronds. There were regular *meke* practices out here, Adi Davila told me, in the afternoons and, in the past, frenzied games of cricket introduced by the missionaries. And in the centre of the green, surrounded by onlookers, the Chief of the early nineteen-hundreds, Ratu Kadavu Levu introduced the most famous Bauan game of all. Faced with the problem of an unusual surplus of shy bachelors and unmarried women on the island, he called them all together and sat them down in two rows facing each other. Each man in turn was given an orange to roll in the direction of the girl he fancied. If the girl failed to roll back the orange, nothing further happened. But when the orange was returned, the couple were married off within a few days and the population of Bau was safely ensured for another generation at least.

Davila talked on of such entertainments, but it was no use. In one's mind the darker scenes overshadowed the bright, just as behind us now the sombre shape of the great Council Hall, built over the framework and foundations of the largest of all the temples, dominated the sunny *rara*, the surrounding *bures*, even the Church itself.

Once inside, up the steep stone steps, littered with cowrie shells, one felt it surround one again more strongly than anywhere else, the unmistakable weight of fear in the air, old and stale now, but still as real as something smelt. Here, it was always twilight, and the Gothic height of the great thatched roof, its sloping corners lost in shadow, gave to the intruder a claustrophobic feeling of smallness. Even Mrs. Smythe, who sat on her campstool sketching in the corner, must have felt it for her scattered groups of Fijian figures are dwarfed by their setting. The ancient reeds and matting of the walls had been welded by time into a single hide-like texture, and the timber of the pillars had grown a patina of age, like grey moss. Deep in the ground, the bones of dead men stood erect beneath them, for every building of importance received in its foundations a sacrifice of slaves or captives who were buried upright and alive supporting in their arms the main posts of the house, so lending *mana* to the fabric and stability to the construction. Here the fates of villages and kings were decided by the councils of elders, the enemy bodies presented for apportioning to the head priest after battle, the widows brought in procession for the ritual murder by strangulation at the death of a chief. Around the corner-post hung a curtain of *masi*, suspended from high up in the roof framing, down which the spirit of the deity descended, and before this the people sat in silence, waiting for Thagawalu, the war-god of Bau, to speak to them through the priest and tell them of the future, the approaching disasters of drought, scarcity, and death, or the promise of success in war and prosperity for themselves and their chiefs.

Among the pictures of persons and scenes from Fijian history that hung on the walls today, the faded face of Tanoa, father of King Thakobau, stood out like a visitation from the past. The sly, wizened features were almost lost in the folds of his turban. On his chest he wore a medal the size of his head made of pearl and tortoise-shell. Nobody knew his age and he said himself that death had forgotten him. Known irreverently to the English sailors as 'Old Snuff', historians recorded him as a vicious and obstinate cannibal to the end, whose greatest delight was to return from tributary isles with the bodies of infants hanging from the yard-arms of his canoes as flags of triumph. On one occasion, he sentenced his own youngest son to death, for a crime against the state, and compelled an elder brother to club him.

This then was the face, scarred, malevolent and daubed with ceremonial black, which confronted the mission ladies, Mrs. Calvert and Mrs. Lyth, when they burst into his private quarters to plead for the lives of fourteen Fijian fisherwomen captured by the notorious slaughterer Gavidi as human meat for a royal feast. Alone with their children at the Mission House on nearby Viwa, the two wives begged a canoe on hearing the news, and were poled over to Bau. The island was full of the sound of the *lali bokola* (cannibal drums), and the firing of muskets, and the Christian Chief who dared to meet them told them, 'Make haste—some are dead but some are alive!'

The Reverend Thomas Williams described the scene: 'Surrounded by an unseen guard which none might break through, the women of God passed among the blood-maddened cannibals unhurt. They pressed forward to the house of old King Tanoa, the entrance to which was strictly forbidden to all women. It was no time for ceremony now. With a whale's tooth in each hand and still accompanied by the Christian Chief, they thrust themselves into the grim presence of the King and prayed the prayer of mercy. The old man was startled at the audacity of the intruders. His hearing was dull and they raised their voices higher to plead their dark sisters' lives. The King said, "Those who are dead are dead; but those who are alive shall live only." At those words, a man was sent to Gavidi to stop his butchery and returned to say five still lived, the rest of the fourteen were killed. Even in cannibal Bau all did not consent to the deed of darkness. Thakobau's chief wife and Gavidi's wife had already secured the life and liberty of two of the victims, and when Mrs. Calvert and Mrs. Lyth left there were others who blessed them for their work of love. What the winning of it cost those intrepid hearts none may know; but their deeds stand in this record above all praise.'

Shortly afterwards, in December 1849, Mrs. Wallis, wife of a visiting American sea-captain, reported Tanoa as wearing a turban daintily adorned with several yards of pink ribbon. Asked where he had procured such a luxury, he announced that it was the ribbon which had tied up the whale's teeth presented by the mission ladies.

Out of all this sombre past, one scene of comic-opera relief re-enacted in my mind, under the tall rafters. It was 2nd May 1867. Amidst a throng of white settlers and native rulers Thakobau knelt to be formally proclaimed King of Fiji, under a constitution designed by the leading Europeans to unite the clutter of petty chiefdoms into one sovereign state, the next best thing to British protection, which had already been refused. Upon his head was solemnly placed a crown of wood, covered with gold paper and decorated with gems taken from penny brooches. It had been constructed by the local carpenter at a cost of four and a half dollars. When this work of art was placed on the King's bushy head the absurdity of the scene, according to the *Sydney Morning Herald*, was irresistible. A titter threatened to develop into unrestrained laughter, and uproar was averted only by the King's natural dignity of deportment. His Majesty's Secretary of State, Samuel A. St. John, Esq., a Californian rover with a Bauan wife and an ardent belief in Thakobau's divine right to the monarchy, hastily led the gathering in a cry of 'God Save Your Majesty!' With a sword in his right hand and a Bible in his left, the King then ascended a platform and took his seat on an armchair suitably draped for the occasion. A salute of twenty-one guns was fired and the national flag was hoisted—a rising sun on a blue ground with a crown in the top corner.

The crown itself, I thought, would have been a cheerful relic in the Council Hall's historical gallery. Davila said she had read of it but never seen it nor heard that it still existed anywhere. I remembered then, as we went out into the sunshine again, the story of Brewster's that after the crowning, with the return of his usual common sense, Thakobau 'threw the bauble of his white advisers away and never used it again'.

We came out on the other side of the *bure*. We would walk, said Davila, pointing past the church, just up to the top of the hill where the old chiefs were buried. That bungalow on the side was on the site of the first mission house.

'The schoolmaster lives here now,' she said, as we passed by the neat terraces and gardens that patterned the grassy slope.

I was interested to know why the abhorred Christians had been given one of the choicest sites on the island. Davila smiled and said that in fact the missionaries were only allowed to build there because in those days it was the most undesirable place of residence in Bau. No Fijian cared to live away from the convenient water level and as a result, the hillside had become the receptacle for all the filth and rubbish of the town. Only the sheer necessity of establishing a base in the capital had induced them to accept at all.

Conversion to Christianity did not bring an end to the tribulations of the people and such primitive hygiene no doubt brought the great measles epidemic to Bau with particular virulence. It was 1875, the year of Miss Gordon-Cumming's visit to Fiji. 'On the king's little island of Bau (the special home of the nobles which is small and overcrowded) all were ill at once,' she wrote. 'Canoes bearing the dead were ceaselessly crossing to the mainland, where the graveyards lie; the cries of mourners and the death-drums resounded day and night. People were starving. They had no strength to go ashore to the mainland for food and many of the finest chiefs and teachers died. . . . A number of the dead have been buried in their own houses and these having fallen, the raised foundation on which every Fijian house is built has now become a platform on which lie the graves of the whole family, marked by the red leaves of the dracaena and other plants.'

These crimson-blades and tall clumps of red ginger, the Fijian flower of mourning, began to mark our climb through the long grass. Gradually the path narrowed, was swallowed up in the undergrowth and we walked through blind bush for the last part until we found ourselves in a clearing on the top.

Now we stood at the height of an English church-tower above the rest of the island. In front of us the limestone cliffs sheered down to the sea under a thick fleece of mango trees—and at our feet lay the Kings of Fiji. It was a small cemetery, closely packed, with the fantastical quality of a Stanley Spencer painting. Victorian marble and brass, expensively conveyed from England and Australia, commemorated the later chiefs—chiselled headstones blurred with rain, the ribs of old railings fretted with rust, domes of glass enclosing the grey crumbs of dried everlastings, while on every side pressed and thrust the living growth of their own land, vines and creepers, ferns and bamboo, wild orchids and rank white lilies with spidery petals and stamen antennae, the strange painted leaves that looked like flowers and flowers that looked like leaves, in all the urgent, greedy profusion of the tropics. On the grave of Tanoa—which lay slightly apart from the others—a rough wooden pillar like a giant's club blackened with age was all that remained of the traditional house built over his tomb, while no memorial of any kind marked the presence of the five wives lying obediently at his side in accordance with his wishes. When the time of his death had drawn near, he gave special instructions that on no account should the women fail to accompany him to the spirit world. The missionaries protested, offered muskets, a whaleboat, even the finger of Mr. Calvert cut off in mourning *Vaka-Viti* (Fijian style), but Tanoa remained obdurate. What prestige or comfort could a chief enjoy in *Burotu* (Paradise) without the ministrations of his principal wives? More important, who would assist him in the many trials of cunning and strength that beset the spirit on its path to this haven? And so the five ladies were dressed with all pomp and new cords placed round their necks as proudly as jewellery. Tanoa himself summoned strength to assist the executioners with only one exception, for it was the privilege of an eldest son to strangle his own mother first. Out of deference to the white men he offered life to the youngest victim, but she refused it and went her way with the others—'not for any love of her cruel lord but simply because it was the custom of Fiji'.

A hundred feet below us the sea crawled and glittered in the sun along the green coast of Viti Levu and the long finger of the Kaba peninsula where the thousand warriors of Bau and Tonga had erupted from the sea on to the rebel garrison and won the last of the great battles of the nineteenth century. Davila and I stood in silence for a moment with the wind rustling the grass, a sea bird wheeling and dipping overhead with harsh, mournful cries. Even the village seemed utterly still and deserted. It was lunchtime, Davila decided. We must go down.

Back at the house, Ravuama and Ronald were deep in a discussion of Bertrand Russell. Books, mostly philosophical and historical, lay open everywhere in the long thatched room which was partly Fijian in style, partly European. Ravuama, a slight balding figure in a shirt and *sulu*, sprang up to shake hands with me, with the smile that was crooked and wide-lipped and an air of impulsive enthusiasm entirely his own. In a way that is as typically Fijian as it is English, he turned back to continue the argument, his profile alert, eyes widened, stroking his clever, Negroid head with one hand as he talked in a characteristic gesture, nervous and passionate. Lunch was served round a small table and Davila talked to me about Fijian women in the elections. It was the first time they had had the vote, and many people had predicted complete failure for this innovation.

'They said we wouldn't even bother to vote,' exclaimed Davila. 'And what happened? The women lined up outside the polling booths as though they had been doing it all their lives. You should have seen them, with their children and their shopping baskets. In the country districts, you know, the votes were taken in a village schoolroom or even a launch. But the women got there just the same, making up parties and tramping for miles together through the bush.'

I told her that Ratu Mara himself had said to me, 'Just because they don't turn up at election meetings, don't think they're not going to vote—and even tell their menfolk how to vote too!'

Davila laughed. 'Well, that is the Fijian way, you know. In most countries they say it's the women who are the conservative ones, don't they? In this part of the world, I think it's the other way round. Often, a new idea, a better way of doing something, gets its first support from the women, who then urge on the men to get things changed. They're so eager for knowledge.'

Women's clubs were a tremendous influence, she went on to tell me. Originally sponsored by the Education Department and guided by Women's Interest Officers from overseas, there were now several hundred of them throughout the islands. 'Women who've never been to school run bazaars to raise money for books and blackboards for the village children, new drugs for the dispensary, a supply of piped water, new paint for the church. Anything in the way of improvement. And as I said, they get the menfolk moving, get them to help with the heavy work like digging new drains in the soggy parts of the village, or arrange with the headman for them to have a day off to look after the children while the women go to their club work. Do you know, one club even gives a cup to the most helpful husband in the village! And then of course there are cookery courses, child welfare demonstrations, needlework lessons, with the experts teaching the learners. You know how Fijian women love their sewing machines, and they'll cart them for miles through mud and stream to learn a school uniform pattern for the children.'

After we had eaten paw-paw, prawns cooked in coconut milk, delicious chestnut-flavoured bread-fruit and roast pork, Davila placed on the table as a final delicacy a dish of tiny, baked *lairo* or land-crabs. 'I will tell you the legend of the *lairo* before you go,' she said, when we had finished. 'At certain times of the year, they swarm down to the water's edge to spawn, almost in millions, in a kind of army. The old people say that on this occasion the leaders can be seen carrying between them in their claws a number of snakes. The snakes are alive but do not resist, and it takes six to eight crabs to carry each one. They are then laid as an offering at the feet of a very old, very big crab who awaits them on the beach and who is said to be the ancestral god of the *lairo*. This presentation is known as *Katundrau*, or one hundred fathoms, for this is the name of the *masi* which is rolled up in bales of the same measurement like snakes, to be presented to a chief. That is the story of the *lairo* which you must always remember you first heard on the island of Bau.'

It was afternoon now and low tide outside, so we set out to walk back to the mainland barefoot over the reef flats as people do crossing to and from the island at this time of day. But they were few, for no tourist comes to Bau and strangers are *tabu* on that hierarchical ground. Undisturbed, the old families live on in the communal pattern of their ancestors, planting their crops and fishing their waters, speaking the language that is to the rest of Fiji what Latin is to the civilized world, drawing together in lavishly punctilious celebrations of the great Fijian ceremonies threads of allegiance that stretch from the Suva jungle of shops and offices to the smallest coastal village of Viti Levu.

I had seen Bau and now, driving back into the city, it was not the past that seemed unreal to me but the present.

12

Savu-Savu Sunday

About fifty miles across the sea to the north-east of Viti Levu lies Vanua Levu—one means Great Fiji, the other Great Land—the second largest island in the group, half the size of Viti and a good deal larger than any of the other 298 lesser specks. Its long lizard shape measures a rough hundred miles from head to tail, approximately thirty across its widest points. Isolated from world airline and shipping routes, and just as remote to many Viti Levu people, Fiji's 'other island' retained something of the mystery it had been to the early nineteenth-century map-makers who preferred to leave it a vague blob on the charts. I was as ignorant as they until an invitation from Adi Laisa to join Ratu Penaia and her on an official tour by launch of Natewa Bay made me fly to the reference books. In addition to the above information, I was delighted to find that the bay in question was the extremely sheltered one, a deep horseshoe near the far tip of Vanua Levu, safely tucked away from the open sea.

Historically, the island lay well outside the shadow of the Bau régime. Not Thakobau, but his lifelong rival Ma'afu ruled on this side of the Fiji Group throughout the crucial years of change of the mid-nineteenth century. Under the shield of a Christian mission to heathen Fiji, this suave and remarkable Tongan chief conquered his way from island to island, using not only the Gospel but the older weapons of club and fire in pursuit of his great dream of an empire stretching from the New Hebrides in the west to Tonga and Samoa in the east, until the Cession to Britain in 1874 put an end to his ambitions. The peak of his influence, especially among the white planters, was achieved as Chieftain Supreme of a Confederation of North and East Fiji, a far more effective attempt at constitutional government than Thakobau's charade of the same period. Yet in their different ways both men were trying to cope with the same tremendous problem of bridging successfully the gap between the old world and the new. One imagined them clearly, each on his island capital, a brief stretch of sea between—the King of Bau with his crown of gold paper and Windsor chair throne, the more wily Ma'afu attending Assembly in black frock-coat, white ducks, patent leather shoes and peaked cloth cap surrounded by his chocolate-soldier police force in dashing blue uniforms, faced with scarlet and white, and on their cap-bands the single stern word *ovisa* (officer).

I was to join Penaia's party at Savu-Savu, the seaside town of copra and planters, at the Hot Springs Hotel. As ever, my good friend Constance had forged ahead of me by the usual ninety years. 'Quite the prettiest place I have yet seen!' she declared. Of the actual hot springs she added, with her customary genius for throwing away a sensational line. 'The water was quite boiling and it was apparently a favourite place for depositing all superfluous babies. They were popped in alive like so many lobsters and treated with quite as little ceremony.' No doubt after dashing this off, Miss G.-C. sat back with a dreamy smile to enjoy the vision of 'dear readers' everywhere falling into swoons of horror amidst the tinkle of breaking china and the popping of sal volatile corks.

We landed on the familiar strip of green, fringed with palms, and a car—new, Australian type—took me to the hotel. It stood on a hill, half submerged in garden, an unpretentious, one-storey, wooden building. There were no visible signs of hot springs, boiling babies or unconventionality of any kind. Inside the entrance a door stood open on an old-fashioned kitchen with a bright fire roaring in a massive black range, and farther on there was a long room with leather-covered chairs and potted palms at one end, dining tables at the other, and an upright piano and a ping-pong table alongside. The row of curtained doorways in the background must have been the bedrooms. There was the smell of small, coastal hotels the world over, a mixture of oilcloth and sea air and vegetables cooking, and from the radiogram in the corner the lazy, easy-going syncopation of Billy Vaughan's Orchestra—favourite of the islands—playing 'Sail Along Silvery Moon'. There was no sign of people at all.

Suddenly a door opened from behind the desk at the far end of the room and a large, sun-tanned man in an old bushjacket emerged.

'Robbie!' came a woman's voice from inside the office. 'Don't forget to ask if those magazines for Lilian didn't come up on the plane, eh? And, if I've told Seti once about putting the chilli salt out on the tables. . . .'

He turned and went back in, then reappeared with a registry book under his arm and a proprietor's smile, cheerful and gap-toothed on his round face. He knew who I was. I hadn't been up to Savu-Savu before, had I? And why not? There was no sign of Ratu Penaia's party yet. 'But', glancing at his watch, 'what about a drink? Just on midday.'

My host disappeared down the passage and I went out and sat down on the steps of the back porch. There was the hot, humid smell of sunshine after rain and things growing. Chickens ran over the grass and scratched in the roots of a red hibiscus hedge. Billy Vaughan changed over to 'My Isle of Golden Dreams'. Then in the doorway appeared a large jug with Robbie behind it. A number of other people drifted in after him, his dark, pretty wife, a few muscular, grizzled men, mostly part-Europeans, barefoot in shorts and flowered shirts.

'Savu-Savu people don't go in much for shoes,' said the wife. 'Except for walking down to the shops and things.'

By now there was quite a circle of us sitting round on the steps drinking cold beer.

'Well, it's not often we get a real stranger up here,' said somebody.

But no one seemed anxious to hear the news from Suva. Savu-Savu talk, staunchly self-contained, rose and fell in pleasant, desultory fashion. Young Len had had another bust-up with his wife, just threatening her of course, but she'd had to lock him out all night. There was an ex-service-men's meeting next Thursday, don't forget, to talk about raising money with a bazaar. The boys on the Weston estate had been caught making grog again.

A double-ring from the hang-up phone on the wall interrupted for a moment. It was repeated twice.

'Gee, that poor old Rosie!' murmured Robbie's wife. 'Her legs must be bad again.'

There was a general sigh of relief when after the fourth ring silence descended. Rosie, whoever and wherever she was, must have made it.

'Of course, you've only got to pick up the receiver to listen in to anyone talking,' his wife explained. 'But not many people bother.'

Someone asked me how long I was staying. 'You won't be here for the Bishop, then?'

Church services, they said, were conducted in the hotel lounge on a Sunday afternoon, and this week-end the Bishop would be present on one of his parish visits. 'We just push back the tables and close the saloon bar,' said Robbie. He grinned. 'Of course, we have our little difficulties from time to time.'

'Like half-way through the sermon when old Daniel stands up in the back row and wants to know where is this heaven they keep talking about—this wonderful place, has anyone actually seen it?'

'And the day when the Bishop thought he heard singing coming from underneath the table. They lifted up the altar-cloth and there was Skippy Thompson just coming round last night's party.

'Joining in "Rock of Ages" as good as the next man.'

A wiry little dark-haired man of about forty appeared in the doorway, wearing old khaki shorts and a faded green shirt.

'Here's Jack! Come on, Jack!'

Nodding over at me, he slipped into the circle. He had a narrow, sensitive face, with the traces of great good looks, carpenter's hands, and a gallery of tattoo marks on each arm.

'That's the famous Jack Morris,' the elderly man said next to me. 'The one who sailed to Australia.'

'Tell her about it, Jack,' urged the rest of the circle.

'Oh, not that old story, it was nothing,' murmured Jack, in a voice that had an echo of a Southern Counties burr in it. He bent his head over his beer, then with no perceptible pause launched into an account of how he had set sail for the Lau Islands in his twelve-foot dinghy—the southernmost islands of the Fiji group—and half-way there, on a sudden impulse, decided to make for Australia instead. 'I just wanted to see if I could do it.' He had with him a crew of two Fijians and a character by the name of One-Arm Jackson. The loss of Jackson's arm, he explained, was the result of an accident incurred as a guest of Her Majesty when, attempting to nick his finger in the circular-saw and so be sent off sick, he over-estimated somewhat and chopped off his forearm. 'Isn't that a fact, now?' inquired Jack of his audience, with a flash of his extraordinary green eyes.

Everyone agreed that it was. 'He did have a wooden arm made for him, remember?' someone intervened. 'But it kept dropping off whenever he got excited, so in the end he preferred to do without.'

'Well, One-Arm Jackson's special job on the trip was to make us all extra clothing,' continued Jack, now fully caught up in his epic again. 'It gets terribly cold with wind and rain when you get near Australia at that time of year. He made us jackets out of old copra sacks and we each wore two or three of them for working on deck. All I had to get us to Australia was a small compass and a couple of maps torn from an old magazine. Isn't that a fact, now?'

It was, said everyone.

'And what should happen but the maps disappeared. Someone used them for rolling tobacco to make cigarettes and I didn't find out till too late. In fact, they were inaccurate as it happened. More than a couple of degrees out over one latitude, according to my calculations, and anyway we got there safely without them in the end.'

This too must be an undoubted fact, the details of which I should have liked to have gone into, but there was an interruption from Robbie's wife.

A message had come for me saying that the launch had been delayed and Ratu Penaia's party would not be in Savu-Savu until the following day. 'So we'll get a room ready for you, shall we, as you'll be staying overnight?'

'Hey, we can't have that!' announced the grey-haired man I had been introduced to earlier as Dave, after producing the usual magic password of our friend Peter France's name. He was a leading planter, one of a number of brothers from an old settler family who all owned large copra estates in the area, a trim, still handsome figure with lean, haggard features, large melancholy eyes, and an indefinable air of distinction. 'She'd better come and stay with us. Take a look at country living while she's here.'

'That's right,' said his wife Betty who was an attractive mixture of German and Samoan, small and plump with long black hair. 'There's always room for a visitor at Belego and we don't get all that many.'

They would pick me up after lunch then, they said. We would be going out by 'put-put', and they'd bring me back tomorrow the same way.

A put-put is the island name for a small open boat, the size of a long rowing-boat, equipped with an engine that makes the appropriate 'put-put' noise. Ours was waiting for us at the jetty, bobbing shell-like on the waves ready to receive its cargo of half a dozen adults, four children and an unlimited number of baskets of food and clothing. Another couple had joined us, the manager of one of the local stores and his wife, a good-looking pair with the warm-hearted, happy-go-lucky ease of manner that enables most part-Europeans to absorb a stranger into their circle in a matter of minutes.

A small, stolid, bald-headed gentleman, very dignified in a shanking white topee and braces, stood slightly apart. Introduced as Betty's father, he came forward and shook hands in the formal old German way, with a bob of his head and a click of his heels. Then one by one we climbed down and settled outselves on the plank seats with Dave at the helm.

'We have to cross the bay and then turn up inland by river,' he said, pointing across to the rumpled coastline in the distance.

With a flick of his wrist he jerked on a cord and the engine shot into life. Slowly we turned round then, vibrating like a bee, skimmed across to the open sea. First few minutes there was sunshine and a silver-and-blue, holiday-poster horizon encircling the little boat. Then suddenly, in the way of Fijian weather, the air darkened and great clouds were lowered out of the sky as swiftly as stage drops. In that moment the scene changed from Polynesian to Melanesian. The other side of Fiji, dark and brooding, now hung over the hump-back silhouettes of the islands with here and there a sallow shaft of light that threw smudges of amber-green and purple across the ridges and valleys of the approaching coast. A hundred yards ahead the white breakers of the reef gleamed phosphorescent against the gloom of the river estuary beyond. As we came closer Dave leaned forward, his hand moving instinctively on the tiller behind him. This way and that we nudged our way forward towards the seemingly unending snarl of surf, stretching from one end of the beach to the other. Then for a moment the waves seemed to open like a

Ratu Thakobau, 1817–83, *Tui Viti* and *Vunivalu* (King of Fiji and Chief of War)

The making of a *Vunivalu* (Chief of War). The Honourable Ratu George Thakobau, O.B.E., great-grandson of the King enters the meeting-house for his installation ceremonies

gate, revealing a narrow lane of clear water, and the boat slipped past like a lamb.

'I smell my way through mostly,' Dave said, when I asked him. 'There's no set passage. It depends on the tide. We do have boats overturned from time to time but only through carelessness or inexperience.'

Once past the estuary the motionless river atmosphere closed in on us, a world of its own. Thick overgrown banks rose steeply on either side. In their shadow the water glimmered bottle-green, pin-pricked beyond the shelter of the trees by the thinly falling rain, stirred here and there by the drop of a leaf. The whirr of the cicadas in the grass was like an echo of the put-put's engine as we glided on in a stillness that seemed to be waiting for someone, something.

'There is something extremely melancholy and yet interesting about Fiji rivers,' I heard Mrs. Smythe murmur. 'They are so still. There is scarcely a sound to be heard except the solitary cry of a water bird or the sudden grating screech of a parrot in the adjoining woods. It is rare even to meet a canoe, but floating gently past you may see a coconut or a shaddock which having dropped into the water from an overhanging tree is slowly making its way down to the open sea, perhaps to sow itself on some distant island. . . .'

A sudden thrill of interest in the boat brought me back again. 'Look, there she is, there's Hetty Pearson,' Betty was saying, leaning over to the children. We all followed her glance to the right-hand bank and saw against the tangled greenery the remarkable apparition of an elderly European woman in ground-length skirts and a battered trilby hat. Her round red face broke into a smile as everyone waved, and she raised her hand in a regal return of the salutations. Cattle grazed in a clearing behind her. At the foot of the bank a slim young Indian girl was tying up a punt.

'That's the Pearson sisters' estate,' said Dave. 'Our Hetty's quite a famous figure in these parts. Her family were pioneers from New Zealand and she's one of the last descendants. They say she's always dressed the same. Apart from the odd trip to Suva, she's never left the island, you see. Hardly ever goes off the plantation.'

'But when she does, it's something to remember,' Betty went on. 'Like the night she turned up at a neighbour's party with her horn gramophone and a stack of old records. She danced every man off his feet with her exhibitions of the Veleta and the Boston two-step!'

When we looked back again for the last time she was still standing there watching us, one hand on her hips, the other against the brim of her trilby, and that is how I always remember her though I never saw her again—Hetty in her world, a lonely yet resolute figure, the dense bush and dark forests of palms at her back, wrapped away in the intense, turgid silence of the river banks and the endless, absorbing monotony of day-to-day living.

'Oh, yes, we have our characters in these parts,' said Dave, leaning back in the helm. 'A lot of them are tucked away on the outlying islands, though. Why, there are old fellows out there that no one even knows about any more, living on gin and bananas in tumbledown shacks with their Fijian harems, and goats and chickens all over the place.'

There was a disparaging grunt from the old man who was sitting bolt upright on the centre seat under a large black umbrella. 'Ve people of the bush!' he remarked, shaking his head with a kind of melancholy scorn.

Farther on, the engine died away and we floated to a standstill alongside a small stone jetty. Black and white ducks bobbed in the shallows like rubber toys. The shallow steps were fringed with hibiscus and white lilies. At the end of a large old-fashioned garden stood the house, a family home, shabby and rambling with wooden shutters opening on wide verandas, the gabled roof of corrugated iron, dark red among the surrounding green.

Inside, the main room was long and low-raftered, full of comfortable cane and mahogany chairs and an enormous rectangular table covered with a heavy baize cloth. With a sigh of relief, everyone sat down. Two Rotuman girls appeared from the kitchen quarters and took away our bags. Two more emerged carrying tea-trays laden with home-made cakes, and carefully polished silver. The milk-jugs were shrouded in white gauze covers, tasselled with tiny shells. I drank my tea and, while everyone talked, stared round at this haven of transported Edwardiana which had travelled so far from home to its unlikely destination in the heart of the Fijian bush. Every available inch of wall and table space seemed crammed with family momentoes. Sepia groups and portraits lined the walls, photograph albums were piled on the lace-covered side-tables, candelabra adorned the upright piano, and in the centre of the sideboard amidst the cut-glass cruet-stands and decanters stood Queen Victoria herself, a twelve-inch high plaster statuette, its original white and gold now dimmed to a sober brown.

'Come on, then! Just time for a game before dark,' Dave announced. Wonderingly I trooped out after the other two ladies and discovered a badminton net strung across the main lawn, the court marked out in white on the grass. A light drizzle was falling with the dusk and the damp river air was breathlessly close and still. But the racquets were handed round, everyone took off their shoes, and we played two sets in a slow-motion, Turkish-bath sort of way before darkness and the mosquitoes sent us in again.

The living-room seemed to be the focal-point of the house in more ways than one. Four or five bedroom doors opened on to it, and the bathroom was situated across a passage at the end. So there was an hour's sociable coming and going with towels and *sulus* before the circle finally settled down again for the evening. By this time, the bottles of whisky and rum, gin and beer, had been set out on the table, and everyone helped themselves while the talk went around, languid, intermittent and familiar, copra prices, fishing stories and local gossip, the men stretched out in the old-fashioned planters' chairs, the women leaning back with easy-spread laps on the sofa, handkerchiefs wrapped round their drinks between perspiring glass and flesh. In the silences a low vibrating trill, like a kettle on the boil, floated up from the frogs on the river bank.

Dinner, a solid, four-course affair, was at ten. Then came the dancing, Rotuman dancing. Singly the girls came in from the kitchen, shaking back their long oiled plaits of hair, plump shoulders gleaming. There was a quickening of expectation in their broad, smooth faces, as the guitars established the rhythm. With ritual movements they began a solemn hula. Then half a dozen young men joined them, plantation workers stripped to their waists, each one facing a partner, and there were more elaborate dances. In these one glimpsed from time to time the hesitancy of a people cut off from the source of such traditions. The words become hard to remember, the voices die a little, the thread of the tune, the pattern of movement wavers. Then someone picks it up again. Once more the hips rotate, the feet keep time in tiny side-steps, bare soles cupped against the polished floor. Between the two sexes there was a perfect counterpoint of movement as they danced, not face to face Western style, but the woman half-turned away, a yielding undulent figure with outstretched hands rippling and weaving, the man close behind her vibrating to the angular, assertive rhythm of pursuit, arms flexed akimbo, knees braced apart, the stomach muscles contracted, heels thudding to the beat of the drum. The bodies never touched. The faces were intense, withdrawn into their separate roles, with now and then the mere flash of a glance between them. Yet the sense of unity was overpowering, and in the unselfconscious, complementary ease that flowed between the masculine and feminine worlds of these people there seemed a kind of state of grace lost for ever to the Europeans.

Now it was the turn of the old man in the long grass skirt who had been sitting in the background. Bashfully he shook his head, his refusals growing more vehement as everyone pleaded with him. Suddenly without another word he was on his feet and loping over to the dancing space. There he stood for a moment shaking his head, his chin in his hand, lost in a confusion of memories while the guitars strummed encouragement in the background. At last, inspiration dawned. With a leap in the air he launched into a spirited prancing dance of his own, head bobbing from side to side, gnarled arms and legs flailing. There was a mounting *crescendo* of whoops, high kicks and whirling skirts. Then as suddenly the impulse fled, the performance broke off and, amidst frenzied clapping, the artiste rushed out into the kitchens to hide himself and did not reappear again that evening.

Retiring to bed in the comfortably solid, farmhouse atmosphere of Belego, it seemed odd to recall Miss Gordon-Cumming's very different visit to a planter's estate in the days of not copra but cotton production. It was the period of the depression that followed the collapse of the world cotton market in 1870, and Miss Gordon-Cumming described them as 'utterly ruined and overwhelmed with debt, with health shattered by privation, living just like the natives on yams and wild pig, knowing no greater luxury than a bowl of *yaggona* and unable from sheer poverty to obtain the commonest comforts of civilized life'.

Even the cheap plantation labour, supplied in the bad old days by blackbirding ships from Tanna and the Tokelaus, the Solomons and the New Hebrides, had come to an end. A popular ditty of the period ran:

Neath a ragged palmetto an old planter sat,
A-twisting the ruin of his Tokelau hat,
And relieving his mind of its terrible load
He hummed the words of the following ode.
Oh for a cocktail and oh, for a nip!
Oh for a digger, and oh for a whip!
Oh for a captain, and oh for a ship!
With a cargo of niggers on every trip!
And so he went oh-ing for all he had not,
Not contented with owing for all that he'd got!

The absurd jingle was still running through my head when I woke in the morning. It occurred to me that perhaps the greatest of all travel pleasures was to lie in bed absorbing the new sounds and smells that were simply part of another day to the people who lived here. It was a large feather-bed, with a tall brass railing at the head and foot. Outside, framed in flounced curtains, bluey-green billows of coconut groves steamed gently in the sun. The black-and-white ducks were splashing in the puddles on the lawn and the dancing girls of last night were hanging out a line of washing, padding backwards and forwards over the wet grass on stolid, brown feet, their long plaits wound sedately round their heads.

We had gone to bed about four. Now it was half-past eleven or round about, they said, as I joined the party at the table for a late breakfast of oysters. Between this and the more serious business of lunch, there was just time for a short stroll down to the new copra dryer, David thought.

By now it was raining again and under large striped golf-umbrellas we set off down a muddy path at the back of the house and were soon hemmed in aisles of dripping trees. Being Sunday, there were no workers to be seen. But here and there in a clearing a bonfire of husks smouldered on from the day before, the blue acrid smoke spicing the sickly-sweet smell of crushed coconut flesh. Split trunks, grassy underfoot, bridged a network of narrow streams and ditches. Through the drizzle to one side of the path the thicker smoke of cooking fires rose above the corrugated-iron roofs of the Fijian settlement.

As we passed faces gleamed in shadowy doorways. Greetings were exchanged and a pack of spindly puppies came snuffling round our heels, two fat babies in singlets tottering close behind until swept up by their mother and carried inside again.

We had reached the river bank again. Alongside a wooden jetty stood a large shed. Inside a long plank floor, oiled to ballroom consistency, reflected a mountain of husked and quartered coconuts that stood at the far end. 'We have some good evenings here from time to time,' David said. 'Taralalas, *mekes*, dancing and so on.'

The new dryer turned out to be a monstrous, black, chimneyed affair, rather like a giant's cooking stove. He patted it on the flank affectionately and said how far superior to the old sun-drying method it was, especially in this sort of weather.

'You can probably understand what it feels like to have made something out of nothing,' he said, pausing on the way back and looking around him. 'Imagine the chaos that faced a family from England when they first stepped out of their boat.' He turned over a chip of copra in his hand. 'Wonderful stuff, isn't it? Not just the nut and the oil, you know, but the whole tree—it's the basis of Fijian life. The leaves for thatch and baskets, wood for bridges and house-posts, husks for sinnet to fix it all together, shells for drinking out of—and fuel. Like they say, *Yaga vakaniu*—useful as the coconut!'

Back at the house, lunch was waiting, a feast of curry, steak and kidney, dumplings and apple pie, which lent stability to everyone else's aim but mine during the target practice in the garden which followed. Strolling across between shots, one of the girls appeared to say that the boat was ready for us. They had taken the bags down.

The beer-can bull's-eye was left in the tree for next Sunday's session, the shotgun propped up in the only living-room corner which didn't already hold either a rifle or a guitar, and David and Betty escorted us down the steps once more. At the helm of the little boat a familiar figure was waiting, the elderly high-kick dancer, his face extended in a toothless grin of welcome.

'Tili will take good care of you,' said David, handing us in one by one, myself, the other Savu-Savu couple and their children.

The river was as still as ever, the water as glassy, but Laura pointed ahead to the white crests beyond the river mouth.

'Pretty rough out there today though,' she said, settling the children firmly among the baggage on the bottom of the boat.

'I suppose we could always turn back,' I suggested feebly, but no one seemed to treat this idea with any seriousness.

The first wave that hit us lifted the bows into the air and slewed us down sideways. For the next few minutes there was a dogged struggle to keep head on to the breakers.

Every wave that swelled towards us looked bigger than the last. Water sluiced in over the edges and the children, who usually sang without stop, sat soaked and quiet as mice in their nests of baskets. Laura sitting opposite me merely looked round crossly, wiping her wet face and baling out with an old tin. Meanwhile I surveyed the leaden coastline that lurched between sky and sea an unswimable distance away, and reminded myself that even the doughty Mrs. Smythe had found herself unnerved by an identical experience—'To hear the pilot say nervously, "Now pull for your lives, lads," and see a mountain wave rushing towards you is *not particularly pleasant*. We got through safely, I am thankful to say, but I would rather not try that passage again. The mouths of these rivers abound in sharks so that in the event of an upset, the danger of being drowned is not the only one incurred.'

Dear Mrs. Smythe, reminding me at this point of the very thing I had been trying so hard to forget! However, by this time, we were past the reef and out in the open sea.

It was a rough crossing. I passed the time composing in my mind a letter home to rival even Mrs. S's epic epistles to her dazzled and envious circle of female confidantes at their cloistered Victorian firesides.

It was almost dark when, cold and stiff, we chugged into Savu-Savu Bay and saw on the hillside the lighted windows of the old hotel shining out through the rainy gloom, as though this were any English harbour on any evening in an English November.

13

The Dead Sea

'You are now in the heart of the Kingdom of Thakaudrove,' said Ratu Penaia, indicating with a sweep of his arm the tide-licked stretch of sand across which we were walking, the blue folds and peaks of the coastline beyond. 'About one-third of Vanua Levu altogether, right across to the island of Taveuni.' He grinned down from his great height. 'And I don't need to tell you, of course, that it produces the best land and the bravest fighting men in the whole of Fiji!'

A jeep had brought us the fifteen miles or so across the neck of land from Savu-Savu and we were making our way now on foot to Nasinu, the first of the coastal villages of Natewa Bay to be visited by the party. From there we would go on by sea the following day. For me this was all an exhilaratingly novel experience. For almost the first time ever I found myself on a Fijian beach not just for an idle stroll but with all communications cut and the necessity of getting somewhere ahead as soon as possible, the only consideration. The simplicity of it was elating—no prearranged hosts, no ministering hotels, only an unknown village at the end of each day's travel along a remote and enclosed strip of land where the few Europeans lived on isolated plantations several miles apart and the Fijians in traditional settlements still sheltered from the seedier encroachments of the outside world.

In close-up, even the scenery looked different—less postcard-picturesque, more physically real. The sand wasn't smooth and marbled. It was muddy and difficult to walk in. There were wonderful shells encrusting the rocks among the shallows and treacherous, toe-stabbing roots under the mangrove trees that fringed the shore. I was in the mood to approve unconditionally for I might so nearly not have been there at all. Adi Laisa was unable to join Ratu Penaia until the end of the week when she would travel straight to Drekeniwai, the last port of call. The two Europeans in the party had been doubtful of the propriety of a stray Englishwoman tagging along on her own on a ceremonial chiefly tour of so conservative an area, despite the fact that one of them was Peter France and the other a charming Scot named Ian Thomson, a senior Government official, also a friend of ours. But Ratu Penaia had prevailed. I would enjoy it. The Fijians would enjoy it. I was his most welcome guest and I must certainly come. Besides, Laisa was expecting to see me at Drekeniwai. So here I was, doggedly trying to match my steps to my protector's giant strides under the eagle eyes of Peter and Ian behind, the three Fijian representatives of the Native Lands Trust Board bringing up the rear—Josua Rabukawaga, an English-trained administrative officer, softly spoken and intellectual, Bula, the tall professional cricketer, and tiny, bespectacled Inoke.

Across our path an inviting-looking, moss-covered boulder came into view. Upon this descendant of the Kings of Thakaudrove sat himself down, motioning me to do the same, and produced from the bag on his shoulder a half-open tin of bully beef and a pocket knife. 'Still having my breakfast,' he pronounced, spearing himself a large chunk and disposing of it in one swift movement. He waved the tin round the rest of the circle. 'Anyone else want some?' He turned to me. 'It's not far now but one's never really sure what time food is going to be produced in a Fijian village.'

About half a mile farther on, the first *bure* roofs appeared through the trees. It had been raining and the thatch lay flattened and sleek like the fur of a wet animal. The path twined upwards now between the houses which lay facing the sea in a sloping semicircle. An elderly man stood waiting on the doorstep of the only wooden house, a square, solidly-built European-style affair in the centre of the *rara*. There was no one else to be seen, but one was aware of that particular hushed silence of people watching concealed from view.

'We are arriving informally here—the ceremonies will come later,' Ratu Penaia told me in an undertone. He had fastened the top button of his bushjacket and his chiefly air, authoritarian, remote and tremendously dignified had descended on him. 'We all just go straight into the house where we are staying. It is the house of the head man here.'

The elderly man crouched quickly as we approached, then stood up, still with his head bowed, to be greeted genially as Sam. Gnarled and serious-faced, he stood aside as one by one the party filed in.

Penaia sat down at the top of the room and leaned forward attentively to Sam's murmurs of greeting and explanation. Everyone else sat down in a circle, the Europeans on chairs, the Fijians on the floor. There was a moment's pause. Sam coughed politely behind his closed fist as though giving a cue. Then in through the door came a middle-aged woman, obviously Sam's wife, moving forward slowly on her knees, her eyes downcast and carrying in her hands a large bowl of *moli*, Fijian mandarines. This she presented to each one in turn, beginning with Ratu Penaia, and when she came to me, raising her eyes and smiling shyly in welcome. Sam supplemented with plates, and the solemnity of our arrival soon melted as we munched away in a fragrant fug of orange peel.

The first offering disposed of, the spirit of formality was quickly restored with the next. Our host delivered himself of another preliminary cough and a delegation of a dozen men came in through the same side passage which is the modern equivalent of the gable door, the commoner's entrance, in a Fijian *bure*. They entered not on their knees but bent almost double, taking their seats cross-legged on the floor, backs to the walls. Except for an occasional whispered conference, the new-comers remained expressionless and silent as did the rest of the circle, everyone gazing thoughtfully down in front of him. I now knew enough about Fiji to realize that an important ceremony was about to take place and to inquire what, even in an undertone, would be the gravest offence of all. We didn't have to wait long. Into the room came another two men, younger and more muscular than the others, dragging between them on a sack what looked like a huge uprooted bush, withered and bare of leaves, the soil still clinging to its fibres. This was placed before Ian Thomson, the representative of the *Kovena* (Governor) while from his corner Sam made a formal speech of welcome; Bula's reply on Ian's behalf was punctuated by the traditional responses of appreciation and handclaps from the villagers. Then, stooping low, they withdrew one by one the way they had come. The ceremony was over, and once again I was moved by the overwhelming air of gravity and meaningfulness of such occasion. The mysterious shrub was in fact the *yaggona* root—*Piper Methysticum*—in all its original nakedness. Trying to connect this with the *yaggona* I knew, a wooden bowl of the prepared liquid, I felt like the imaginary Cockney child introduced to her first cow.

Lunch was served for the four of us in a small inner room presided over by the rumblings of a large kerosene fridge which, Sam told us, was his wife's pride and joy. While we ate a gourmet's meal of village produce, crab and chicken, lobster and prawns, he remained standing at one end of the table, his wife kneeling at the other, both of them waving fans gently and continuously over the food to keep away the flies. The Fijian contingent were being entertained elsewhere, I was told. When we had finished, Ratu Penaia decreed a period of general rest. Nudged forward by Sam, his wife came up to me and touching me by the arm led me into one of the small outer rooms. There were curtains of *masi* over the window, white hibiscus in a jug on the tiny old-fashioned dressing-table. In the corner stood a narrow bed, covered with a neat white counterpane and a pillow embroidered with the words 'Sleep Well Sweet Heart', an instruction which I faithfully obeyed for the next two hours.

When I awoke it was to the sound of Ratu Penaia's voice through the open door. They had just come in from a *bose*, a meeting with the villagers at which the intricate problems of land boundaries between the different *toka toka* (closely related family units) had been discussed. Ian and Peter suggested a walk as far as the house of a neaby planter and together we set off again along the path that led on through the village to the creek. A tall young boatman with a handsome moustache poled us across in the village punt. Helping us out on the opposite bank, he announced that he would accompany us as our guide. But first the boat must be returned to the other side of the river. He put his hands to his mouth and called out to a group of children playing in the mud outside the *bure*.

'Evi!'

Immediately a little girl of about six came forward. With a single quick movement she bent over and peeled off her ragged little scrap of a dress, then folded it up and placed it carefully under a stone. The next minute Evi had plunged into the water wearing a pair of small blue knickers. With the strong overarm stroke of Fijian children she swam gracefully across the current. Then with a leap she was inside the boat, smiling away from us with a modest flick of her head, and poling back to the other side again.

At first we walked beneath the mangrove trees and the wild hibiscus on the edge of the beach, circling cautiously round a hornet's nest hanging from one of the lower branches. There was crisp, white sand underfoot. But gradually the path twined round into the bush again, muddy and overgrown and blocked by slippery dips and boulders. From behind, a muscular pair of arms scooped me up beneath knees and shoulders with gentle competence and I found myself, without a word being exchanged, carried by our boatman for the next hundred yards or so. The same thing happened whenever the track became difficult and after a while I stopped feeling guilty about it, ignored the taunts of Ian and Peter, and simply enjoyed the feminine luxury of being swept off one's feet by a strong silent male on whom protests are wasted. There was also the added pleasure of feeling one up on Miss Gordon-Cumming about something, anyway.

Round the next bend in the coast the public footpath came to an end at a turnstile. A straggling line of rusty wire railing divided the bush from a private plantation though there seemed little difference between the overgrown ground on both sides of the fence. There was no one to be seen and over the tin shacks of the estate workers, the shabby bungalow beyond, the broken hulks of old boats on the beach in front, there hung an air of resignation, I felt. It was raining, a fine, lethargic drizzle. In the distance two bony horses cropped among the fallen coconuts, descendants no doubt of those first horses brought to Vanua Levu by the missionary Hazlewood in September 1851, when the natives ran into the bush, climbed trees or fled to the reef to escape such monsters.

At the entrance to one of the huts a face of startling beauty appeared. A young Indian woman with a baby on her hip, a tawdry shawl over her head, leaned against the doorway to watch us pass, then with a shy, vivid smile withdrew into the shadows again—a glimpse of vitality and grace that seemed strangely incongruous in this bleak, lonely setting. From the steps of the bungalow came shambling an old Fijian, in ragged shorts and shirt, who gestured us inside. The boss had gone out in the launch to one of the islands, he told us in guttural pidgin-English, the smell of rum on his breath. Maybe come back soon. We wanta wait, eh?

He led the way into the veranda room, pulled forward three of the circle of faded canvas arm-chairs, then shuffled out again, scratching his head. We sat and rested for a while, waiting for the rain to stop. His daughter, who was of mixed blood, was married to the owner of the place, also a part-European, Peter told us, explaining the old man's oddly proprietorial air. He worked as a kind of overseer on the estate. They were what was known in Fiji as bush-planters. There was neither road nor telephone within a distance of several miles. The launch in fact was their only contact with the outside world. I looked around at the bare furnishings, a few rickety tables with torn lace mats, an old radio set, a picture of Princess Margaret tacked on the wall—the assorted flotsam and jetsam of the European way of life—and thought that nothing could have been more different from the solid, thriving background of my hosts of last night.

It had stopped raining, our guide announced from the steps outside. Besides, soon it would be dark. The old man had disappeared and we left unnoticed, singing to raise our spirits as we followed the track through the bush again. A party of fishermen rounding a bend to meet us froze in their steps and stood gaping after us at Ian's arrangement of 'Over the Sea to Skye'. Otherwise the path was deserted at such an hour.

Back at the creek Evi was waiting with the boat and our guide poled us across to the village. Dusk was falling, interwoven with the blue haze of evening fires. The silhouettes of women with pots and pans criss-crossed like moths around the flaring hearths of a dozen small thatched cooking-houses. Higher up the hill, lanterns were being lit and carried from *bure* to *bure*, floating sparks in the misty half-light, and above the dark shapes of the bread-fruit trees, the first stars glimmered in an opalescent sky. Young men in *sulus*, gleaming from their bathe in the creek, gave us low murmurs of greeting as they passed. The oncoming darkness seemed to sharpen the smells of the sea and wood-smoke and cooking food, deaden all sound except the crackle of flames and the voices of the women talking together in a soft and rapid sing-song under the eaves. In the *vakatunaloa*, the open-sided Council House of palm and reeds built specially for the visit, the old men were still sitting round the *yaggona* bowl. We joined them for a few minutes on the mat, where even I, in my turn, received the coconut shell of milky liquid amidst polite hand-claps—condescendingly exempted on this informal occasion from the tradition that women do not drink in such circles.

Back in the house, the room was soft with the shadowy, yellow light of lamps. Changed for the evening into shirts and *sulus*, such as Ratu Penaia was wearing, the men sipped their first whiskies, discussed the day's findings, glanced through a couple of old copies of the *Fiji Times*. Then Sam and his wife summoned us once more to the fabulous prawns, crab-meat and chicken, and it was once more Ian's turn to say *masu* (grace) before we ate. Afterwards, we sat in our cane-chair circle again and someone started to sing a hymn.

'We always sing in the evenings in the bush,' said Peter. 'Usually hymns.'

Sam brought out the black Methodist hymn-book owned by every Fijian household, and the rest of the party were called in. Josua, I learned, was a composer and choir-master in his spare time. Under his guidance we harmonized our way lustily through most of the traditional tunes, singing the Fijian words for 'Rock of Ages', 'Guide Me O Thou Great Jehovah', 'The Church's One Foundation' and the particular favourite, the Scottish 'Belmont', with Josua's professional tenor weaving a Welsh-style descant in the lead, as he sat beating time in the centre of the circle.

Ratu Penaia and Ian went to bed early but, from the seclusion of the front porch and in *pianissimo* key, we sang on. In between hymns Josua talked to me about life in Taunton, where he had taken his course in government administration. Then when everyone had left, Peter and I sat on looking out to sea, a sudden cool breeze ruffling the lantern flame, the palm trees clacking overhead, while he told the stories of some of Ratu Penaia's nineteenth-century ancestors, who had fought and ruled along this coast from their island stronghold of Taveuni. The most famous Tui Thakan of all, for instance, wielded almost as great a power in the land as Ratu Thakobau at Bau, his alternate rival and ally. European travellers of the 1830's and 1840's described him as a fine specimen of a Fiji Islander, tall and manly, with a head fit for a monarch. Among his most treasured possessions were an English chair, two chests and several well-polished muskets. Like Thakobau he had collected a court of European advisers and also boasted a 'Secretary, Interpreter and Collector of Customs'. This was an American sailor by the name of Hoyle, a survivor of a wrecked whaling brig, who married a half-caste girl, and in return for such varied services as the mending of muskets or the writing of letters to naval commanders, was given land, a large house, and labourers for his food-gardens, though his salary was often in arrears. As a very old man, the King was buried before death had actually taken place, a Fijian custom which was then regarded as an act of service both by family survivors and the sick man himself. The horrified missionary, seeing that he still moved and coughed, protested in vain. His father's spirit, the King's son assured him, had already left his body.

It was for this son, Tui Kilakila, Peter went on, that Bau's most notorious feast was prepared—and never eaten. The occasion was the formal investiture of Thakobau as Vunivalu in 1853, and Kilakila sailed across in state with his retinue to attend it in a fine new ship the *Packet*, chartered from an Australian, William Owen of Adelaide, in return for the ownership of an off-lying island. Fourteen bodies were already lying in the earth-ovens of Bau in preparation for the next day's celebrations. But in the morning Owen, appealed to by the missionary Calvert, told the chiefs that if the bodies were not given up Kilakila and his people could find their own way home. As a result, Owen appeared at the Christian island of Viwa a few hours later bringing for decent burial a cargo of eighty-four well-cooked portions of *bokola* (human flesh).

Less than a year later, Kilakila was murdered while asleep on his mat, at the instigation if not at the hand of his own son. That son was killed shortly afterwards by his brother to avenge their father's death, and the avenger was himself murdered in 1857. The historians called this a classic example of the dangers of polygamy in association with the Polynesian system of rule by high chiefly families.

'Sounds more like Shakespeare to me,' was Peter's remark, as we went in again to bed. 'Pity he couldn't have done the Kings of Fiji after he'd finished with the English lot!'

Next morning there was a business-like air about the party again. After an early breakfast, all seven of us assembled outside the house and Ratu Penaia led the way down to the water's edge. Now we could see, riding about fifty yards out in the sunshine, the trim blue and white outlines of the *Turaga Levu*, the Fijian coat-of-arms fluttering from the mast. A rowing-boat was waiting in the shallows to take us out. I was just taking off my shoes to paddle through when, as on the day before, I was lifted up and carried over before I knew what was happening. This time my faithful gillie—as Miss G.-C. would have put it—was an even brawnier Fijian in a pair of faded shorts, a member of the *Turaga's* crew, who was introduced to me as Johnny-the-Boatman. Accepting my thanks with a benign smile, touched with condescension, he took up the oars from the centre seat and pulled us out with long swinging strokes, his handsome head half-turned over his shoulder, his broad, oiled back flexing with easy grace. As we drew alongside, a small figure appeared in the cabin doorway.

'Jo!' called Ratu Penaia, with his deep laugh. 'He usually comes round with me on these trips,' he said to me. 'And he much prefers to sleep on board with the crew than come ashore.'

Two other Fijans helped us on board as the little boy came running up the ladder with the agility of a ship's cat and clasped his father firmly around the knees. Josua, Bula and Inoke swung themselves up on to the roof among the sacks of coconuts and baskets of yam and dalo, while the rest of us sat round on the narrow padded benches in the open stern of the launch. The gleam of white paint and polished brass, the well-scrubbed deck, established the *Turaga Levu*, if not in a luxury class, as a suitably natty and workman-like craft for a chief to travel in. The engines started up and, bucking a little against a sudden fresh wind, we turned to the open sea. Although we were in an enclosed bay, the coast of the opposite peninsula was about ten miles distant, they told me, and it could sometimes be rough in these parts.

'The Fijians call it the Dead Sea, anyway,' Penaia said reassuringly. 'And we're keeping close to land all the way.'

Our first stop came after half an hour or so. Here the party would call at a village and walk up the valley for a few miles, taking a look at land development. It had started to rain, so I was even happier to stay on board and do some writing. In the cabin below there was a folding table, wall-seats, and four neat bunks on the topmost of which I lay with my notebooks for another half an hour.

Then the light from the hatchway was blotted out by a burly frame.

'Cig'rette?' inquired the voice of Johnny-the-Boatman.

'Well, no, as a matter of fact, I haven't!'

There was a flash of white teeth. 'No, no! You like to come smoke with us, I mean!'

Up forward around the wheel the three of them were lounging

Indian patriarch

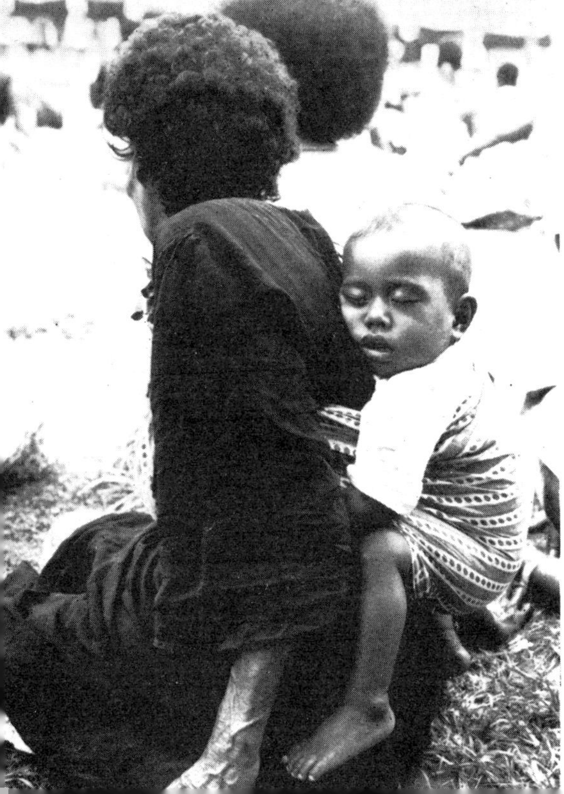

Spectators at the *mekes*

The Cagi-mai-Ra (Wind-from-the-West)

Sunset from the launch

comfortably over tea and cigarettes, while Ratu Jo squatted fishing at the rails. The tall, shy one was Samisoni (Samson) the cook. Tomasi, the engineer, was a bright-eyed, snub-nosed youth who spoke the best English and when we had finished drinking and smoking the others left the conversation to him.

'Pretty good place, eh?' he said, sitting down in the doorway next to the cushion they had hospitably provided for me. He nodded towards the sandy bay and green hillsides around us. 'Yea, I'd like to have a look round the rest of the world sometime, but I'd always come back to Fiji. Back to these parts, I mean. The city's no good for living. Here we are free. Even if a man has no money, he can grow enough to eat, live the village life. Of course, in the villages there are many laws to be learned, many customs to be kept. But that's right. The Fijian customs are very strong. I think they can never die, whatever happen.'

Was it true, I said, that some of the young Fijians thought little of the chiefs these days? He laughed, mockingly.

'Ha! Don't let anyone fool you by saying a chief means nothing to the young men of the town! Let them come face to face with him and they will be on their knees, wanting to please him, their hearts beating out of their bodies if he is angry with them. Of course,'—he nodded judiciously—'a chief must keep respect too. Some drink and talk too much with the ordinary people. The best ones are those who keep to themselves. We don't want them to mix with us. It is not the right thing.'

There was a pause for a few minutes while he jerked at his line experimentally, wound it up round his bottle, then seeing the hook empty, reached in a jar for fresh bait. He grinned sideways at me. 'Not that I'd want the old days back again. You heard all about those, I suppose? People cutting off their fingers and hanging them up round the houses when someone dies, burying a man in the ground to hold up the *bure* posts.' He finished baiting his crab-leg and whirling the line round his head, threw it half a dozen yards out from the launch. He seemed to be enjoying the conversation as much as I was. 'And you know, that man mustn't cry out—just bear it, or it would be shame for his family. Well, that's all gone. But one thing perhaps you people wouldn't know. Even now, if Ratu Penaia should get mad with one of us men on this boat and told us, jump in the sea—well, that man would just have to jump in and try to swim till he get to the shore! Don't worry, he don't do anything like that ever!' he added. 'But see, a chief can still ask for anything to be done, and it must be done—by the people of his tribe that is.' He swept his arm round the circle of crowding hills and sweeping valleys, his face suddenly glowing. 'And Ratu Penaia is the richest of all the chiefs. All this land is his, all the people too, and it's the best land and people in Fiji, I can tell you!'

I asked him about his family, and he shook his head, smiling. 'Oh, my grandfather! He was the one! He lived till he was ninety-five and he used to sit and yarn to me when I was a little boy about all sorts of things—even back to the days of eating men. I suppose he could just remember them himself. I never forget him telling me that the toughest part of the human body was the shoulder, for that was where burdens had been carried during the man's life and the muscle there made it very poor meat.' We both laughed. 'He was a great big man, my grandather, nearly seven feet tall. When he was very old he grew a beard because he was too tired to shave and his hair was long too, all white and bushy. Sometimes if we children were naughty he would bring out his old war-spear and threaten to cut us up and eat us. But I think he was only joking to frighten us. Human flesh, though!' He shuddered. 'I think I should feel sick to eat a man's body!'

Someone had switched on the radio telephone and at that moment there was a crackling sound and the voice of the woman operator in Suva repeating a cable for someone at Levani. Then a second voice came in ırom somewhere else with a message for Suva. Briskly Tomasi looked at his watch, then flicked on another switch and reported the exact position of the *Turaga Levu* in Natewa Bay. The voice from Suva confirmed the report.

'Over and out!' called Tomasi, in best R.A.F. style. 'We have to do this at a certain time every day,' he told me. 'Just to be on the safe side.'

A companionable silence fell again broken by the soft slapping of the waves as we rocked idly at anchor.

Samisoni's face appeared in the hatchway. He was becoming anxious about our lunch. The people from the village were to send it out to us. All we had on board was the *walu* in the fridge that Tomasi had caught yesterday. Perhaps he'd better put it on to cook though. The party would be back soon and if . . .

A shout from Ratu Jo interrupted him. A boat was coming out from the village. The next minute, a tiny canoe was floating alongside. Amidst much laughter and chaffing the two men and two young girls in it handed up baskets of cooked bread-fruit and chicken. Then the two girls, one about ten the other younger, climbed on board with their final basket of bananas, and with widened eyes had a rapid *sara-sara* (look-around). The sight of an Englishwoman in trousers was obviously still a novelty, despite the wives of district officers and planters who had been this way before, and while Samisoni was unloading the baskets they squatted down on the deck a few feet away and surveyed me in detail, smiling, but much too shy to talk. To bridge the gap I brought out my usual party trick, a powder compact-cum-musical box. Delicately, the elder one took it in her hands and together they peered over the hidden tinkling sounds with muted exclamations of delight and whispered consultations not forgetting, being female, to peer quickly at themselves in the glass before returning it. They were still chattering as, springing down into the canoe again they glided away, waving, to the strains of 'The Blue Danube' on its fourth wind-up.

I wondered how they would describe it to their families and thought of the old woman Lavinia who 160-odd years ago had run back to her village not far from these parts at the sight of the wrecked sailors of the *El Plumier* and reported, 'They must be gods for they are biting live fire and have their ears wrapped up in red cloth.' Just as strange as the pipes and naval caps of those first Europeans, bound for Sandalwood Bay, were the casks of gunpowder which some of the old men hid away to use as black paint for their bodies. The ramrods they used as scratchers for their heads. Mirrors, too, the mysterious 'magic frames', came into the old *mekes* composed to celebrate these encounters, and now found only in scraps in people's memories or the historian's pages, as queerly touching as pottery fragments in a museum case.

At dawn, at dawn, a foreigner appeared again.
Anchored she lies off Nukuthagina.
We of Nawarowaro run towards her,
Board a canoe and go off to her.
We traffic while the sun is up.
You snatch the magic frame

And hold it in hand before your eyes to look into.
'Tis true, the sickness that is reported.
The people are wasted by it on all sides,
The men are wrecks, and bent.
They droop like the daiga (*arum lily*),
They go down to na Thibathiba (*place of departed spirits*).
Oh, alas, alas!

The sickness was *na lila balavu*, a strange new wasting disease which the crews of the *Argo* and *El Plumier* brought with them to the islands. 'Its progress through the Group was fearfully rapid and destructive; in many places it was with the greatest difficulty that persons could be found to bury the dead. Those who were seized died in agony.' Combined with the awesome appearance of a great burning comet in the skies in the same year and a fearful storm of hailstones which the people thought were fallen stars, the whole sequence of events was regarded by the Fijians as a visitation from the gods in their wrath, heralding perhaps the end of all creation.

However, here we still were in the middle of the twentieth century, off the Natewa coast of Vanua Levu, with Samisoni bemoaning the lateness of the party's return when the food was all ready and growing cold. It was now mid-afternoon and we all went up on the cabin roof to look out for their approach. It was still drizzling and the tide was going out. Suddenly, out of the mist appeared a string of isolated figures, slowly advancing across the mud flats to the water's edge. Even at that distance we could see how wet and tired they were, the Englishmen in their shorts and bare legs, the Fijians in their *sulus*.

In a moment, Johnny had drawn the boat alongside and swung himself down. Now he stood in the centre, legs apart and balanced to the movement of the water, black rain-cape flapping in the wind, as he neatly peeled a banana, devoured it and flung away the skin before taking his seat. As he pulled away the thin whistle of his favourite tune, 'British Grenadiers', floated back to the launch. Somehow or other, all six men managed to pile in for the return trip, surmounted by the tall figure of Bula the cricketer straddled across the middle. As they came closer, a full-chested rendering of 'Belmont' rang out across the bay. Then they were bumping alongside, the Englishmen mock-gallantly raising their sodden bush-hats, Ratu Penaia clowning the gesture with a tug of his wiry crown of hair.

By the time we had finished eating the rain had stopped so out we went on the roof again for the short journey back. From below, someone emptied a bowl of *yaggona* over the side, a rapid, unacknowledged gesture.

'Grog for Dakuwaga,' said Peter. 'They still do it around these parts, just to keep on the right side of things. After all, he only lives just round the next bay, you know!'

When he had been on a trip with Ratu Edward in another part of the Group another such moment had impressed itself vividly on his mind. Their boat had been passing through the reef and one of the crew was about to throw a load of refuse overboard until smartly stopped by Ratu Edward. 'No rubbish here!' was all he said in Fijian, explaining to Peter that this was a place that was sacred to the spirits of his ancestors and therefore must be treated with respect.

We were not far away from the village when Johnny-the-Boatman leaned up and pointed out an island, small and overgrown, quite close to the coast. It looked deserted, though, as we chugged past a flock of white birds came swirling out from a cleft in the rocks. This was supposed to be the birthplace of the Natewa tribes, he told us. Did anyone live there now, I asked?

'Yes,' boomed Ratu Penaia who had been listening to us. 'A giant has his home in a cave there. He is eight feet tall and covered with feathers!—Well, that is what the legend says!' he protested, laughing, as we drowned him with cried of disbelief. 'I'm only telling you what people say!'

Back on shore again at the village, the men walked on to the creek for their evening bathe. Women were not allowed there and back in my room I found a bowl of warm water, sponge and soap carefully laid out for me on the mat. When I had changed I went out to the kitchen and found Sam's wife who told me in smiling, hesitant English that after dinner, some of the women were to do *mekes* for Ratu Penaia. These would be *vakamololo*, sitting-down dances. They were very difficult to do well. I would be interested to see them perhaps.

For this occasion a row of armchairs had been placed at the far end of the room and as soon as we had eaten we took our seats, Ratu Penaia in the centre, leaning back expansively, drawing on his cheroot and watching the proceedings through the narrowed eyes of a connoisseur. It was all very decorous. First came the elders of the village, serious, wrinkled men with old pin-stripe jackets over their *sulus*. Stooping, without any loss of dignity, on to their hands and knees they made their way past Ratu Penaia, and sat themselves as before, with their backs against the walls, their legs tucked elegantly beneath them. Then half a dozen men carrying *lalis* and sticks crept quietly in and squatted in a circle at the other end in a kind of arched alcove. Finally, the performers themselves appeared, six stolid matrons crouched low with bowed heads who took their places in two rows, in front of the musicians. Someone pumped up the hurricane lamp in the corner. There was a low, steady hiss, the whitish glare shining on watchful eyes, throwing long shadows across the ceiling. No one spoke or made a movement and the women sat gravely cross-legged in front of us in their bright cotton *sulus* and overdresses, with rustling garlands of leaves at the neck and wrists and ankles, their eyes lowered, their hands loosely clasped in their laps, until there came from behind them a single voice chanting the opening of the *meke*. Slowly the theme swelled as the others joined in and the staccato clicking of the *lali* took up the rhythm. With a single sweep of movement the women raised their hands, pink palms vivid in the lamplight, and began the first *vakamololo*, arms weaving and twisting, hands twining and arching, threading the invisible tapestry of the story. Sharply, their heads moved from side to side, up and down, in time to the beat, while a pair of eyes followed each pair of hands, the upper half of the body swaying gently on its solid base of folded thigh and calf. Only once or twice there was a mistake, marked by a suppressed giggle or a nudge, a human moment amidst so much perfection which made Penaia smile to himself. Each *meke* ended with a brisk double slap of the palms on the floor, then a resumption of the passive pose of before, hands clasped, heads bent. There was no applause simply, at the conclusion of the item an appreciative '*Vina'a, Vina'a*,' from Ratu Penaia, dropping his k's in the approved Thakaudrove fashion, and nods of agreement from the rest of us. At the end of the performance, the ladies smiled modestly then shuffled out backwards one by one, followed by the musicians, and lastly the elders.

We parted for bed but the rest of the village remained awake for some time. At intervals throughout the night one was aware of the various sounds of village life—the drone of chanting round the *yaggona* bowl in the *vakatunuloa*, the hollow handclaps that followed each round, shattering the stillness, like Chinese crackers or distant machine-gun fire, the light stipple of rain on the iron roof overhead. Somewhere a dog yelped, a rat scratched in the rafters, a cockerel crowed a false dawn. Behind it all, whenever one stirred, half-dreaming, half-waking, one heard like a soft, continual murmur of approval, the lull of the sea-tides on the beach.

14

Ceremonial

For the first time the next morning the sky was cloudless. The three men were up early, shaving with propped-up mirrors under the honeysuckle out on the porch. The *Turaga Levu* was to take us farther up the coast to a village called Drekeniwai where we were to spend the last three days of the trip.

That day, in the brilliant sunshine, the coast looked idyllically like the tropical-paradise advertisements as we walked down the path to the sea for the last time and called our *mothés* back over the widening strip of bright water to Sam and his wife and the cluster of villagers on the beach. Lying out on the cabin roof with the towels and dark glasses and sun-tan lotion, one tended to petrify into the tourist image, disconnected and self-contained, the Thakaudrove peaks and lush green hillsides flicking past as impersonally as someone else's travel slides.

Somehow, too, it was more difficult to conjure the comings and goings of the past than in brooding, cloudy weather. The clear-cut twinkle of sunlight varnished over such ghosts, slipping a two-dimensional screen between then and now, fixing the present for ever in a series of picturesque, smiling poses framed in the blue *passe-partout* of sea and sky. Did one of the longest wars in Fijian history really take place along this sleepy peninsula? Was it on these forgotten villages that a fleet of 5,000 warriors came swarming down from Tavenui in their outrigger war-canoes, drums beating, long flags of *tapa* flying from the bamboo breastworks, to fire and pillage the rebel tribes of Natewa? It was a war of revolt that had started in 1842, over a case of adultery, it was said, and this grand invasion by the combined forces of Tui Thakau, Ratu Thakobau and the Tongan chiefs was planned as its turning-point. Defeat was unthinkable. The Thakaudrove king had invoked not only the assistance of Bau and Tonga for his purpose, but the even more powerful approval of his tutelar god. A presentation of 10,000 yams,

30 large turtles, 40 roots of *yaggona*, and 50 large clams had been made to the priests, apart from a quantity of land crabs, ripe bananas, water-melons and drinking nuts. The warriors themselves had for three days gone through the frenzied ceremonials of *bole-bole*—the boasting challenges to the absent enemy—and had built a new temple for their lately-neglected war-god who promised success. The net results of it all were surprisingly modest—half a dozen dead on each side and for the cunning Thakobau a lion's share of the plunder and a fat new province in addition. It was not until two years later though that five double canoes, each carrying 150 men, set sail from Natewa deeply laden with tribute of *tapa*, coconut cordage, and the symbolic baskets of soil, to make the formal peace-offerings to their overlords and put an end to eight years of bitter fighting and privation.

The opening bars of 'Guide Me O Thou Great Jehovah' brought me back to the solid, Methodist present. Josua had formed an improvised choir in the stern with Bula and Inoke, and the three crew members gathered round the black hymn-book. Operatically rich and resolute the harmonies went throbbing across the bay, in a setting as far removed from chapel gloom as could be, while the *Turaga Levu* cleaved on through the transparent blue water.

Afterwards Inoke, diminutive and clerkly in his dark grey *sulu*, white shirt and horn-rimmed spectacles, came and sat next to me and told me the legend of the turtle-callers of Koro.

'I can call them myself,' he said. 'It is a kind of chant with very old words. But when the turtles rise up to the surface to show themselves one must never, never point towards them. Otherwise they will disappear again at once.'

The turtle was sacred on Koro, he said. Almost every tale and tradition centred around it. There was even a tree that bore a kind of hard fruit exactly the shape of a turtle, and it was found nowhere else in Fiji.

The rattle of the anchor broke in on those stories. Unnoticed, we had glided into another sheltered bay with the *bures* of a large village crowning a white, sloping shore.

'This time there will be welcoming ceremonies,' said Penaia, helping me down into the rowing-boat. 'At Drekeniwai we arrive officially.'

As if to mark the solemnity of this announcement, Ian began to remove his plimsolls and don instead a pair of long socks and brown polished shoes. Even Peter straightened the brim of his battered green bush-hat before replacing it at an impressive angle over his eyes.

'Wouldn't it be better if I waited on board?' I suggested, tentatively eyeing the reception committee of elderly beetle-browed men on the beach and trying to pull down my wave-splashed shirt as far as possible over my rumpled trousers.

'No, no. It will be interesting for you to see, I think. Just keep at the back of us.'

I needed no urging on this point, though the handshake of the village headman was reassuringly firm as he listened to Ratu Penaia's brief explanation and eyed me piercingly from under his brows. These greetings over, the old man stepped aside. Behind him we saw that the pathway up to the village *rara* was lined on either side by silent, seated figures, the men in front, the women at the back. Slowly, Ratu Penaia strode on ahead, his hands clasped behind him. The moment he was within sight of all, there went up from them the unforgettable sound of the *tama*, the ceremonial greeting of allegiance accorded only to the highest chiefs. It began with a shout, low, fierce and staccato. Slowly it died away on a long sigh of awe and wonderment. Then came the triple handclap of obeisance. According to custom, Ratu Penaia made no formal sign of acknowlegment, but simply walked on with a measured, dignified tread between the ranks of bent heads.

In the centre of the *rara* was the usual long pavilion of plaited palms and reeds. One by one we stooped under the eaves of the centre doorway. Through the greenish dusk inside gleamed the accumulated scrutiny of the village council, thirty or forty elderly men, who were already seated cross-legged around the walls. There was a murmured chant of welcome, then silence again as we took our seats on the four upright chairs at the far end, Peter motioning me into the one just behind Ian, the three Fijians settling themselves in a circle on the ground near by. Penaia was seated in the centre and I noticed that the air of strain he sometimes wore had fallen away. His whole face and bearing, though solemn, seemed fortified and relaxed as though secretly nourished by these ancient and private communications with his people. Leaning forward, his eyes followed intently the suppressed shuffles of preparation among the inner ranks. Equally absorbed, the old men watched his face then, with a hardening expression turned their gaze on to the main actors in the rituals that followed, impartially relentless as judges in a show ring.

First came the presentation of three *tabua*, the first to mark our arrival by sea, the second for our landing and the third for the entering of the council chamber. Each was presented individually by a different representative, each was accompanied by a short speech of welcome and accepted by Ratu Penaia who then handed them over to Bula at his side. Next, a file of young men stepped forward, and laid at Penaia's feet one by one the heap of fine mats that, after a sea journey in olden times, would be required as change of clothing.

Now, in the long dim tent of leaves, airless and heavy with coconut oil, the atmosphere of dedication settled more closely still over the watchful, tight-packed ring of faces. Solemnly the mats were lifted to one side and in the clearing was placed a large *tanoa*, a wooden bowl on four legs, its plaited cord hung with white cowrie shells laid out towards Ratu Penaia. The climax of the ceremonies, the preparation of the chiefly *yaggona*, had been reached. The powdered root lay ready in the bowl, together with the bundle of hibiscus fibre for straining the liquid. A small fierce-faced man took his place cross-legged before it. Crouched behind him with blackened faces and skirts and garlands of leaves, the cup-bearers waited with lowered eyes. When all was ready, the silhouettes of two tall warriors appeared against the gold of the doorway. Over their shoulders they carried long tubes of bamboo. At a sign from the little man, they came forward one by one, removed a plug of leaves from the top of the stem, and tipped forward into the bowl a stream of fresh water that was quickly stopped at a further signal from the *yaggona*-maker. A measured chant, rhythmic and slow, began among the onlookers, first with a single voice, then swelling to a wailing, melancholy descant punctuated by hand-clapping, while with an air of almost mystical intensity, the dark-faced little man raised and lowered his hands in and out of the liquid, straining and re-straining it through the mass of hibiscus fibres. Then with a final twist, the used bundle was thrown over his shoulder to the man behind him. Swiftly, someone else crept forward and wound up the plaited cord. The chanting stopped and an intense hush fell as the premier cup-bearer came forward and received in both hands the first bowl of *yaggona*. It was the ceremony's moment of truth, a climax of almost unbearable nervous tension. Turning to face the chief and holding the cup with arms fully extended, he slowly lowered his body until his knees were fully bent and every polished muscle was taut. The *meke* had begun again, softly, insistently. At the appropriate line, the man straightened and approached Ratu Penaia, stooped again to fill Penaia's own personal cup, then squatted before him as the *yaggona* was drained at the prescribed gulp.

With a neat twist of his wrist Penaia spun the cup back across the mat. '*Matha!*' (Empty!) cried everyone. A second cup was filled and drunk amidst applause, and then it was the turn of the others in order of precedence, from Bula, as Penaia's personal *mata-ni-vanua* or herald, to Ian and Peter and then round the rest of the gathering. The urgency of the central moment had drained gently away, although the performance of each serving remained as perfect as ever. This was, to me, the secret of the ritual's power, the clear-cut definition of each man's role, his own sureness and pride in it, and the still-vital meaningfulness of it all to everyone present.

By the time the *magiti* (the feast) was presented, the atmosphere was almost relaxed. Approving eyes watched the carrying in of several baskets of cooked yams and bread-fruit, two roast sucking-pigs, and finally the *pièce de résistance*, an enormous turtle about four feet long and three feet across which had been baked in its shell and was now dragged in on its back by the two muscular water-carriers. An elaborate speech was made by one of the elders, excusing the poorness and smallness of the offerings. An equally elaborate one followed, in which Bula, his hand resting on the flank of one of the pigs, protested that on the contrary such gifts were overwhelmingly large and generous and much appreciated by all the party.

The meal itself, Peter murmured—or our portion anyway—would be eaten in the house where we were staying. The ceremonies were at an end. Amidst relieved smiles and murmurs of approval, Ratu Penaia led the way outside again. Here a broad-shouldered Fijian with a military moustache and businesslike manner, was introduced to us as our host. He had been a major with the Fiji military forces in Malaya. The pride of place in the living-room into which he led us was given to a carved Malayan chest and a fine pair of silver-mounted daggers on the wall. There was also a handsome suite of bamboo chairs, which gave the room the look of fashionable suburbia that made one expect to see rows of semi-detacheds through the windows instead of the unending colonnades of waving palms and the blue Pacific beyond. It was the usual four-square wooden bungalow that every village seemed to boast, however remote, for its headman. It was Lockerby, the mate of the American ship, the *Jenny*, who claimed to record the first of these European novelties while on a visit to Sandalwood Bay in 1809. The King of Bua, he wrote, had been presented with the first wooden house in Fiji as a gift from a Botany Bay trading company. The old man, however, noting that some of the boards had been split during the journey, firmly refused it and said such a thing was good for keeping out neither sun nor rain, and the white men could keep it.

Over the dining-room table hung a black-and-gold clock with a glass-cased pendulum, which our host told us was a trophy from Singapore. Around the walls there were coloured pictures of the Queen, surrounded by family snapshots, regimental groups, photographs of visiting officials of the past. In this sedate setting we sat for a while and talked near the breeze of the open doorway until the wife of the headman came in to tell us that food was about ready. She was a young, pretty woman who spoke excellent English and greeted her guests with a calm poise of manner acquired no doubt from her travels in Malaya with her husband. Her name, she told me, was Ruve, which was the Fijian word for a pigeon. Gentle, plump, and soft-voiced, it was one which suited her well, I thought. From between the household Bible and the hymn-book on a nearby shelf, she brought out a faded blue exercise-book on which she had printed the words *Visitors' Book*.

'We bought it for the visit of the Governor and his wife last year,' she said, opening it on the first page where the vice-regal names stood alone in pristine glory. 'It is time someone else wrote in it.'

Gravely we each signed ourselves in, watched by Ruve and her husband and the small group of leading elders who had sat themselves down in the doorway to keep in touch with what was going on.

'We've someone here who knows all about handling Governors though,' said the ex-Major, laughing and nodding in the direction of a very old white-haired man at the back of the circle. 'Eh, Joeli?' He translated himself into Fijian. Every one else began to shake with laughter except the old man himself who merely permitted himself a sardonic smile and a nod of agreement. 'Shall we tell them about it then?' Another nod and this time a broader grin. 'Well, Joeli, you see, comes from a small island quite close by. He's the big fellow there, the headman, so when the Governor pays them a visit on his way past, he's the one to receive him of course, guide him round and so on. This is good few years ago, by the way, so it could be any Governor we're talking about! Anyway, the great man arrived and the first thing he did was to give the people a long talk about how the Fijians must learn to take their place in the great big world outside. He even drew it in the sand for them. Fiji was just a dot on the map, he said, and this little island of theirs was an even tinier dot. Well, then he said he'd like to have a look at the other village before he left. And what does Joeli do? Instead of taking him straight there—it's only half a mile away—he leads him off in the opposite direction so that by darkness they're still walking, and they have to camp for the night. They finally reach the village the next morning, having gone right round the whole island. Of course the Governor finds out, but all Joeli says, very dignified, is, 'Your Excellency, I only wanted to show you just how big a dot can be.'

At this well-known climax even Joeli chuckled amidst the general shrieks and thigh-slappings.

'Then the next V.I.P. comes here—a very important professor sent from England to tell us how to build better villages—says to Joeli he's very sorry he won't be able to go any farther to look at the new *bures* because it's raining. "Well, you're not made of salt, are you?" asks Joeli. After that the professor walked on all day, rain or not.'

There was renewed laughter. Now firmly established in his sceptic's role, the Voltaire of Drekeniwai edged himself farther forward into the limelight and quaveringly embarked on yet another epic of defiance, but with a courteous gesture our host cut him short. 'Another time, Joeli. Food is ready and our guests are hungry.'

Good-humouredly the old man shuffled to his feet and with a dignified stoop of acknowledgment to Penaia, went on his way with the rest of the elders. At a loaded table, the array of feast dishes was dominated by a strange-looking mound of spiky skin and dried flesh.

'Ah,' said Penaia, rubbing his hands. '*Pito!* The part of the turtle that only a chief may eat.' With elaborate politeness he passed on the dish to Ian. A minute later Peter looked up from the battered Victorian pocket-dictionary he always carried with him and announced with a scholarly frown that the only translation of the word he could find was either lower bowel or umbilical hernia. Ian's first forkful froze in mid-air. Tactfully, plates were changed and the mysterious delicacy removed for the consumption of lesser men outside.

'Laisa should arrive about three if all goes well,' remarked Penaia, changing the subject. 'We shall be at the *bose* with the men, but you will be here Tiune, with Ruve?' he grinned. 'Better have plenty of mats ready. She's probably had a rough crossing according to the weather reports.'

It was, in fact, after five when the *Turaga Levu* glided back into the bay. Watching from the veranda, I saw a familiar figure in elegant emerald green climb down into the little boat to be rowed ashore by Johnny. There were to be no formal ceremonies of welcome, but Ruve and half a dozen senior matrons of the village were seated together on the beach waiting to greet her as the boat was pulled up into the shallows. Adi Laisa's final descent from the prow into the remaining two inches of water was as polished a lesson in deportment as the emergence of English royalty from a motor-car, and ten times as difficult. One hand raising her long black *sulu* to just above her ankles, the other extended in greeting, she swayed gracefully across through the ripples to the waiting group. The women clapped their hands and remained seated, looking up at her while she stood speaking to them for a few minutes. Then slowly they came up the white sandy path together, Laisa in front, the others stooping behind her, the sunshine dappling their flower-coloured dresses through the branches of the mango trees, glinting on sleekly oiled arms and faces and haloes of jet hair.

This time it was I who awaited her on the doorstep.

'*Ni sa bula*, Adi Laisa!'

'Bula! Tiune!' The greeting was as warm as ever, yet tinged faintly with the restraint of a public occasion. The women watched us smiling, then crouching to clap again, withdrew. In the cool of the living-room Ruve brought in an elaborate tray of tea, then also left us to talk together for a while.

'*Sobo!* But what a journey!' Laisa heaved a sigh of relief and lay back in an armchair. 'Wait, I'll tell you.' From her handbag, which like herself was large, brown and handsome, she drew first a tiny lace handkerchief with which she dabbed her forehead, and then her cigarettes. She lit up, took a sip of her tea, smoothed down her emerald silk draperies, and went on, 'You see, to get from Taveuni on to Vanua Levu you have to cross the Somo—Somo Strait. One goes by put-put and normally it's about an hour's trip. Today it took us three and a half hours! And, of course, it would be today that I had visitors with me—two young nurses from Canberra who looked after me so well while I was in hospital there. They've been staying with us at Taveuni and had to be back at Savu-Savu this afternoon to catch the 'plane. Well, to begin with the engine broke down, twenty times at least. Then this terrific wind got up, with breakers coming at us from every side! Often we drifted right off course towards the open sea, and the sky overhead was as black as pitch, with the rain coming down in sheets. Of course, the poor girls were terrified! One of them, a Catholic, was on her knees praying. I can tell you, I was praying myself, when I'd got any breath left from baling out.' She laughed suddenly. 'I kept telling them, "This nothing. This is calm by our standards!" But underneath I was really frightened. I don't think I've ever been so glad to see land in my life when we finally got to the other side and there was the jeep waiting since morning to take them on into Savu-Savu. As for me—well, the trip round to Drekeniwai in the *Turaga Levu* was just a joy-ride after that!' She finished her tea, then got up and stretched herself. 'And now I shall have my bath and rest for an hour. Did you know this house has a shower?'

I said yes, Ruve had showed me.

'And as for the other matter—' Laisa went over to where a china fish was hanging on the wall, reached into its mouth, and brought out a large, rusty key. 'I suppose she showed you this, too? Did you find it all right? It's quite a long way up the hill at the back of the village if I remember—good old Fijian style!'

I said on the contrary I was delighted I didn't have to walk out on a shaky old jetty over the sea, as in some places.

'Well, we'll walk up together, at night-time, anyway,' Laisa said firmly as she left. 'It's quite a rough climb in the dark even with a torch and we don't want any Naiserilangi accidents here!'

It was almost seven when we met again in the *bure* opposite where Ratu Penaia and Laisa were staying. It was the home of the village schoolmistress who was away at the time. Amongst its possessions was a portable radio around which Penaia, Ian and Peter were gathered, their meeting over, awaiting the seven o'clock B.B.C. news relayed through the Suva station of the Fiji Broadcasting Commission. It was the beginning of a winter's morning in England now, I thought, people sleepily putting a match to the gas-fire, rubbing at misted windows, switching on the radio as we did here in this thatched room in the lamplight, silent except for the susurrations of the reef and through the open doorway the tall palms rustling against the stars. Bleakly the Greenwich pips came cheeping through space. The detached, muffled tones that followed with news of the latest bomb tests, air disasters, floods, famines, race riots and a warning from the Prime Minister, seemed even more unreal than the thought of an English winter. Not involvement, but embarrassment at the misfortunes of the world and its ugliness was what one felt at this Olympic distance, and sadness too that this was the very world that the young schoolmistress and her pupils leaned forward so eagerly to embrace, urged on, of course, by escapees like ourselves. I shut out the voice from my mind and looked around at the family pictures pinned on a strip of *masi*, at the soft mats that covered the beds fringed with loopings of coloured wool, the mosquito-nets above them embroidered with patterns of flowers and elephants. On the shelf alongside was a row of paperback books—the schoolmistress, I had been told, was much respected in these parts for her fine English. At the far end of the *bure*, a neatly ranged food safe held her provisions. Everything from the fine white mats underfoot to the polished gables overhead, reflected a feeling of optimism and self-respect combined with a loving regard for one's background and one's past. To me it seemed the exact opposite of the bush-planter's house we had seen a few days before. There, a final surrender was taking place, purpose was petering out. Here life was only just beginning. Perhaps this very contrast was a neat lesson in not turning one's back on the world after all.

Mercifully at this point a loud burst of static heckled the announcer into oblivion and the set was turned off. Ratu Penaia, with that enviable gift of complete and unself-conscious relaxation unknown to Europeans had stretched himself out on the floor, lying flat on his back with outspread arms and legs like the illustration of Gulliver tied down by the Lilliputians. Now he bounded to his feet beaming and refreshed and stretched expansively, throwing titanic shadows on the wall behind. It was time for soup, he declared. They had a long evening ahead of them and the meeting should start as soon as possible.

Laisa had already planned our after-dinner entertainment. First an extra benzine lamp was brought in and pumped up until it roared and sizzled like a ship's boilers. Whisky and water followed, while Ruve and I settled ourselves on the floor on either side of her and from the familiar handbag she produced two packs of cards.

'Canasta! And if you don't know how, you can soon learn.'

The next two hours sped by as Laisa with her usual energy alternately reminded me in English of the conditions of 'melding', instructed Ruve, a beginner, in the basic rules in Fijian, and in a combination of the two languages entertained us both with a round-up of the latest news from Suva where she had been last week.

When we finally retired the men were still at the *bose*. From the *Vakatunaola* just outside the house drifted the slow rhythmical murmur of question and answer. This was the sound that coloured the whole of the following day too—the husky sibilance of the villagers' voices and Ratu Penaia's gruff authoritative tones, broken occasionally by the Scottish burr of Ian's Fijian and Peter's theatrically accurate reproduction of the slurring Thakaudrove dialect. Mingled with this came the bee-like drone of children repeating their lessons in the schoolroom and, regularly marking every hour, the roll and thud of the village *lali*.

After breakfast I went across to Laisa's *bure* and found her winding herself into the long black length of material that is worn beneath the European dress of every respectable Fijian lady so that they are decorously covered from ankle to neck. Tucking it in at the waist with a final twist, she then sat down on the bed to arrange her hair. I watched fascinated as the thick wooden prongs of the long-handled Fijian comb flicked the wiry strands upwards until the outline of the head stood out as neatly rounded as a well-clipped ornamental bush. Then we went out together for a walk through the village. In the *bure* schoolroom, the children were reciting tables, sitting at old-fashioned bench desks. Next door stood the church, a tall wooden building with a corrugated-iron roof, gabled and painted red. Once a week for the Sunday services it generated its own electricity—so the old man weeding the garden proudly told us, pointing to the small shed alongside also surmounted by a rough wooden cross. He also told us, and Laisa translated, that the hum of the generator tended to drown the sermons, but on the whole the people felt that the advantage of a good light for hymn-singing outweighed any drawback to the system. Almost every *bure* was surrounded by well-kept flower-beds and grass patches and we went in and out of half a dozen houses during the morning talking to the women and drinking tea.

Soon after lunch the final meeting ended. There were to be ceremonies on the *rara*, Laisa told me, and together we took our seats on the row of chairs placed for us along one side of the grassy arena. Crowds of people were already waiting in a deep square all around. When Ratu Penaia appeared and took his place in the centre of the row with Ian and Peter a sudden hush fell. In this impressive silence, without further introduction a long line of men and women came walking slowly towards us, carrying in their arms gifts of the land, a yam, or a bundle of *dalo*, a string of coconuts, a bunch of bread-fruit, which in turn they placed on the ground at Ratu Penaia's feet. Soon a small hillock of produce had mounted in front of his chair by the time the last of the procession had finally wound away. This was the presentation of the fruits of the soil, Laisa told me. In olden times such first-fruits would be presented at the shrines of the *Kalou vu* (ancestral spirits) before the crops were harvested.

Then from the far corner of the green, like the unfurling of a coloured fan, came the dancers, about fifty women in long white *sulus*, pink blouse-tops, and thickly bunched overskirts of black white and brown patterned *masi*, white flower garlands swinging from their shoulders. Already the singers were gathered in a close circle to the right of us. In the centre sat their leader, a stocky Lloyd-Georgian figure with flowing white mane and moustache, impressively arrayed in a black Sunday jacket and a large pair of horn-rimmed spectacles. Peter informed me in a whisper that he was, in fact, the local sorcerer and the reputed descendant of the feathered giant in the cave. At a flick of the sorcerer's upraised finger, the opening phrase rang out followed by the slow surge of supporting voices, the irresistible click and tap of the *lali.* I looked more closely and saw that in addition to the usual canoe-shaped gongs, one of the men was beating out the rhythm with a pair of clappers in the form of two shaped sticks and three more struck the ground with stamping tubes of closed bamboo.

Silhouetted between the grass and sky the women arranged themselves in double file and glided into the first *meke.* The steps they took were so slight, sideways and forwards, that all the movement of this dance came from the swaying of their bodies, swinging gently this way and that like something growing and blowing in the wind, hands and arms weaving swiftly, *masi* streamers fluttering behind them, to the intricate rhythm of *lali* and voice. They were not, by European standards, graceful figures. The outlines were too solid, too thickset. Yet they perfectly conveyed those qualities which characterized all Fijian acts of ceremony—an awe-inspiring, coarse-grained nobility, an almost religious intensity of concentration and devotion to detail in every moment made, every sound produced.

As Miss Gordon-Cumming expressed it in the Victorian idiom: 'No high-bred English duchess could carry herself more nobly than these born ladies leading their minuet.'

Lockerby, too—'Massa Lombe', as the Fijians called him—saw these Vanua Levu *mekes* sixty years earlier when, in the pagan tradition, they were performed at night-time and probably in a less restrained form.

'The moon shining, we joined them in dancing; it being a part of their worship to dance while the moon shines. The men and women dance in separate bodies. They keep excellent time with their song during which some play on a hollow bamboo which they blow with their nose; it produces a sound somewhat like our fife.'

The nose-flutes of the Fijian musicians had vanished into history, but their timing was as excellent as ever. Despite the closeness of the link between them though, neither glance nor word was ever exchanged between these singers and dancers. Each were remote, enclosed in their own separate worlds, yet intercommunicating on the most subtle level. Nor, according to the same etiquette, was the appreciation of the onlookers expressed by anything more than a lordly *vinaka* among the senior villagers, as the lines of the dance broke up and interchanged with each new chant, the figures sometimes strung out like printed notes of music, sometimes twining into a Catherine-wheel circle or folding back again into a single unbroken arc.

Too soon it was over. With the light rustle and ripple of a flock of settling birds, the women sank to the ground. For a moment everything hung against the evening sky—the cloud-banks of dark, massed faces on either side, the low-spreading wings of the great *ivi* trees, the line of children's heads beneath where they sat waist-high in the long grass. Then, this being Fiji where emotion is expressed in symbol, there came one final ceremony to mark the gratitude of the guests to the performers. Gravely Bula stepped forward and, on behalf of Ratu Penaia, bent to present the white-haired old man with a *tabua* on its cord of sinnet. Solemnly Lloyd George put on a second pair of spectacles over his everyday ones and intoned in a rich rhetorical wizard's style the thanks of the performers for the honour of such company and their apologies for the meagreness of their talents. There was a formal volley of clapping and after a while everyone drifted home.

At the Major's house that evening there was a farewell party. In addition to our own group there were some new-comers—Atu Maitonga, the handsome young Roko Tui of Mathuata, a Fijian agricultural officer; and Lionel Bentley, the doyen of one of Fiji's pioneer families and a connoisseur of boats and boat-building, who regaled us with a flow of local stories laced with the lovely island names—Komo, Kabara, Fulaga, Totoya—and full of those racy expressions adopted by the part-Europeans often from the Australians and now spiced with their own individuality—'You can put a ring round that, I said, . . .' 'Had a yarn with the cobber, . . .' The mosquitoes came up like sand in the wind . . . ."

After the stories came the songs and finally the dancing, this time a *taralala*—the pidgin expression for a European-style barn-dance. Two guitars supplied the music and half a dozen village ladies were invited in to provide sufficient partners for the gentlemen. A kind of foxtrot shuffle, danced sideways on with one's arm encircling one's partner's waist was the most popular step. Whenever a change of company was desired, the lady simply went over to the gentleman of her choice, bent down, and touched him on the ankle in meek invitation—an ingenious combination of the submissiveness and the relentlessness of the female character, I thought, following suit with enthusiasm.

The real entertainment of the evening, however, started up as we were all retiring to bed. In the *Vakatunaloa* had gathered all the singers of the village. Their duty was to serenade us through the night, fortified by rounds of *yaggona* served by the women. A stirring composition based, I was told, on Ratu Penaia's ancestral motto (English translation: 'Never Say Die') was the first contribution. After that, everything blurred into one sonorous reverberation of sound, and I fell asleep.

At six o'clock the next morning, they were still singing, rather more raggedly perhaps then, roused by our leave-takings to a final farewell burst. Ratu Penaia and Adi Laisa who were staying on for a few more days were already waiting on the shore to see us off, Penaia in his flowered *sulu*, Laisa in a flowing Hawaiian *mu-mu*. Preceded by our baggage we made our way down the path, blinking in the bright sunshine. From behind the last *bure* appeared three young girls with *salu-salus* in their hands.

'*Tulo*,' (Excuse me) each one murmured in turn, slipping the garlands over our shoulders and sinking to the ground with a swift shy clap of the hands. The traditional clusters of fine bark-shavings hung crisp and light against the skin. The men's were the natural cream-white colour but mine had been dyed a deep wine-red and indefinably scented.

Then we were in the boat, pulling out to the *Turanga Levu* across a blue and glittering sea and looking back for the last time as departing travellers do—at the diminishing line of figures on the shore, the green clustered hills behind and among the *bures* the silvery feathers of smoke rising from the first fires of a new day.

15

The Siege of Thau-murė-murė

'The village is called Saivou,' said Josua Rabukawanga, the musical administrative officer of the *Turaga Levu* party. 'I have chosen it because it is in the very heart of the interior, quite remote. The hill tribes there are a completely different people from the Fijians of the coast. Also', he added, in his mellifluously Edwardian English, 'I am well acquainted with the headman there. I know they will be extremely pleased for you to visit them.'

While we were still in Natewa Bay, Josua had told me that I should see more of Vanua Levu before returning to the mainland and Suva—something of the island country first, then perhaps an expedition by sea up to the northernmost tip of Udu Point. Of course I was delighted to agree to this suggestion and to find someone kind enough to put it into operation for me. Back at Savu-Savu a Fiji Airways plane made the giant's stride across the island to Labasa, the steamy river-mouth town where Josua was District Officer. Labasa was mainly Indian in population and character, and centred around one of the thriving mills of the South Pacific Sugar Mills Corporation. Now we were driving away inland, leaving behind the narrow streets and tin-roof settlements, the rambling wooden front of the Grand Eastern Hotel where the smooth-faced, Gujerati business men sat over their four-o'-clock beers in the lounge to talk of exports and imports, profits and losses, and the latest injustices of the Customs Department. The single-line track of the sugar trains curled away through the cane-fields. Small, dark-skinned southern Indians moved among the feathery plumes with a flash of cane-knives. An engine whistle tangled in the distance with the blast of a ship's hooter from the river. Under a tree in a wayside clearing there was a glimpse of a Hindu shrine, a tall stone smeared with red and yellow powders and garlanded with marigolds.

'Most interesting of all,' Jo went on, 'there is at Saivou a very old man who relates a true story from history that only he is left to tell. If he agrees to do so, Mei will translate for you.

Adi Mei, Josua's wife, sitting next to me in the back, nodded with a smile—the only part of her that was visible beneath layers of head-scarves, dark glasses, cardigans, and her husband's tweed jacket over her knees. The soft, lilting voice that emerged from this cushiony outline in the corner informed me that she felt the cold, especially when out in the car. As we drove past an outlying store we stopped to do some shopping.

'Bread for our breakfast—you may not feel like *dalo*—and some *yaggona* for the *turaga-ni-koro* (village chief),' she explained as Jo returned with the parcels, an authoritative figure in his dark grey *sulu*, white shirt and Royal Commonwealth Society tie.

'Of course not!—you are our guest,' they protested, when I attempted to pay. Finally they allowed me to pay for the *yaggona* and some cigarettes as my present to the chief.

Soon a strangely ambivalent countryside began to take shape—hunks of savage red clay and sprawling bush interspersed with neat little Government projects—a grove of young eucalyptus trees, a cluster of new white clapboard offices on stilts, a chicken farm. Stones flew up from the rough, twining road.

On our right a signpost pointed to Naduri town, but we continued towards the hills. Gradually the scenery grew wilder and more deserted. All around the land was broken up into abrupt humps and crags. Beyond, the central mountain range of Vanua Levu reared a jagged dinosaur spine against the sky from which the last light was now fading. Huge rounded stones, grey and smooth, lay among the long grass at the side of the road, reassuming in the twilight something of that primaeval mystery for which they were venerated by Fijians in the past, as the abodes of the gods or reincarnations of a deified ancestor. Even the trees of these parts loomed larger, denser, than the trees of the plains and coasts, great arching domes of shadow that swayed and strained in the wind like black-sailed galleons at anchor.

'Many of the older people round here have never seen the coast,' Jo said. 'From earliest times they were split up into little communities of three or four houses. Right up to the present century they were as cut off from the mission and the Government as if they were in another country—even though they were supposed to be *lotu*—

officially. Which is the reason for what happened in Saivon in 1895, just twenty-one years after Cession.'

Amidst a slither of loose stones we turned off down a side-track. 'It's not far now. This is the country of the Seagaga tribe, and the uprising was known as the Seagaga Revolt.

'The trouble began when the Roko demanded extra supplies of the timber with which the people paid their taxes. The people felt they were being unfairly treated and declared a revolt against the Government.

Any villagers who refused to join in were burned out of their *bures*. Two of them killed and cooked for eating.

'Ancestral spirits were invoked by the pouring of *yaggona* on their graves. The gods of olden days appeared in the forms of animals, and so on. Then the rebels entrenched themselves for a siege in an old hill fortress called Thau-muré-muré. The Governor himself sailed across in his yacht and marched inland with a military detachment. A party of traitors led them up a way at the back of the fortress and the battle was short and sharp, as you can imagine.

'Taito, the old man, who was a young boy at the time, escaped and eventually returned to his village to tell the tale as he has been doing ever since, through three generations! As I hope he will tonight!'

Bundles of yams and *dalo* began to dot the verges of the track. The villagers left them there on the way home from their food gardens ready to be loaded on to the market bus at first light, Adi Mei told me. Occasionally we passed a man still making for home, a basket and cane-knife in either hand, or against the last glimmer of landscape a woman trudging bent beneath the load of firewood strapped to her shoulders, a hump-back silhouette that turned to flash a smile, raise a hand in the flare of the headlamps.

Then suddenly the track curved round a grassy mound and came to an end. Above us clustered the peaked outlines of a dozen *bure* roofs. 'Just a small village, as you see,' said Jo, as we all climbed out. Under a *baka* tree, a lantern fluttered and someone moved forward to meet us.

'This is Petero, the *Turaga-ni-kora*,' Jo said. A heavy-jowled, handsome face with a small clipped moustache, hovered smiling in the circle of lamplight. 'You'll be staying in his *bure*.'

I refrained from asking where Petero would spend the night,

which would have been a serious lapse of etiquette. Any Fijian of substance possesses two or three *bures*, seemingly interchangeable for all purposes.

Petero and his lantern lead us across the *rara*, up a ramp of small cobbled steps and into an unpretentious *bure* which boasted none of the European additions acquired by people living near towns. There was a side door of rough timber, but no windows. The only furniture was a large squared bed-frame, looped round with green cotton curtains, and covered with brightly fringed mats. Two old suitcases stood on a shelf behind. Under the floor mats, silky surfaced with age, the mud floor was packed with dried ferns which lay deeply piled up to the reed walls. Jo would drive back for us the following morning, he said. This evening he had a meeting to attend in Labasa.

When he had gone, Mei made our presentations to Petero who excused himself to go and see to the supper arrangements. Speaking in Fijian—his English was 'little', he explained—he turned to ask Adi Mei something from the doorway.

'He says, are you sure you wouldn't rather eat at a table? He has one, if you would like one.'

Petero's face assumed a politely vacant look, gazing into the middle distance during this interchange of English, then turned with a pleased smile when Adi Mei repeated in Fijian my assurances that no such thing was necessary.

Left to ourselves, Adi Mei produced from her basket a minute transistor radio and drew up the aerial. Then she removed her scarves and cardigans, and lay down on the mat with a luxurious sigh, her arms folded under her head, a plump, pretty woman with a turned-up nose, smooth skin and perfect teeth. 'Now we can stretch our legs,' she said, as the voice of Pat Boone joined us with 'Friendly Persuasion', Adi Mei humming an alto descant, otherwise there was a companionable silence as we rested in the lamplight. From time to time Petero reappeared crouched in the doorway with questions about our meal. A European woman would have automatically sat up to talk to him. Adi Mei, however, seemed able to conduct a conversation from her prostrate position with the poise and dignity of a Roman empress, rolling over slightly on to one side, one hand beneath her head, in the most natural way possible.

After a while, a young girl and a youth of about fourteen came hesitantly in, carrying a cloth and a pile of crockery which they laid out on the floor in front of us. There were whispered conferences about the placings of knives and forks, salt and bread. Then came the food itself—a delicious meat broth, baked pork, spinach-like *roro* in coconut milk and fried bread-fruit. While we ate, our two attendants sat cross-legged facing one another at the far end of the cloth, occasionally passing dishes or pouring out fresh water. They looked like brother and sister with handsome broad-boned features. Once or twice I asked them questions about the village to which they gave brief, whispered replies with lowered eyes and bashful smiles. Otherwise they were silent and solemn apart from a suppressed nervous giggle when one of them made a clumsy movement or dropped a spoon. Half-way through, a small boy appeared with a note. It came from Petero next door. In a flourishing hand he apologized for the humbleness of the food. His wife was away and he was supervising the cooking himself. If we would excuse his absence at the meal, he would join us later. Adi Mei produced a fountain-pen and wrote a neat reply. The small boy disappeared with it, the attendant cleared away the dishes, and we were on our own again. Outside, the wind had begun to blow with an intermittent patter of rain. Even with both doors tightly closed the little room grew suddenly cold.

'These nights up in the hills at this time of year!' shivered Adi Mei. 'It is like a foreign country!'

We put on sweaters and scarves again and pulled down pillows from the bed to make a stockade around us. The ever-efficient Miss Gordon-Cumming would, of course, have brought her Scottish rug with her on such an occasion, along with all the rest of her travelling impedimenta. There was that little scene of hers entitled, appropriately, 'Quite Alone in a Mountain Village'. 'Having hung up my green plaid curtain, one kind woman has brought water in a bamboo and therewith filled my big brass basin (the old companion of my happy tent-life in the Himalayas). Now a party of laughing brown children are holding up small torches of blazing bamboo, by the light of which I am writing. . . .'

Here in our mountain village there was no sign of either laughing brown children or the aged survivor of the Seagaga Revolt.

'Perhaps he will be coming presently with Petero,' Adi Mei said.

Fijian arrangements were like this, I reflected—vague and timeless—and to press for action would be considered the height of ill-manners. Meanwhile, Adi Mei began to talk of her life on the island of Bau where she was born and lived until her marriage to Jo. It had been a formal Fijian wedding with close observance of all the old customs. *Tabuas* were exchanged, and at the close of the Methodist church service, the *masi* trains of bride and groom were presented to the minister. Afterwards had come the ceremony of spreading the mats (*i tevutevu*) when in the couple's new home sleeping-mats were laid down by women relatives in strict order of precedence, the bride's mother spreading the last mat on top of the pile. A ritual four days' honeymoon was spent in the *bure*. Food was cooked and handed in by the women of the families at discreet intervals. Otherwise the couple were left strictly undisturbed, nor were they allowed to leave the house except to bathe each morning. On the fourth day the bride was taken out for a ceremonial fishing and bathing party by her female relations and friends, and after that life returned to normal once more.

'Apart from weddings, funerals were the great ceremonial occasions, of course. As a small girl, the one thing that stayed in my mind was the song that the old women used to sing on the fourth day after a death. As they sang they used to tap with their fingers on the mat in front of them to imitate the rising of the maggots in the dead body.' Adi Mei leaned forward and drummed lightly with her finger-tips on the ground. 'The day after, the spirit was free to start out on its long journey to Burotu, Paradise that is, and everyone had to make as much noise as possible to send it off—beating the *lalis*, banging on tin cans, blowing the conch shells. It was all very frightening for a small child.'

I knew that Burotu was believed, in the old days, to be an enchanted island lying to the south-east, invisible except for calm days when it might be seen shimmering in the distance. Some people thought it might even be a kind of Atlantis, beneath the sea. On Vanua Levu the jumping-off place for the spirits was Naithobothobo Point at the western tip of the islands, on Viti Levu at Vuda at the end of the Kauvandra mountain range. In all parts of Fiji the spirit world was believed to lie in the direction from which the original migrations came. Departing spirits retraced the path followed to Fiji by their ancestors. The journey overland made by the spirit to reach the jumping-off point was one beset by trials and dangers.

I asked Adi Mei if she knew some of the old stories about it. As a staunch Methodist she seemed a little doubtful of this, then said she could remember some of the old people's tales—and, of course, Josua was an expert on such legends. 'There was the god *DdroHro-yalo*, the Pursuer of Shades, who would attack the approaching spirit with stones, and the Dread Fisherwomen who would try to sweep him up in their nets and bite off his head. Then there was Taleya, the Dismisser, who lived in a great *baka* tree. His duty was to ask the spirit if he died a natural death, or by club, strangling or drowning. If he had died naturally he would be sent back in shame to re-enter the body and return to life. This is how the Fijians would explain a trance, I suppose. After a while the spirit would come to the Pandanus Tree that he must aim at with his whale's tooth. If he missed his throw, this was a sign that his wives were not to be strangled, or that they had been unfaithful to him in life. There was one very sad part, I remember. This was Naililili—the Hanging Place where the shades of little children who had passed on would hang like bats from a *vasa* tree. 'How are my father and my mother?' the child would ask the approaching spirit. If the reply was, 'The smoke of their cooking-fires is still upright,' meaning they were in their prime, the child would weep to be still an orphan. If it was that the smoke of their fires hangs along the ground, the child would rejoice that it was soon to be joined by its parents after waiting so long. There are many other parts to the journey, I know. Finally, I think, the spirit comes to the Place of Wonder where it takes its final look on the pleasures and sorrows of the living world before it passes on to Burotu.'

We sat in silence for a few moments. There was the rustle of a rat or a bird in the eaves, and outside the wind was rising on a melancholy note. I thought of the wonderful Lament of the Shades to the Gods of the Spirit Path:

My Lords, in ill fashion are we buried,
Buried staring up into heaven.
We see the scud flying over the sky.
We are worn out with the feet stamping in the earth.
The rafters of our house are torn asunder,

The eyes with which we gazed on one another are destroyed,
The nose with which we kissed has fallen in,
The breast to which we embraced is ruined,
The thighs with which we clasped have fallen away,
The lips with which we smiled are fretted with decay. . . .

Then, through the wind and rain, we heard the sound of voices just outside the *bure*. There was a low knock on the gable door. The next moment it was pushed open by Petero, a lantern in his hand, who turned to help inside someone behind him. As if blown in like a leaf, the tiny shrivelled figure of a very old man stepped over the threshold. For a moment he stood leaning on a long staff, gaining his bearings. The old European jacket of a dark, heavy cloth that he wore over his *sulu* hung from his shoulders like a scarecrow's coat. His har was cropped close to the skull. He had a small nutshell face, wizened and hollowed, with jutting brows and cheekbones, and when he turned towards us the lantern caught the nacreous gleam of blind, wide-open eyes. Petero guided him to the wall at the far end where with a sudden, surprising nimbleness he sat himself down, folding his stick-like legs beneath him and laying his staff in front of him.

'This is Taito,' said Petero.

In a sharp, piping voice the old man delivered himself of formal greetings, with an unfamiliar accent I had never heard before. He looked older than anyone else I had ever seen, yet when he spoke he radiated a fierce, crackling kind of vitality, a pungent personality, heat-dried, as it were, and perfectly preserved. Settling himself more comfortably, he shielded his face with his hand and with a touch of irascibility, asked for the lantern to be moved to one side as it burned his eyes.

'That is all he can see,' Petero told us. 'He was blinded by the juice of the *sinu* tree while he was chopping wood twenty years ago.'

The little *bure* soon filled up with other villagers. An elderly couple were crouched against the wall on our left, the woman haggard and tousle-headed with an elegant simian profile, the man of humbler appearance, wild and unkempt-looking, huddled in a blanket like a cave-man. Both had the flattish, primitive features of hill-people, and an air of animal remoteness in their manner.

Our two attendants were seated opposite, and another young girl with her smaller brother were squatting in the doorway with rounded glistening eyes and open mouths.

Silence fell. Then folding his hands in his lap, the old man gave a short preliminary cough and launched into the opening sentence of his saga.

'At the time of which I am speaking, the Roko Tui of Mathuata was a very hard man. . . .'

For the next two hours, in Adi Mei's soft English, I heard how the provincial tax for every family in those days was thirty logs of *bua-bua* wood a year. Twice in succession the load presented from Saivou was deemed unworthy for the construction of the Roko's new house and ordered to be returned, a trip of some fifteen miles. This was an insult. A council-of-war was held by the elders, and the old hill fortress of Thau-muré-muré was selected as a retreat for the rebels. Three *bures* were built near the summit—one of them a temple to their war-god—stockades were erected and thirteen pigs were killed and put in the *lovus*. Then, one by one, each of the surrounding villages received a *tabua* as an invitation to join in the revolt. Refusal was indicated by the return of the whale's tooth and on these villages the rebels descended, firing the houses and threatening the inhabitants into agreement. Taito named the 'villages of the cowards', one by one, in a tone of scorn.

Suddenly the old man scrambled to his feet and swung both arms downwards, as if driving a heavy blow. 'In every *bure*, crack went the clubs of the warriors across the bamboos! Spilt water was the sign of war!' He made a jabbing movement towards his stomach. 'One of them ran outside and a spear got him here. He trod on it and broke it. He was dead. Another was struck here.' He spun around and violently thrust at the small of his back, a wild little dervish figure grotesquely shadowed in the lamplight. 'He pulled it out but one of our clubs was ready for him. He begged for mercy. The reply of the chief was "Close his eyes!" He died.'

An enjoyable shiver ran through his listeners, who turned to watch me writing it down, word for word, in the English translation.

'Back in our village, my father kissed my mother and we climbed up to Thau-muré-muré with the others. My grandfather was there already. He had been preparing food in the *lovus*. When he unwrapped it, I thought it was the leg of pig.' Adi Mei paused for a moment, then moistening her lips continued with a tremor in her voice. 'Except that the fat was yellow. My grandfather ate the meat alone and I asked him why he took no *dalo* with it. "If you hate sombody," he replied, "you need no relish with him." I realized then that the food in the *lovus* was the arms and legs of the dead men. My grandfather gave some to my father saying the god had told him, "If you are frightened eat pork. If you are brave you will eat human flesh and be victorious in battle." My father ate some in the end, but he had to run away to be sick afterwards, though no one knew this except myself, so he was not shamed.'

There were visits from the gods, Taito went on. One spoke from the rafters of the *bure*, saying his name was Levi of the Bible story, and warning them of the approach of disaster to Thau-muré-muré. The god took his departure walking slowly across the mat—the old man placed his hands one after the other on the ground in front of him. The people could hear him though they could not see him. Another god appeared as a shellfish who stood upright at the *yaggona* bowl and drank with them—this was a favourable omen. Still more came at night-time as they were performing *mekes* by the light of reed fires. These took the form of humans armed with fans and axes. They told the people they had become jealous of the Christian gods and would show their power by giving them victory in their battle against the Government.

Here Taito paused. He had reached the climax of his tale and everyone hung on his words. Nudged by his wife, the man on our left who had been lying down shrouded in his blanket, sat up and curled himself into a cross-legged position. The lantern flame flickered in the wind under the door. In the far corner the young girl crouched holding her brother, her expression rapt, a silver crucifix rising and falling in the open neck of her dress.

'Then came the Government soldiers in their white *sulus* and black shirts,' the story continued, Taito's voice dropping to a sibilant whisper. 'The Governor was with them in his fine uniform. He wore spectacles, I remember, a new sight in those days. From the stockade we watched them drilling on the *rara* below—as a boy I thought it a strange kind of war-dance for fighting men. We laughed up there in Thau-muré-muré. There were just on a hundred of us wearing the black paint of war and skirts of leaves. We were armed with spears while the enemy for all their fine clothes, carried only long sticks over their shoulders. We had blocked the pathway up the cliffside and we were ready for them. But the next morning, two women came running to tell us that the soldiers were coming from behind the hill.'

The old man leaned forward, his face strained as though listening for something.

'Suddenly there was a great bang, like a thunder-clap. My grandfather gave a cry and raised his hand to his forehead where something seemed to be *stuck*. Then he fell forward over the stockade, rolling right down the hillside. The noise grew louder. Soldiers appeared through the trees, with smoke coming from their sticks. Men fell all around, my father among them. Blood was pouring from his chest as he lay there. He told me I must run, get away as fast as I could——'

For the first time, he seemed to falter, staring past us into nothingness, his lips moving without sound. Then I saw gleaming on one cheek the almost unnoticed, rheumy tear of old age. With a sense of shock I realized that he was not here with us at all but back on the stockades of Thau-muré-muré, a frightened boy crouched among dying men, the noise of thunder in his ears, and the air full of the unknown stench of gunpowder. Vaguely, Taito smudged the back of his hand across his face. Clearing his throat, he went on, 'I said good-bye to my father. I wrapped myself in a blanket, took up a piece of baked *dalo* and made my escape down the side of the hill. I ran till I got into the bush. I slept and walked on again the next day and reached at last a village in Thakaudrove Province where some of my father's relatives were living. There I stayed until it was safe for me to return to Saivon. . . . I have been here ever since.'

It was the end of the story. Five hours had passed in the telling of it. The old man bowed his head and sat motionless, his hands folded in his lap. No one spoke for a while. Finally the man and the woman said together in low, heartfelt voices, '*Vinaka, vinaka!*' (Well done!)

'*Vinaka*!' murmured everyone else in turn, regarding the old man with expressions of awe. Soon there would be no one left to make such tales as these, and they wanted to remember him, his face and his way of speaking.

Nodding to himself, Taito returned the courtesies. When I asked him, through Adi Mei, how he was able to remember in detail the events of so long ago, he looked surprised. His reply was, 'But it is all there before me as though it were still going on. To tell of it is just like the reading of a map.'

I thanked him again. With a sigh, he picked up his staff and got to his feet. Raising his hand in farewell, he made his way out on Petero's arm with the dignity befitting a survivor not only of war but of history.

When the others had gone Mei and I retired to sleep. Despite all my efforts, she insisted that I should have the bed and she a pile of mats on the floor. There were no blankets but I rolled myself in one of the bed mats against the cold which, for Fiji, was intense. Shivering, I watched through the bed curtains the dying lamp flicker over the rough wooden beams and piled ferns, the dark shape of a rat slipping between the rafters, the rain swishing down on the thatch overhead—a woodcutter's cottage from a Grimm's fairy-tale with just the same unreal mixture of the cosy and the frightening about it. The wind that surged round the walls seemed to fade into a distant *meke* chant, deep and monotonous and dully menacing. Singers or wind, wind or singers, I thought hazily as all at once the flame went out and I fell asleep.

The next morning we went down to the stream to bathe before breakfast. The men of the village were setting off for the food gardens with baskets and knives, the women busy over their cooking fires, the smaller children clinging to their skirts. Pale shreds of mist still clung to the slopes of the valley below. After we had eaten, Petero called us outside and pointed out a volcanic tower of bush-covered rock, jutting up from the horizon about a mile away.

'That's Thau-muré-muré,' he said.

'Does anyone go there nowadays?'

Petero replied to Adi Mei in Fijian, then added something else with a grin. 'Only ghosts,' Mei told me. 'Besides, Petero says, what reason would the villagers have to go up there now? The Seagaga people pay their taxes and live in peace nowadays!'

Then the car was hooting at the bottom of the hill and it was time to collect our things and make our farewells.

Back in Suva, the records I looked up in the Government archives exactly confirmed, detail for detail Taito's account of the Seagaga Revolt of 1895. Writing twelve years later, Basil Thomson reflected: 'The siege of Thaumuremure will not loom large in history. The garrison numbered at the most one hundred persons; they had no arms but their spears while the besiegers carried Martini-Henry rifles. But the garrison bravely blew their conch-shells and danced the death dance to the last. It was all over in a few minutes. Nine men were shot dead and the rest took to their heels, to surrender a few days later, while the Government force could boast but three spear wounds. . . . The outbreak is interesting in that it shows how the Fijians confuse Christianity with the Government, and cannot throw off the one without repudiating the other; and how cannibalism was a religious rite and not the mere gratification of a depraved taste.'

But more clearly than the scholarly tones of all the historians, I heard and shall always hear the thin, cracked voice of Taito relating the last battle-saga of old Fiji through the eyes of a boy who was there.

16

Wind-from-the-West

'So-and-so tourists, I call these people who want to come along for the ride. So-and-so cameras clicking all day.' Miss Johnson, a tall rangy woman in her forties with piercing blue eyes and a knife-edged Australian accent surveyed me with a sardonic grin. The Government health sister at Labasa, she was about to embark on a sea trip to the northern-most point of Vanua Levu dispensing polio vaccine to the village children, with me as her passenger. 'But when the D.O. asked me to take you on, what could I say?'

I smiled ingratiatingly and said that at least I didn't have a camera with me.

'It'll be terribly rough, it always is,' she ground on, ignoring this. 'When the forecast says moderate seas it means a heavy swell, and when it says rough it's a real hurricane. The last time I took some people along, they were seasick all the way. What sort of condition are you in?'

'Not too bad I don't think—oh, except for my Achilles tendon.'

There was a gruelling silence as I demonstrated a Byronic limp around the hotel room.

'You'll never make the Steps,' Miss Johnson announced finally.

What exactly were the Steps, I asked, with a sinking heart.

'Well, most of the time the weather's too bad to land on the beach at Thikobia, so we have to go round the other side and climb a kind of iron pole with rungs that goes up through a hole in the cliff. If you're no good at heights you'd better not look down behind you either. Then there's a climb up the rock face that's pretty tricky in wet weather, and after that it's quite a walk through the bush to get to the village.'

I had always been determined to get to Thikobia, the last tiny island in the Fiji group going north-east, if only because—like the explorers Tasman and Wilson, neither Miss Gordon-Cumming, Mrs. Smythe or Mrs. Wallis had actually landed there and I would have outstripped them all at last. Europeans I had spoken to seemed equally vague about the place, isolated as it was from the mainland of Vanua Levu by a thirty-mile stretch of reef-strewn sea.

A sudden friendly clap descended on my shoulder. 'Don't worry —we'll make it, I expect,' remarked Miss Johnson briskly. 'Anyway, we're going across to Kia first and then up along the Udu coast and that's easy. You'd better get yourself packed.'

An hour or so later, primed with Grand Eastern gin-and-tonics and a good dinner, we walked down to the little jetty in front of the hotel. A trim white craft was drawn up alongside with the glamorous look of all island boats at night, yellow windows mirrored in the water, white rails glinting faintly above, a glimpse of brown faces round a hurricane lamp, the plunk of a guitar. We climbed aboard and a leathery, astute-looking little man stumped forward to meet us with a smile of Puckish charm. This was Poasa, the captain Miss Johnson said, as we shook hands. Behind him three other people got up from the game of cards they were playing round the wheel, a hulking giant in overalls who was Likini the engineer, his assistant Vilaime (William), a youngish man with the golden skin and classical features of the Lau people, and the ship's cook, a sort of coloured Harry Seacombe by the name of Waisea.

Inside the tiny dining cabin a middle-aged Fijian woman was sitting at the table reading the Fijian paper, *Volagauna*. She stood up and took off her glasses as we came in, a small stocky figure in her nurse's khaki skirt and white blouse with a face of great character and intelligence.

'And this is Taina, my offsider,' drawled Miss Johnson. 'Eh, Taina?'

'That's right, Sistah,' replied Taina, with a grin. The two women exchanged glances of good-humoured affection.

From outside came the rattle and clink of the anchor chain. The engine sneezed into life and slowly, imperceptibly we began to move. After Taina had shown me the little two-bunk cabin I would have to myself for the trip, I went up on deck for a few minutes. With a regular snore the *Thagi-mai-Ra* was gliding down the river towards the sea. The water flapped gently under the bows as we slid past the lamp-lit outlines of houses and shops. Then there were only the tangled shadows of the banks on either side shrouded in bush, a twining mangrove root or overhanging branch illuminated for a moment by our passing before slipping away again, folded in darkness. Ahead of us, the lights of a sugar boat twinkled in the estuary.

'Waiting for the tide,' said Miss Johnson at my side. 'They anchor here for the night, like us. Then with first light tomorrow we'll be on our way to Kia.'

It was the sudden throb of movement that woke me early the following morning. Outside the sun was sparkling on a calm sea and after breakfast I climbed up on the cabin roof with some books. One of them, a travel diary by the Victorian archaeologist and explorer Alfred Maudsley, who along with a number of other interesting personalities formed an eighteenth-century-type court around Sir Arthur Gordon, Fiji's first Governor, had provided me at last with a pen portrait of my Miss Gordon-Cumming.

'She is a very tall, plain woman,' wrote the ungallant Alfred. 'A regular globe-trotter, wonderfully good-tempered, no tact, very pushing when she wants anything done, and yet one of the best-natured creatures in the world. She is sufficiently clothed in suits of brown holland or blue serge and wears an enormous pith hat. . . . I'm afraid we all tease the poor woman a good deal, but then she does rise so beautifully and besides is quite capable of taking care of herself.'

This description made it even easier to imagine her in the situations in which I found myself. For, of course, Constance had made this very journey to the island of Kia that the *Thagi-mai-Ra* was now embarked on, and as usual, 'the whole coast with its fine mountain ranges reminded me strongly of Argyllshire, the *noko-noko* (casurina) trees taking the place of the birch.' At Kia itself she had spent a happy day breakfasting with the Chief on a canoe-sail under a tree, searching for specimens of the finely woven mats, carved bowls and stone axes which were the traditional products of the islands, and sketching from a canoe with a 'cute, sturdy little fellow' of a boatman. The night was spent on mats in the *vale in lotu* of church house, 'my big sun hat acting as my pillow'—no doubt the pith helmet noted by Mr. Maudsley.

She made no mention, though, of the mysterious cannon which is still supposed to stand on the highest peak of Kia though how it got there no one knows. When finally the island came into view it seemed quite natural for such a thing to crown the extraordinary, scarred facades of stone flecked with bush that rose from the sea like the ruins of a medieval castle. I asked Poasa if he knew the site of the gun. He waited for a moment standing alongside me at the rail, as the boat swung past a jagged outcrop of rock. Then he pointed quickly up to a tiny v-shaped cleft in the topmost range. 'There, just there it is.'

'Is it still there, though?' I asked, peering at clumps of trees through the glasses. I was thinking of the well-known English District Commissioner whose private passion had been his collection of ship's cannons picked up in outlying parts of the Fiji Group.

'Yea, yea, it still there. All covered with bush though now and nobody climb up there nowadays. You ask the King. He tell you all about it maybe.'

'The King?'

'The King of Kia. Likini and Viliame take you to his house when we land. He story you about the cannon.' Poasa turned his back to the rails and surveyed his ship with a smile of pleasure. 'You like the *Thagi-mai-Ra*?'

'Very much,' I said.

'It mean Wind-from-the-West.' He spread his arms as if to embrace the horizon. 'A nice name, eh? *Thagi-mai-Ra*,' he repeated with a nod, then still smiling, turned and descended the steps to the wheelroom to supervise our landing.

Round the rocky bluff of the island a scene of gentle contrast had pivoted into view. Tarpaulins flapping in the breeze we were chugging towards a smooth sloping beach framed in green hills. The long shadows of coconut palms with the sun behind them lay across the white sand in a palisade of light and shade, reaching down to the water's edge. Thatched roofs clustered silvery-brown under the trees. From the wooden schoolroom behind the beach came the sound of children singing. Along a grassy bank had been lined up in white painted stones the words Kia District School. It was like drawing up at an old-fashioned village railway station in England on a hot summer afternoon.

'It is called Brown's Island from an American of that name who lived there while preparing a cargo for one of his country's vessels,' wrote the first and perhaps the strangest European visitors to Kia. These were the Brethren, half a dozen missionaries bound from Tahiti to Canton who with their wives and families set up a kind of

Robinson Crusoe establishment here in 1809 while repairs were being made to their ship. Usually inhabited, the island was vacant at that time because of recent massacres along the adjoining coast. 'It is about half a mile in circumference, has several trees on it and some coconuts, the leaves of which we intend to thatch our hut. The soil is sandy and the heat is very great,' noted the Brethren.

Despite the heat there were the usual prayer meetings and dogged readings from the works of a Doctor Dodderidge and the Reverend Burder's 'Village Sermons', punctuated by meals of salt pork brought from Tahiti and taro, fish and coconuts purchased from passing canoes. Not much love seems to have been lost between the Europeans and their Fijian callers. The Fijians apparently referred to them as *sa bati kadi* or grasping, while the Brethren described the natives as 'very hard and cunning in their dealings, more so than any of the islanders we have seen'.

These visits also aroused alarm in the hearts of the Brethren for the safety of their womenfolk, who must undoubtedly have been the first white women in Fiji. 'They have great curiosity to see our women and would no doubt, if they could, seize them and take them. . . . We understand that polygamy is common here among the chiefs, if not among the common people.'

This problem, however, was solved by sending the wives on board a neighbouring American vessel collecting sandalwood, while the men continued on the island. Occasionally they were disturbed by strange lights near the shore and conch shells blowing 'which we know are used in war'. But there was no open trouble and when their ship was ready the Brethren sailed peacefully away and were never heard of again. One wonders though what the natives made of the somewhat original selection of farewell gifts they left behind —'medical apparatus such as amputating, dissecting, trepanning, cupping, teeth-drawing and midwifery instruments, and *a case containing apparatus for restoring suspended animation*'. (The italics are mine—the Brethren obviously saw nothing odd in this.) It is only to be hoped that full use of the last item was made by the local sorcerer to enrich his reputation among his tribe.

A group of women were waiting for us on the beach as Viliame and Likini pulled the little rowing-boat up on to the sand. Likini explained to them that I would like to pay my respects to the King. An elderly lady nodded and led us towards a path alongside the village while Miss Johnson and Taira set off in the direction of the school with the rest of the women. Under the bread-fruit trees two large *bures* came into view, well-built with neat cobbled doorsteps.

'This is where the King lives,' said Likini. The elderly lady disappeared through the back entrance of the first house, and at the same moment through the front door emerged the King. He was a smally wiry man of about sixty, barefoot and clad in a pair of old white shorts and a khaki shirt. He had a face that reminded me of photographs of Picasso, with a high forehead of a rich mahogany polish surmounted by a thatch of silver-grey hair. He approached with dignity and we shook hands. I then presented my passport to respectability—a large green folder containing a registry of all the families on the island which Doctor Verrier had asked me to take with me for the Tui Kia. Now a warm smile was added to the handshake and we were ushered inside. There were white mats of an unusual fineness on the floor. A length of *masi* decorated the centre beam with the word Welcome printed in the middle. A coloured photograph of Prince Philip hung on the wall, an oil lamp on either side of him. A young man in a *sulu*, sitting in the corner, got up and was introduced as the King's son.

These formalities over, the King seated himself at the head of the room and gestured to us to join him in a circle. Likini, who had established himself as my *mata-ni-uanua*, presented our gifts of cigarettes and *yaggona*. Then with a frown of concentration on his heavy, good-natured face, he explained that I would like to ask some questions about Kia if His Majesty had no objections.

His Majesty acquiesced with a stately smile and, with Likini as interpreter, proceeded to tell me that there were about two hundred people on the island. The Kia people were famous fisherman—not reef or shallow fishing as in most parts of Fiji but deep-sea fishing. They took their catches to Labasa market, also mats and baskets to sell, because the weaving of the Kia women was well known for its fine quality. I said I had heard of this, also of their pottery. Was this still to be found? The King shook his head, shrugged his shoulders. Alas, no longer. It was the same with *masi*. The women were too lazy to make it nowadays and preferred to buy cotton cloth from Labasa.

I was mentally forming a question about the cannon when Likini put in with a grin, 'But they were not always lazy, I think.' A remark obviously designed to remind the King of a story. It did and the story, laced with laughter and gestures, was how long ago the crew of a visiting whaling-ship were looked after, fed and housed by the people of Kia while they hunted the surrounding waters. In return for this hospitality, the captain presented to the Tui Kia of those days a cannon from the ship as a memento of their stay. Although the people were unable to operate it, being without either the ammunition or the knowledge, they were most proud of the gift and were only anxious to keep it where no one else could take it away. After much discussion it was decided to place the trophy on the topmost crag of the island, about eight hundred feet above ground. The ascent proved more difficult that they had ever imagined, as a troop of the village's strongest men tugged and hauled the cannon on ropes of sinnet up the precipitous slopes. Half-way up, they gave in. And who was it who took over and finally got the cannon to the top? Why, the women of the island, of course. Or so the story went.

'Perhaps she would like to meet some of the ladies of Kia?' the King suggested. I said I would like to very much and with involved exchanges of courtesy we took our leave. Outside the elderly lady was waiting for us again, and led us over to one of the village *bures*, where a circle of women were gathered in cosy gossip. One of them spoke English, she said. With some relief Likini and Viliame sat down to wait outside and smoke a cigarette.

'Please sit here,' said my hostess, indicating the bed in the corner of the room. She was an imposing woman who looked well capable of hauling a cannon to the top of a cliff, with long, heavy features and shrewd, close-set eyes under a pair of beetle brows.

I said I would prefer to join the circle on the floor and that nothing could be softer than the mats of Kia. This seemed to amuse them, not necessarily as an expression of truth but as the kind of formal flattery which the Fijians themselves like to produce on such occasions. We discussed children and families in the usual way. 'But where are you going? Why are you going?' they kept asking, and seemed puzzled with the idea of a trip made not for necessity but pleasure, especially detached from one's family or relations. It seemed a very well-stocked household, I thought, looking round at the kettles and frying-pans in the corner, the row of tinned food and jars of tea and sugar on the shelf, the *sulus* hanging from nails in the wall. When I said so, expressing it politely, there was a roar of laughter.

'But, you see, this is the store!' cried the beetle-browed proprietress, producing from the shelf a weighing-hook and a cash-box. 'We are the town of Kia in here!'

The joke lasted several minutes, after which they produced an envelope of photographs to entertain me. Likini and Viliame were invited in, with much giggling and shuffling round, to inspect these. They were mostly old snapshots taken by visiting officials, but among them was a more recent one depicting the visit of the Governor and his wife the previous year. Enshrined in flowers they were being carried ashore in the traditional way on a huge double litter of bamboo. Viliame seized on this with a crow of delight. 'This is the picture the Russians were so mad about, eh? I read about it in the *Fiji Times*. They put it in their papers and say that you British are the conquerors and make us your slaves.' He threw back his handsome head and laughed, then looked quickly around us, his eyes flashing. 'And what do they know of us? How could such people understand that we do such things because we wish to, because they are our customs and right for us. Most of all, because they make us happy.'

All this was rapidly translated by the proprietress and greeted with explanations of first disbelief and then irate agreement. Calm was restored by the appearance of a clutch of small children in the doorway who were pushed forward one by one by their mothers to shake hands. Their expressions of wavering trepidation changed to incredulous delight when they received instead a palmful of toffees.

Then it was time to walk back towards the boat. The sand bleached and powdery was hot under our bare feet as we followed the path that wound between the trees and the tall grass fringeing the beach. Inside a kind of wooden corral some women piling up coconuts in neatly stacked pyramids straightened to wave to us as we passed. Out in the bay the launch's hooter sounded twice across the ribbon of blue sea. The echo died away in the cool darkness of the bread-fruit groves behind us, where canopies of huge fan-shaped leaves gleamed above the pale green globes ripening beneath. The air was full of an indefinable flower smell. I understood how Miss Gordon-Cumming felt when she sat on this beach, ardent in her dark-blue serge, and wrote, 'I only wish it were possible to convey to you all the impressions of delight of such a day as this—all the thousand details of beauty which give such light and gladness to the life I find so fascinating though it sounds so dry and dead when I put it into words. . . . A calm glittering blue sea, white coral sands sparkling in the sunlight, ourselves in the deep cool shade of dense glossy foliage whence bunches of rosy, silky tassels float down with every breath of air as playthings for tiny brown children in lightest raiment. Close by are the graves of successive generations of these hardy fishers who have lived and died on this tiny isle without an aspiration beyond it. Now the graves are overgrown with tangles of marine convolvulus with lilac blossom, while the starry white convolvulus hangs in light drapery from the rocks beyond. And beyond the sea rise the blue mountain ranges of Vanua Levu in ever changing light and shadow. . . .'

Schoolchildren lined the sand outside the school as we rowed back to the *Thagi-mai-Ra*. Miss Johnson said they had enjoyed their 'lollies' as they called the sweet-tasting drops of oral vaccine. Some had tried to rejoin the queue for a second helping but Taina had been prepared for this and had promptly sorted out the offenders.

Back on board there was a short conference between Poasa and Miss Johnson.

'Poasa says it's too late to make much headway this evening, so we'll do some fishing instead,' she announced finally. 'Okay, boys?' The four men grinned and nodded. 'Good, Sistah,' said Waisea. 'Then we eat *walu* for supper tonight.'

Ten minutes later we were back round the far side of the island. Dusk was falling as we dropped anchor, and from the rocks exploded a cloud of white gull-like birds, screaming and wheeling up into the darkened air.

'*Dre*,' said Poasa. 'Wherever they come, there is plenty of fish.'

Two lanterns were lit and the little boat became an enclosed world of its own, rocking gently in a pool of gold, ringed around by the black mass of the land and the white breakers of the reef away on the horizon. Everyone chose their favourite spot round the edge of the deck and let down their lines, baited with meat, in sacramental silence. In less than five minutes there was a shout as Likini landed the first catch, a giant *walu* who came up lunging and fighting on the line, teeth bared, eyes rolling with a look of almost animal hatred at his captor. In a final defiant flash of strength he grazed the skin on

Likini's arm with his struggles before he was finally flung on to the deck. Miss Johnson caught the next. An hour later, the well of the boat looked more like a fishmonger's slab, ankle-deep in the shiny, slippery silver flesh, gills flapping, mouths gaping, the light gleaming on scales of garnet, green and blue. Some were long, thin, sinister specimens, others large and flat and good for eating, while in a bucket a dozen tiny striped morsels, bright as paint, swam round and round like clockwork toys, waiting to be used as bait. Cane knives were soon hacking up fresh steaks for dinner and the delicious fragrance of frying came wafting up from the kitchen.

After we had eaten, glutted with the sight, smell and taste of fish, we all went up to the little top deck and wrapped in blankets, sat cross-legged under the canvas awning in a cage of moonlight, singing and singing until it was time to go to bed.

17

David of the Reef

The next morning as we prepared to move on again, there was the sound of a worried conference outside on the bows between Poasa, Likini and Viliame.

'The anchor stuck in the coral, Sistah,' reported Poasa. 'Viliame gonna go under for him.'

A short *salu* twisted round his thighs, Viliame stood poised in the sunshine on the edge of the deck, a bronze Mercury on a museum pedestal. Then with a war-cry, the statue plunged down in a spectacular dive and disappeared under the water. After a moment, he reappeared and shaking his head, grasped the edge of the boat breathing hard, the water beading his oiled skin. The third try he came up with a beam of triumph.

'Okay! I pull him loose! We go now!'

There was no sign of life on the cliffside of the island. But as we drew away a line of people came into view slowly picking their way across the rocks, about a dozen men and women moving with an air of solemnity across that barren landscape.

'They will be going to the feast,' said Taina. 'They told us in the village that today is the tenth day since the death of one of the old men of Kia, so there are ceremonies to be made by his family and his friends from all parts of the island.'

Then slowly, Kia was gone, a dissolving speck of green in the blue of sea and sky. We were turning into the coast of Vanua Levu now, following the chain of honeycomb peaks, green sloping hills, and white-looped bays that tapered away to the tip of the lizard's tail at Udu Point. These shallow seas of Mathuata had once been the richest fishing grounds in the whole of the Group for the *bêche-de-mer* ships of the nineteenth century. Staring out in the hypnotic haze of midday one saw, not the war-fleets of the Thakaudrove coast, but an even vaster army of 12,000 men who in January 1852 sailed over this horizon in a great shoal of eighty long canoes to catch *bêche-de-mer* for King Thakobau. One thousand *piculs* had to be produced to pay for the fine new American vessel ordered by the King from Captain Wallis. The King sailed in state in the *Thakobau,* as it was named, at the head of the expedition, and set a strenuous example by diving and fishing industriously himself. But despite its size the enterprise was a disaster, defeated by the passive resistance of the Mathuata people and their chiefs who refused to be bullied into working-parties by the Bau warriors and regarded the whole thing as piece of Thakobau impudence unsanctioned by custom and therefore doomed to failure. The unfortunate captain never received his payment. He left the ship to Thakobau though, and cutting his losses went off in disgust to find cargo elsewhere.

Seven years earlier, he and his wife had sailed the Mathuata coast themselves and from a diarist's point of view this was Mrs. Wallis country as noted in her journal *Five Years Among the Cannibals.* From now onwards Miss Gordon-Cumming was almost left behind, replaced by this sturdy New England lady, also plain and of middle-age, who met the trials and perils of that still barbarous period with a typically American spirit of enterprise and independence. Tacking in and out of the village ports in 1845, as we were now, one glimpses her sending ashore a pair of muskets as a plea for the life of an erring wife of the chief, chatting persuasively with heathen priests who threatened them with hurricanes, embroidering sashes for the Mathuata ruler Ritova, sailing the meantime 'through placid lagoons, past golden sunsets, sparkling waters, fleecy clouds and dusky natives . . .'.

Later in the afternoon I was joined on the cabin roof by the dusky native who had that morning extracted the anchor from the coral.

'You like I should write down some of the songs we sing last night for you?' Viliame inquired, with a smiling mixture of delicacy and bravado. 'Then you can sing properly with us.'

I said I would like it very much and handed him my notebook and pencil. Squatting down on his heels, he carefully wrote out in a clear, round hand a selection of favourite verses, translating them for me as he went along. 'This is a love song—"Please Come Back To Me". . . . This is a sad one—"Good-bye To My Island".'

When he had finished, he sat down on the other end of the roof opposite me. 'You like I story you about my family?'

I said I would like it very much and for the next half-hour he told me about life on the island of Vanua Vatu—which meant Stone Land—in the middle of the Lau Group, far away to the south-east of Fiji's two main islands, where the people are mainly Polynesian descent and closely linked with Tonga. Poasa and Likini both came from another Lauan island, he told me, Kabara about forty miles away. Life in Lau was quite different from the rest of Fiji, Viliame said. 'It's the place for fun—lots of singing and dancing all through the night. 'Not like Suva,' he added, turning down his mouth. He had been there working as a P.W.D. engineer. Now he was working for the administrative department and living in Labasa. 'I'm gonna go back to Lau pretty soon, nothing to worry about there.'

I asked him if he had a big family. Six brothers, two sisters, he told me. His father was a carpenter. His face changed as he spoke and he hesitated for a moment as if making a decision. 'A younger brother died,' he went on looking out to sea. 'He was sixteen. Something to do with his heart. When he got ill, my family sent me to the bush-doctor—witch-doctor like you people say—to get something done to make him better. They thought it was the work of an enemy that he had fallen sick. I took the old man some *yaggona*. Well, first he "talked to the *yaggona*", then he sent me back with a medicine made from leaves. My brother got worse. When the A.M.O. came he said, "It is too late." That is why since then I can never believe in *drau-ni-kau*. I don't want anything to do with it, man.' He turned to face me again his expression drawn-looking and said earnestly, 'But one thing's for true—it still goes on.

"This boy I knew in school. His father died. He didn't have any sickness, he just got weaker and weaker, so everyone knew it was *drau-ni-kau*. The week after two men enemies of his father took the boy by force to where his father was buried. There they drove long sticks into the grave, many times. Then they ran away. This was to stop the spirit coming back to haunt them. They took the boy with them as protection.'

Suddenly he sprang up and pointed alongside. A school of flying fish went skimming over the water as light as dragon-flies, then disappeared again beneath the surface. On our left a small solitary island with a crown of palms and a strip of white beach receded into the distance like a mirage of happiness.

'Why don't you stay in Fiji and live on an island like that?' asked Viliame, jumping down on to the deck again. He shielded his eyes with his hand, and looked up with a grin. 'We can bring you your food by boat and Likini and I will build you a house and cut down your copra for you! You could be peaceful there—not like in England with all those moving stairs and televisions!'

We looked again but the island had slipped down over the rim of the sea, lost in the yellow glow of approaching sunset. The *Thagi-mai-Ra* had put on speed. The village of Visogo was our next port of call and we were due to arrive before dark. It was still twilight when we finally turned into the little bay and dropped anchor. Within a few minutes, small boys in home-made canoes came gliding past close to the windows to inspect the cabins. They told us there was to be a big wedding tomorrow. Everyone in the village was busy making preparations.

'Well, I shall still be there at the school with my lollies, first thing,' declared Miss Johnson, wagging a warning finger.

The bullet-headed group grinned back at her, as Taina translated, then waving, poled gracefully away again. The contrast between these easy-going exchanges and Mrs. Wallis's arrival at this village more than a century ago was striking.

'This morning a canoe filled with natives came off to see the "lioness", a white one never having been seen by the natives of this part of Fiji. The wonder was gazed at and every motion watched with the most intense interest. . . . One chief when he saw me, actually screamed and called his followers to see the *Marama ni Papalangi* (Woman of the Europeans).' Gaining courage, one of the chief's wives later asked Mr. Wallis why he did not bring more of his wives with him. When told that he had no more, the lady expressed disbelief, exclaiming, 'But why? You are a *Turaga-Levu* (Big Chief) are you not?'

'Ah, the white men make gods of their wives!' another observant *marama* had remarked on coming aboard the captain's schooner.

'Yes,' said her husband, with quick presence of mind. 'Because the white women are wise, but Feejeean women are foolish.'

So Mrs. Wallis reported in her journal, at least.

From the shore lights sprang up one by one through the darkness —not the fixed illumination of electricity but the wavering glow-worm twinkle of oil lamps set in narrow doorways. Lazily supine the

P

half-moon drifted up again behind the trees. The sheen on the water was as smooth as if we were on an enormous lake, land-locked with the black, indented ramp of the hills almost encircling us except for a furrow of silver behind that led to the open sea. Nothing, I thought, was so intense as the silence of a boat at anchor at night in a sheltered bay after the throbbings and tossings of the day. Very faintly, like the ring of glass, the sound of a guitar came over the water.

'You want to go ashore?' asked Likini, after supper. 'Come! We go!'

I gave him some money to buy *yaggona*, collected a carton of cigarettes and four of us climbed down into the boat, Likini, Viliame, Taina, and myself. Waisea was fishing. The dining-table cleared, Miss Johnson and Poasa had settled down to a game of cards.

The Visogo landing was a long jetty of loose-piled stones. We tied up the boat and got out, walking in single file through a mirror reflection of the village that lay on the surface of the water on either side, clear-cut as an etching—two aigrette palms on tall curved stems, the silhouetted ridge-poles of the high old-fashioned *bures*, pinpricks of lanterns, the dark blue of the night sky beyond, and the low-hanging tropical stars. Shadowy figures moved over the grass. Someone carried a brazier of fire from one house to another, an orange glow in a nimbus of golden faces.

When Captain Wallis landed here to inspect the *bêche-de-mer* house, Mrs. Wallis insisted on coming, too, announcing that if it was safe for him, it was safe for her. Fijians with clubs and muskets lined the beach but made no move towards them. Inside the hut a deep trench had been dug along its whole length and filled with burning logs of wood for curing the fish. 'The glare and heat from such an immense fire, surrounded as we were by nearly naked savages numbering perhaps fifty in all including women who had joined us, sent a strange sort of thrill through my frame. . . .'

At the end of the jetty a small neatly-dressed Fijian with a tooth-brush moustache was waiting to meet us with a lantern. He was the local schoolmaster delighted to welcome me, he told me in a precise English accent. Likini and Viliame and Taina, he was well acquainted with from previous visits. A volley of hand-claps burst from the meeting-house as he hurried us past. 'A bit of a grog-session going on there, I'm afraid,' he explained.

Likini disappeared into a wooden shanty opposite and emerged a minute later with a bundle of *yaggona*.

'Now let us pay our respects to Ratu Elisoni,' said Master, as the others called him. 'He is the *Tui Visogo*, a very fine old man I think you will agree!'

Stooping, he led the way into a tall, narrow *bure*, raised high off the grounds on stilts. Inside, a circle of elderly men were seated cross-legged round an open lamp. As we filed in through the door a tall, prophetic-looking figure stood up to greet us. Bent and thin, he had a striking face, light-skinned, with the jagged ruins of small, handsome features surrounded by an aureole of stiff, white hair. Most extraordinary were his eyes, wide-set and milky-blue, with the staring, opaque appearance of approaching blindness and it was perhaps this that gave him an air of tragic grandeur; a Lear drawn by Blake, despite the old serge jacket and faded *sulu*. With quiet dignity he shook hands and directed me to sit in the only canvas chair in the room. The rest of our party settled themselves alongside on the floor, facing the circle of elders. One by one, the old men who had remained motionless and expressionless until now, came over in crouching attitudes to shake hands. There is a solemnity, I thought, about shaking hands with someone to whom this is an unfamiliar action. It is done slowly and at length with a concentrated attention on the correctness of the grip. The Chief who, after receiving the languidly extended forefingers of Colonel Smythe, whispered, 'Why did he only give me two fingers instead of his whole hand?' was quite right to complain. 'It seemed to me that I had the hand of a little boy instead of a great chief come all the way from England,' the old man had commented witheringly.

After the handshaking a formal silence followed. Eventually it was broken by Likini who pushed forward our *sevu-sevu* of *yaggona* into the centre of the mat and made a speech of presentation full of sensational pauses and perorations. Ratu Elisoni in his reply, spoke of the pleasure they took from our visit and the regrettable humbleness of the surroundings. Exclamations of *Mana! Dina!*—True! Yes, indeed!—punctuated these formalities. At their close, a beautiful girl of about eighteen appeared in the doorway and stooping, came forward towards us.

'This is the Chief's daughter,' Taina stage-directed in a whisper. 'You shake hands to her. She has a present for you.'

With inexpressible charm and grace the girl bent in front of me and handed me two long-handled fans made of cock's feathers, one white, one black. Then with a quick hand-clap and a sudden brilliant smile, she was gone again.

'This is the kind the women make in these parts,' Ratu Elisoni said. 'You will keep them as a memory of Visogo.'

Then through the schoolmaster he went on to tell me in a tone of pride, that the people of this village came originally from Bau and were closely related with that island even now. Some time before Cession, it seemed, their ancestors came over from Bau in two canoes, sailing along this coast in search of a new home. They saw a good piece of flat land and decided to settle here.

What was the village famous for, I asked him. Its mat-making perhaps, a special kind of fish or shell?

'Its warriors,' replied the old man simply, with a flash of vigour in his voice. 'Whenever the Labasa people wanted good fighters, they had to come to us!'

The elders cackled gleeful agreement, nodding their heads.

He would tell me a story, Ratu Elisoni said, handed down by his great-grandfather to his grandfather, and by his father to him. When the canoes came from Bau they also brought with them two goddesses to look after the people. Their names were Adi Wassa-Wassa and Adi Marama Rua and they lived on the hill above the village in a great *baka* tree. Under the tree was a stone shaped like a bowl and in this the people placed gifts of shells so that they might be victorious in battle. Round the tree of the goddesses grew a creeper which the young men tied to their spears so that they might never miss their mark. Whenever people dug too near the roots they would find blood in the soil. For this was the tree of the warriors, and Adi Wassa-Wassa and Adi Marama Rua were the Goddesses of War.

'Even nowadays, people may see their sign, a very bright light that moves swiftly down the hill, then disappears again in darkness,' the old man concluded. He looked down at his hands. 'When this happens it means that a chief is going to die.'

There was silence again. Two of the elders murmured together. From outside the *bure* came the sound of voices. Ratu Elisoni said something to the schoolmaster, picked up an old canvas airline bag and a torch and went outside.

'The relatives of the bride have come from their village to make presentations of food for tomorrow's feast,' Master explained.

'Hadn't we better leave then?'

'No, no. This is not ceremonial. Merely a brief handing-over, a few courtesies. He will be back in a minute, he says.'

From just behind where the Chief had been sitting a bundle of mats seemed to stir. A small hand was flung out and the bundle subsided again to the sound of quiet breathing.

'It is the grandson of Ratu Elisoni,' murmured one of the elders, smiling. 'He is always by his side, night and day.'

Conversation was desultory as everyone was trying to listen to what was going on outside. We heard the Chief speaking, then the voices of his visitors, low and humble, and the rattle of hand-claps. Suddenly there was the violent squealing of young pigs, followed by chickens cackling, and finally a wild, flapping sound like a giant bird beating the air.

'Those are the turtles,' someone said.

By the time the old man returned, *yaggona* was being prepared. Water was poured in from an iron bucket, though the *tanoa* itself was a beautifully carved specimen in the shape of a turtle. I was given a small coconut cup and according to protocol we progressed through five dignified rounds. Over the *yaggona* we talked of things of the present. I asked Ratu Elisoni what was the greatest need of the village. He said the Governor himself had asked him this on a visit last year and he had told him a road through the village. But in fact, what was needed most of all was simply some cement to make their jetty a properly built affair. The loose stones were too dangerous and many accidents had been caused. He had omitted to mention this other matter at the time otherwise he was sure it would have been attended to.

The elders sitting opposite nodded agreement, four upright old men with deeply lined faces, the skin drawn tight across the cheekbones, folded slackly around the dark bright crevices of their eyes. The strange assortment of hand-me-down rags which they wore—a frayed waistcoat, an old seaman's sweater, patched khaki shorts and ancient shirts—together with the iron bucket in the corner were the only things in the room to show that 'civilization' had indeed visited them. The graceful and ceremonious courtesies with which they embroidered the threadbare framework of existence certainly owed nothing to European influence. There was no unseemly eagerness to find out about us, few signs of curiosity even. Wrapped in dignity, the elders were quite sure of the way things should be done and would always be done. What more was necessary, except to receive one's guests with the hospitality decreed by politeness?

I asked Likini to tell Ratu Elisoni that we would disturb them no longer. But I would like to stop for a little while and hear the singing in the meeting-house that had been going on in the background through our visit. There was a slight ripple of concern among the elders as this was translated.

'I'm afraid it's neither the most civilized nor comfortable of places,' said the little schoolmaster.

'They say to tell you it's Rubbish Hall over there!' Viliame put in with a grin.

'A chair must be taken over for her, then,' Ratu Elisoni decided.

I said perhaps such a formality might inhibit the singers and I would be happy to sit on the floor with the others.

'Well, a mat at least,' the old man finally decreed with a smile. He disappeared into an inner room and returned with a new, brightly fringed mat which was handed to a boy at the door to be taken on ahead.

One by one we all shook hands, Ratu Elisoni holding mine between his two for a moment, looking humorously down at me. He had enjoyed talking to an Englishwoman, he said. I must promise to come again soon, and he would have some more stories for me.

In the moonlight we picked our way past two enormous piles of yams and dalos which now stood outside the *bure*. Two primeval upturned shapes each about four feet long broke into a wild, helpless flapping of fins as we passed. 'They always do this with turtles,' Viliame told me. 'They can't kill them till tomorrow because the blood must be drunk fresh as soon as the veins are cut.'

Over in 'Rubbish Hall', a long shabby *bure* with ragged thatch and two or three doorways, a song died away and a ring of shadowy faces looked up as we came in. I saw that my mat had been laid out next to a very old man at the top of the room.

'You sit over there, please,' someone said politely.

Master followed close behind and took his seat next to me, while Likini and Viliame squatted down near the door. These were the only empty spaces for all round the room the walls were lined with men, sitting with legs crossed or outstretched in front of them, and at the side of each one a tin of black tobacco and a piece of dried banana leaf for rolling their cigarettes. Everyone watched us settle down, smiling broadly if one caught their eye. Then the entertainment continued. The singers sat in a circle with their backs to us in the far corner of the room. First there would be softly-pitched humming on different levels—a kind of practice run. Then the guitar would set the key, the ukulele establish the tempo, a single alto voice plunge into the opening lines, with all the others pounding in afterwards, a roaring torrent of noise made up of tenors, basses, and the wailing high falsetto that is the substitute for women's voices, all strung together on the rhythmic, hollow handclaps of the audience. It was typical untrained Fijian singing, strident and unmodulated. But it generated a vitality that was overpowering in itself. First, in my honour, came a song about the coronation of Queen Elizabeth ('All the world has heard about her,' roared the basses and tenors—'A lovely and powerful woman,' trilled the falsettos—or so Master industriously translated in my ear). Then there was one extolling the fund raised by Lady Garvey, wife of a former Governor, for the Fijian troops in Malaya. This was followed by a serenade to Aperisa, a Labasa policeman once stationed in the village who had ordered a *meke* to be written about him when he left. I was delighted to hear that another song celebrated my friend Jack Morris from Savu-Savu and his achievements in sailing his ketch to Australia.

'He is a Vanua Levu man, you see,' Master told me. 'All the people on this island are proud of him.'

Between songs he told me something about himself. He originally came from the same island in Lau as Likini and Poasa, but his job took him all over Fiji. His name, I learnt for the first time, was Tevita Thakau, David of the Reef. I told him this was almost a Welsh name and related for my part the story of David of the White Rock. The very old man on my other side had been listening with interest and now felt it was his turn to contribute something. He gave me a tolerant wrinkled smile, and leaning forward spoke in a quavering voice to Tevita.

'This old man', said Tevita finally, in a low tone of respect, 'is a survivor of the great measles epidemic of the eighteen-seventies.

Perhaps you'll have read about it. It killed off about one-third of the population they say. Our old man was a very small boy at the time but he remembers his mother dying of it and the graves being filled with three or four bodies at a time.'

The old man watched Tevita as he talked, like an ancient hawk, gaunt and beaky with a noble head, outlined against the lamplight. He spoke again, closing his eyes.

'All the sick were burning with a terrible heat,' Tevita translated. 'To cool the fire in their bodies, they fled to the sea or to the rivers to bathe themselves. And this was the way in which many of them met their death.'

The old man nodded and sighed to himself, then held out his hand for me to shake.

From the doorway Likini made our presentation of cigarettes and, as usual, they were accorded the ceremonial thanks worthy of a roast pig. The singers had sung for me all my favourite songs. It was late and we had to leave. David of the Reef came with us down to the jetty and as we glided back across the bay to the *Thagi-mai-Ra*, laden with feather fans, torches, baskets of yams and dalo, we saw his lantern swinging to and fro in farewell through the darkness.

Anchored for the night off Visogo, Mrs. Wallis and I shared, at last, an identical experience, 'We were visited last night by a tribe called *Namu.*' She wrote, 'They were all armed with a short, sharp instrument and attacked us most ferociously. Their numbers were so numerous that we found it impossible to defend ourselves and we suffered exceedingly from their poisoned instruments. The English name for this hostile tribe is Musquitoes.'

18

Farewell Island

Now we were skimming along the tail itself of Vanua Levu with only two more stops before we reached the point and made the crossing to Thikobia. The first was a village called Thawaru. To reach it we turned a sharp bend in the coast and suddenly found ourselves in a macabre blend of lunar landscape and a mad sculptor's workshop. The whole of the bay was dotted with tiny islets of a strange, smooth stone which rose from the sea in a fantasy of different forms, some mushroom-shaped and squat, some tall and spiralled like frozen waterspouts. The largest of this surrealist archipelago shelved away in layers, like a cluster of *bure* roofs, brown on top, a creamy-white beneath. One near by was the exact shape of the map of Australia, one carved like the prow of a ship, yet another whittled away to the convolutions of a Henry Moore abstract.

Though this strange gallery the dinghy nosed its way up on to a patch of bone-white sand, screened at either end by a living trellis of twisted mangrove roots. A cliff of sandstone, warmer-coloured and shadowed with palms and hardwood reared up behind the beach. The village, Miss Johnson said, frowning back at the cliff and settling her bag on her shoulder, was right at the top. But it was a hard climb, so why didn't we stay here and have a look round until they came back. They'd only be gone an hour.

Waving, she and Taina set off on the rough track that wound away in an almost perpendicular spiral through the bush. I turned and for a moment of odd panic thought I had been left alone. But laughing, Viliame stepped out from behind a slab of rock that jutted out of the sand.

'There are other beaches farther along,' he said. 'I'll take you round in the dinghy.'

We followed the coast for almost a mile and still the strange stones grew out of the sea, fungus-smooth boulders, great ribbed awnings of rock, squat weathered forms like headless idols. Through this Dali landscape, sharply shadowed by the morning sun, the little boat floated with the unreal, timeless felicity of dreams until, as in dreams, the strangeness became normality, part of the flowing sequence of scenes and people conjured out of nowhere by the Wind-from-the-West. Such a moment, I thought, transported yet effortless, was one of the rare rewards of travel, cancelling out the disappointments, discomforts and, however brief, crystallizing in the imagination the mysterious essence of the whole journey. Once we got out and stood in the eye of a needle-shaped spur on the fringe of the water. Farther along we walked in the shade of a canopy hollowed by the wind to an almost encircling tunnel.

'These stones are bewitched,' said Viliame, as we moved away. 'Like at Vunikodi where we stop this afternoon. There is a *tevora* there, a devil who lives in a big flat stone. Men who have been refused by the women they want, go there secretly to put tobacco leaves and *yaggona* on the stone. "She doesn't want me, so you have her," the man says to the devil. And in the night the *tevora* comes to the woman's house and bewitches her, and she is cursed from then onwards.'

Out in the sunshine of the bay he talked about himself again. He wanted to travel before he settled in Lau. Most of all he would like to see Europe. 'I want to meet a European girl, you see.'

'Why?' I asked him.

'So that she can teach me how to love,' he said soulfully. 'Like in the films and the books. Fijian girls can't be like that. They laugh and talk too much about such things.' He screwed up his eyes in a moment of intense concentration. 'I want to love so that if there was a medicine to cure it not all the medicine in the world would be of any use for it!'

It seemed a curious reversal of the European dreams of love in the South Sea islands.

After a while Miss Johnson and Taina reappeared on the cliff-side path. It was only while rowing back to the *Thagi-mai-Ra* that I suddenly realized Miss Gordon-Cumming had been with us on this visit after all.

'We landed on a beach of fine white sand,' she had written of an unnamed point along this part of the coast, 'shadowed by palms and rich hardwood and enclosed by high sandstone cliffs of warm colours. Here we had supper and hunted for sleeping quarters. We found an overhanging rock just like the rock-temples of Ceylon where the sacred images of Buddha are carved; and I really thought we looked rather like a row of Buddhas as we lay beneath this rock-canopy.'

It was a memorable farewell glimpse of my friend, an angular elongated figure in blue serge, pillowed on her pith hath, reclining in the moonlight among the bizarre silhouettes of the Thawaru stones.

Vunikodi was not much farther along the coast and time went even more quickly as, after lunch, Likini 'storied me' about a small green island we had passed called Silivakatini. 'That means Ten-Times-Bath,' said Likini. 'You know why? Well, Captain Cook was taking not just one turtle like everyone knows to Tonga but two, as a present for the King. But one of the turtles escaped on the way and he sent people looking for it all the way from Lau. Then they heard that someone seen it near this island. So they stay on the island for a while to look for it. But each time they set out in the boat, a storm gets up and drives them back again to land. They are cold and wet and must bath and change their clothes. They do this again and again and on the tenth day, they change and bath for the last time and decide to forget about the turtle and stay on the island for good. And these are the people of Silivakatini.'

If Thawaru had been extraordinary, Vunikodi was the perfect, conventional image of a Fijian coastal village. From the deck we saw a white sandy bay scooped out of the last green hills of Vanua Levu. The dinghy took us almost to the shore and we waded through rainbow shallows on to the sand that was pale and sugary and studded with coloured shells. In the background was the familiar up-turned boat, the odd hut thatched with coconut leaves, the tin-roof store and a winding path to the village under the palms. As ever a lean old beldam in a ragged *sulu* was waiting to lead us there, surrounded by an advance party of shouting children and barking dogs. As we came through the ring of houses on to the *rara*, there was a cry of greeting. A young man bare-chested and wearing an old pair of khaki slacks and a flourishing new moustache came forward and welcomed with exuberant hand-wringings and slaps on the back, first Poasa then Likini and Viliame.

'This is the *Tala-tala*, the Methodist minister,' Viliame said. 'He also comes from Lau. He wants to know if you would like to visit his house.'

It was with an air of ceremony the *Tala tala* ushered me into the more sophisticated atmosphere of the wooden bungalow opposite. A round bevelled mirror hung from one wall, from another a coloured picture of Jesus blessing the children. There were rows of shabby books on shelves, mostly nineteenth-century titles by forgotten authors and a few paperbacks on religion and psychology. A portable radio was booming out Stravinsky from the Suva station. I noticed some very fine Lauan mats on the beds, with two-feet-wide coloured borders of fringed wool of the sort Fijians call *vaka-bati* (like teeth).

'And here are some pillow-cases my wife makes,' said the *Tala tala*, producing a suitcase from under the bed. He brought out a pile of vivid green cotton squares, edged with lace and lovingly embroidered with flowers and the favourite mottoes—'Sweet Dreams', 'Mothé Vinaka'. My own favourite was the one that read 'Rest in Peace'. The *Tala tala* shook his head irritably. 'I told her this was not right for a pillow-case. But it was too late. It was already done.'

We sat down in neat canvas chairs and talked above the Stravinsky.

A thin, elderly man came stooping in through the doorway—how old it was impossible to say, as like most Fijians his hair was dyed a glossy jet-black. 'He is a church worker,' my host explained. 'He speaks no English.' The church worker gave me a stately, toothless smile and took his seat on the floor near the door, listening with apparent interest as the *Tala tala* told me about the five villages that were under his ministerial care. 'I travel round them through the week, visiting the people. Then on Sundays I preach my sermon here. It is usually based on a passage from the Bible. Or sometimes', he added, pursing his lips, 'I decide to speak about something wrong that has been done in the village during the week—should that be necessary.'

He had never been out of Fiji, he told me. Most of all he would like to visit New Zealand.

The Stravinsky came to an end. In the pause, the sound of singing drifted across the green.

'I think they have prepared some music for you—shall we go over?'

In a large empty *bure* on the other side of the *rara* sat a cheerfully improvised group of performers, a guitarist, a young man who had set up his cane-knife as a double-bass, tapping on it with his finger-nails, another who brushed out the rhythm with an empty cigarette packet on the floor, and a squatting circle of singers and onlookers.

'I told them you like Fijian songs,' said Viliame, ushering me into one of the canvas chairs drawn up at the top of the room. 'I want to tell you about the beauties of my coast,' translated Viliame. 'The long white sands stretch right to the point of the colony. . . .'

The third verse drifted into silence as through the door came an extraordinarily striking-looking man, the *Tala tala* at his side. Immensely tall and stout with white curling hair he was so light skinned that he looked more Italian than Fijian. He wore a working singlet and shorts, yet surveyed the gathering with his tawny slit eyes in an unmistakably authoritative way. He was simply introduced as the Chief and, the *Tala tala* added, he spoke no English. Vilame, who had been standing, crouched down with a hand-clap for permission to speak, telling him about my journey on the *Thagi-mai-Ra*.

The Chief scrutinized me quickly, smiled, and without shaking my hand, sat down next to me. Throughout the singing he kept a keen eye on all that went on, noting for example my involuntary expression of concern as I was presented with my fifth cup of *yaggona* and indicating with a brief flick of his head that this was to be the final offering. He had a Tahitian look, I decided finally, not only in colouring but in caste of feature. There was also an unidentifiable feeling of mystery about him which was more than his manner of cautious reserve, but any hope of further conversation disappeared when Poasa announced in polite undertones that it was time for the *Thagi-mai-Ra* to leave. Miss Johnson was meeting us on the beach.

The party, however, was not yet over. The young man picked up his guitar—he was the son of the Chief, it seemed—the double-bass stand-in swung his cane-knife over his shoulder, someone poured the rest of the *yaggona* into a bucket, and escorted by the whole company of singers, we went down to the beach. There under the palm trees, the Chief's son flourishingly removed his crepe-paper *lei* and placed it round my neck. There was a final round of *yaggona* as Miss Johnson and Taina joined us. Then with the delightful mock-sentimentality of a bunch of gondoliers producing 'O Sole Mio' for the tourists, they broke into 'Isa Lei', waving and laughing, as the dinghy pushed away. It was almost the South Seas in fancy dress, an animated travel poster, that final shot of blue sea, white sand, and a group of brown young men under the palm trees singing to a guitar a farewell song that faded away behind the regular rattle and swish of the oars.

There was still a patch of coloured shirts on the beach when the *Thagi-mai-Ra* turned to the open sea half an hour later.

'Probably go on all night now,' said Miss Johnson, with her sardonic smile. She shrugged her shoulders. 'Ah well! If they've nothing else to do.'

After dinner I sat on for a few moments longer, listening to Taina talk about her childhood in Wainibokasi. Her father had been a minister and she was one of nine children so had to stay away from school a great deal helping her mother at home. One day a European nursing sister came to the village who took her under her wing. Taina begged to be allowed to train as a nurse. Eventually she was given permission, took a brief course in obstetrics and general medicine, and began the work round the districts that she had been doing ever since. She was fifty-three, she told me. She could read and write in Fijian, but not in English. 'Too late to learn now, I think. Never mind!'

We said good night and she stumped away down the stairs to the cabin she shared with Miss Johnson, a resolute, wiry little figure in her nurse's uniform, her bush of iron-black hair combed defiantly up over her white collar, her khaki skirt flaring over muscular chestnut calves.

Soon after first light the *Thagi-mai-Ra's* steady rhythm had changed to an ominous tossing and heaving. Breakfast over, I went up on deck and clung to the rails, closing my eyes. Deckchairs ricocheted from one side to the other with each swoop of the boat and even standing became an athletic feat. Down below, Poasa was poring over an outspread navigation chart. 'This where we are now,' he explained, pointing with his compass needle to an alarming rash of darker-blue blotches and whirls which he added, with a cheerful grin, were the reefs. Think of Tasman who discovered this passage in the February of 1643, a famous month for hurricanes, I reassured myself—sailing round from Taveuni without even a map, let alone a marine chart. The hilltops of Vanua Levu along to Udu Point he took to be distant islands. Passing close to Thikobia he reported more accurately that it was but a small portion of what was once an extensive island, but encircled it only long enough to record that it was clear of reefs near the suface. A sunken reef though extended far to the south-east, the edges of which were from fourteen to forty fathoms deep.

Scylla Reef was the foreboding name added to the chart of these waters by Captain Wilson in 1797. Another map direction of his noted in elegant copperplate 'upon these small reefs there is scarce a ruffle of the sea to apprize of the danger'. This remark was the result of the *Duff* striking such a reef on its journey to Thikobia. 'We knew that the Feejees were cannibals of a fierce difpofition,' wrote Wilson in his log of this disaster, 'and who had never had the leaft intercoufe with any voyagers; confequently we could expect no favour from fuch. Imagination, quick and fertile on fuch occasions, figured them dancing round us while we were roafted on large fires. However it was not time to indulge thoughts of this kind, but to try what could be done to fave the fhip.'

Saved it was, and following land far removed from Bligh's sightings either in the *Bounty* or the *Providence*, Wilson observed, 'Where we paffed clofe we faw many inhabitants and have no doubt that they are all well peopled; and they muft be an improved people in the favage ftate for the natives of the Friendly Iflands who are unwilling to give place to any acknowledge that the Feejees excell them in many ingenious works; that they poffefs larger canoes and are a braver fighting people; but abhor them for their deteftable practice of eating their unfortunate prifoners.'

Mrs. Wallis, I thought at this point, crawling on to my bunk, would have been ashamed of me. To the howl of a headwind and cries of, 'Get out the fore-topmast studding-sail!' she had followed her daily round undeterred, entertaining the King of Mathcuata to coffee though sensibly declining with a curtsy a request to shave His Majesty with an American razor, lecturing the natives on the evils of cannibalism ('Do the Americans eat each other? No, we know better.'), and on calmer days exploring by open boat for twelve hours at a stretch without food or drink, 'sheltered from the rays of the sun by an umbrella', or descending at friendly villages to plant slips of rose-bushes and geraniums as momentoes of her visit.

Yet even the adventurous Mrs. Wallis had baulked at the idea of going on to *Jekombia* (Thikobia). In support of the island's evil reputation she told a tale of how five Europeans on a turtle-shell expedition had been slaughtered while sleeping on board their boat anchored just off the island. Soon after another boat-load had narrowly escaped with their lives. A native invited them to land, saying he was a Christian teacher. The white men did so but when they heard the name of the island, they returned to the boat, sent the natives away in search of a large stone for anchorage, then rapidly cleared the boat and set sail. The missionary Williams relating the same story, added, 'Several bullets passed through the sail but the savages aimed high and the party escaped uninjured.'

It was more than physical relief then, to look out half an hour later and see a hundred yards away a peaceful-looking mass of grey rock rear itself out of the sea. The tall honeycombed cliffs were draped with tangled greenery. Of houses or people there were no signs, nor was there a beach in sight. Several huge fragments of rock had fallen to the bottom of the cliff, where they had worn by the tides to humming-top shapes. Round these the waves seethed and swirled, curdling the humming-water to dazzling onyx shades of green and white.

'But how?' I began, following Miss Johnson numbly into the boat. With a grin, she handed me a pair of glasses. On one of the slabs of fallen rock I saw a rusty pole transfixed with a half a dozen rungs leading up and apparently disappearing into the cliff face. I gulped —then looked again. A surge of relief swept through me. Two of the rungs were missing. 'Well, that's it then!' I explained.

'What do you mean, that's it?' demanded Miss Johnson. 'We can make it easy!'

The next minute we were out of the boat and clinging together on the tiny slab, slippery with the last tide. We were standing in a sort of cave. The steps disappeared through a hole in the roof, leading to sloping ground above.

'On your shoulders, Waisea,' directed Miss Johnson. Obediently, Waisea squatted, wrapped his arms around the pole, and squared his massive back. Viliame went first, then with a nimble swing, Miss Johnson, too, had bridged the gap and was clambering aloft, hand over hand, followed by Taina.

Waisea and I were left on the slab. Through the hole peered a ring of anxious faces. 'Take it slowly with that ankle,' Miss Johnson instructed. 'And remember not to look down.' Concentrating hard I did both these things then slowly, with an Alice-like feeling, felt my head emerging into the open air. Helping hands reached down and hauled me out. A semi-sheer cliffside stretched above, knotted with bush. Several feet below, the waves slapped briskly around the rocks. Without another word, Viliame crouched down and indicated his back. Leading the way, he scrambled surely and steadily up—a foot placed in a crevice there, a hand grasping a vine-rope there, with a pause for breath now and again and a silent prayer from me.

Suddenly we were at the top—with a reassuring pat, Viliame slid me down. From now on the ground rose and fell in gently slopes as we followed a pathway shoulder-high in undergrowth. Occasionally we came to a clearing where copra fires smoked and an old man held out his hand to each of us as we passed. Bony dogs came snarling and wagging at our feet, young men rose from the bush with grins of welcome and a waving of cane-knives. After we had walked for about an hour we came to a village. A white wooden building on stilts stood clear of the other houses and outside this some fifty children were waiting in a line, neatly dressed in green cotton uniforms, while mothers with babies watched from the surrounding doorways.

'The school,' Miss Johnson said. 'You'll be able to see what goes on today—and I'm afraid that's all there'll be time for, too.' She grinned. 'You must come again sometime.'

'I will,' I said, for I already loved the wildness and remoteness of the place.

The schoolmaster, a handsome young man in a white towelling shirt, showed us into the classroom. Beneath poster pictures of the Palace of Westminster, English Road Communications and Books of Britain, Miss Johnson assembled her syringes and bottles on one of the ancient desks. A canvas chair was pushed forward into a spectator's position for me, and supervised by Taina the procession began—toddlers who marched proudly alone, shoulders erect, babies carried in by anxious tousle-haired mothers, older boys and girls, nudging and giggling all obediently opening their mouths for the three drops of 'lolly'. One or two had to have booster injections by needle, but there was little crying, only a quick intake of breath and a smiling flash of quick sympathy from the women.

As they filed past the schoolmaster brought in his baby son to show me. He pointed to a boy in the line with a face of startling beauty, the wide-set eyes and golden-copper hair and skin that to a lesser degree most of the Thikobia children seemed to have. 'My oldest son. He's just eleven.'

He sat next to me and gave me the island's statistics—four hundred inhabitants, four villages, four horses, eleven cows, some forty pigs, and a few goats. Health was the great problem, he said, in such an isolated place. The sister called for regular inspections, but in the case of serious accidents there was only the boat. If petrol ran out, they must wait till another boat called on them. There was a store on the island. If stocks were scarce people lived on the land. Everyone had their patch of dalo, yams, kumala. They had money for their copra. Some built wooden houses with it. Otherwise they were not much interested in anything beyond their immediate needs. Many people had never left the island. The Sister or District Officer were the only Europeans they saw.

'It is a peaceful place and the children are healthy.' He looked round the little schoolroom with pride, the sums on the board, the pile of handicraft mats, the cut-out pictures of the Royal Family pasted on cupboard doors. 'Most of the children are taught in English from the age of eight onwards,' he said, 'though some learn it right away. The difficulty is to get them to speak it at home.'

Noting a poster of Wales on the wall, with pictures of Llangollen, I told the schoolmaster it was quite close to where I lived. He gave a delighted smile and passed on the information to the older children standing round us. 'Thlan-goth-len,' repeated the children with a truer accent than any English attempt as he tapped out the pronunciation with a cane on the blackboard. A buzz of interest ran through the room.

'Isa!' exclaimed the women, clucking their tongues in sympathy for the homesickness they knew I must be feeling. Everyone peered more closely at the harp-playing ladies with tall black hats and red cloaks depicted in the picture.

'They want to know if this is a *meke*,' said the schoolmaster.

I said indeed it was. Like Fiji, Wales was the land of *meke*, though it was the singing rather than the dancing at which they excelled, and the making of poetry, too. Wasn't it true, I asked the schoolmaster, that in Fijian tradition the island of Thikobia was supposed to be the home of the goddess of poetry?

He said he had heard how in the old days a certain woman was possessed with the power of visiting the spirit-world where she would be taught a *meke* by one of the divinities and then returned to repeat it to the people of the island. Her mother had done so before her, and her grandmother before that, for it was a hereditary gift. But he knew of no present-day descendant. People spoke less and less of such things nowadays. 'Though the *mekes* performed by Thikobia people are of a very high standard,' he added, 'as anyone will tell you.'

Returning to more mundane matters, Miss Johnson told him as we left of the two missing rungs on the steps. The schoolmaster merely smiled with a look of slight surprise—obviously this was a minor hazard to people who had scrambled up and down these cliffs barefoot, often in the rain and darkness, all their lives. 'The hole in the rock is better though,' he suggested.

'Seems bigger,' Miss Johnson admitted.

'The F.M.F. Band,' replied the schoolmaster with a pleased nod. 'They came here when they were touring Vanua Levu recently and some of the instruments wouldn't go through so we had it enlarged.'

Off we set down the path again under a huge mango tree where on a rough wooden stand the children's lunch-boxes and bottles were ranged in the shade out of the way of the ants. A bevy of small boys returning with buckets of water from the spring stepped aside with military salutes as we passed. We were crossing to the beach on the other side of the island, Miss Johnson told me, relieving me of nightmare visions of a descent down The Steps. There the dinghy would be waiting to take us back to *Thangi-mai-Ra*.

A charming elderly Fijian in shorts and vest emerged from the bush and joined us on our way. Tucking his cane-knife and a bundle of *roro* under his arm, he shook hands all round while Taina introduced him as the Minister of Thikobia. Continuous exchanges of church news, farewell tea-parties and extension funds, accompanied us as we plunged through the muddy undergrowth, he and Taina following behind, chatting together in Fijian. Gradually sand and grass appeared underfoot, the bush thinned out and we emerged into another village with the sea beyond. There was a brief call at the dispensary, a rough reed shelter with wood-shavings on the ground and shelves lined with giant bottles, mysteriously colourec and labelled.

'Anyone could walk in and take them but no one ever does,' said Miss Johnson, who was binding up the infected arm of a small girl waiting with her mother. There were a few more injections to be performed under the cynical gaze of a withered crone squatting in the doorway and the admiring scrutiny of two teen-age village girls who told Miss Johnson they would like to be nurses but they were both getting married next year.

It was getting dark. A cold wind blew in from the sea. As we made our way to the beach people came out to see us go. Under the eaves of one of the kitchens, where a bright fire flickered in the shadows over iron pots and pans, the *Tala tala* and his wife stood watching for us.

'She has something to give you,' the *Tala tala* said to me. Shyly the elderly woman at his side handed me a ceremonial Fijian fly-switch with strands of coconut fibre as long as a horse's tail. We both smiled at the pleasure of the moment and I made my thanks.

'It is an old thing. One does not see them any more made like this,' said the *Tala tala.*

Together they followed us down on to the sand where the broad figure of Likini was waiting. Through the dusk the lights of the *Thagi-mai-Ra* glimmered on the horizon, an unnervingly long way away. One by one we packed ourselves into the dinghy. Between the little boat and the big boat rolled a desert of inky sea, barred with white breakers.

'She's too far out,' said Viliame, pushing off and climbing in at the back. He pointed to a sheltered passage behind the headland. 'Can't she follow us there?'

The first of the offshore rollers swept towards us, lifted us up and half-swamping the bows, dumped us down again. Likini gestured to another ahead. Hunched over the outboard motor Viliame faced him following his directions, steering the boat through the reef, turning it to dodge the current or take a swell three-quarters on. By now, we were all drenched through.

'Better to be wet than have someone hurt,' Viliame grunted, his face gleaming, teeth clenched with effort.

At that moment the *Thagi-mai-Ra* began to turn, moving across in the direction of the headland, though as in a nightmare the distance between us never seemed to change except when her lights seemed farther away than ever. Once Taina stood up and furiously waved a long white scarf. Likini put his hands to his mouth and shouted. Then gradually she was closing in with us until at the limit of safety the engines stopped again and she waited motionless, rising and falling with the waves. It was pitch dark by the time the dinghy lurched alongside and Poasa and Waisea leaned over to haul us up the ladder.

'If we had gone out to where the boat was first we should all have been drowned for sure,' Taina summed up solemnly after dinner as Miss Johnson and I sat up on deck over our hospital brandy.

The wind had dropped and the sea was calm. Thikobia lay on a raft of moonlight, a long black silhouette circled by the white smoke of the waves on the reef.

'Towards the east the island wears a better aspect; and at this part there were natives and houses on top of the hill. Probably there is low ground on the fouth-weft fide where we intended to anchor; but coming to the north-weft point we faw a fhoal clofe to us and a large flat ran S.W. of the ifland; upon which we hauled our wind and as this was the laft we faw of this dangerous group, it received the name of Farewell Island. . . .'

Thikobia was still the last of Fiji's three hundred islands. For Wilson it had marked farewell to the mysterious, half-hidden shapes of an unknown country. Setting a new course he had sailed on for China. For me Thikobia marked the limit of my present travels. Tomorrow we, too, would be changing course, making not for the east but for home again, and home was Fiji.

THE END

References

A History of Fiji by R. A. Derrick (Fiji, 1946).
The Hill Tribes of Fiji by A. B. Brewster (London, 1922).
Fiji in 1870 by J. Britton (Melbourne, 1870).
My Colonial Service by Sir G. W. Des Voeux (London, 1903).
Fiji Times: Files of the Paper.
Fiji Times and Herald: Files of the Paper.
Two Years in Fiji by L. Forbes (London, 1875).
At Home in Fiji by C. F. Gordon-Cumming (Edinburgh, 1881).
The Discoverers of the Fiji Islands by G. C. Henderson (London, 1933).
Lockerby's Journal by Sir Everard Imthurn (Hakluyt Society, London, 1925).
Polynesian Reminiscences by W. T. Pritchard (London, 1866).
Ten Months in Fiji by S. M. Smythe (London, 1864).
The Fijians: A Study in the Decay of Custom by B. Thomson (London, 1908).
Life in Feejee: or Five Years Among the Cannibals by M. D. Wallis (Boston, U.S.A., 1851).
Fiji and the Fijians by T. Williams and J. Calvert (London, 1860).
A Missionary Voyage to the South Pacific Ocean (1796–98) in the Ship 'Duff' by J. A. Wilson (London, 1799).
The King and People of Fiji by J. Waterhouse (London, 1866).
Fiji's Indian Migrants by K. L. Gillion (Melbourne, 1962).

The unpublished notes of Mrs. Emma Small, by kind permission of her granddaughter, Mrs. McHugh.